SEA CHANGE

PRAISE FOR *SEA CHANGE*

"An upbeat portrait of a revitalized global fishing industry. Readers looking for a climate change narrative shot through with optimism will find this does the trick."

—*PUBLISHERS WEEKLY*

"Finally, some good news! An uplifting read that will leave you hopeful about people, our planet, and the power of working together."

—CAROLEE HAZARD, Kepler's Books

"Leland and Workman make a convincing case that empowering fishermen to work together, even as they compete, can create miracles."

—BILL MCKIBBEN, *Here Comes the Sun*

"*Sea Change* reveals how those most tied to the sea can, must, and are becoming its greatest protectors. This book will change how you see the ocean—and those who live by it."

—CARL SAFINA, *Alfie and Me*

"The greatest environmental success story that no one's ever heard of."

—ERIC POOLEY, *The Climate War*

"The game-changer we didn't know we needed; an eye-opening, exhilarating story of how bold, pragmatic solutions can revive our oceans and redefine the future of seafood."

—RICK MOONEN, James Beard Award winner

"*Sea Change* is both an antidote to environmental gloom and a fair, deeply informed, and fun read."

—TINA ROSENBERG,
Pulitzer Prize and National Book Award winner

"*Sea Change* reveals one of the great environmental turnarounds of our time. It's essential reading for anyone who cares about the future of our oceans."

—BRUCE BABBITT, former US Secretary of the Interior

SEA
CHANGE

Unlikely Allies and a Success Story of Oceanic Proportions

James Workman
Amanda Leland

TORREY HOUSE PRESS

T<small>H</small>P

Salt Lake City • Torrey

Torrey House Press

First Torrey House Press Edition, September 2025

Published by Torrey House Press
Salt Lake City, Utah
www.torreyhouse.org

Hardcover ISBN: 979-8-89092-040-9
Paperback ISBN: 979-8-89092-028-7
E-book ISBN: 979-8-89092-029-4
Library of Congress Control Number: 2024952874

Cover design by Kathleen Metcalf
Interior design by Lark Washburn and Eryon Shondíín Greenburg
Distributed to the trade by Consortium Book Sales and Distribution

Torrey House Press offices in Salt Lake City sit on the homelands of Ute, Goshute, Shoshone, and Paiute nations. Offices in Torrey are on the homelands of Southern Paiute, Ute, and Navajo nations.

To Teagan and Simon, Camille and Louise. May the lessons of this story inspire more people to work together for this blue planet and all it provides.

CONTENTS

Full fathom five thy father lies.
Of his bones are coral made.
Those are pearls that were his eyes.
Nothing of him that doth fade,
But doth suffer a sea-change
Into something rich and strange.
Sea-nymphs hourly ring his knell.

—William Shakespeare, *The Tempest*

PREFACE

A commercial fisherman and an environmentalist walk into a bar...

Sounds like the setup for a joke about familiar antagonists, right? The bitter rivals—on land you could swap in a logger, rancher, miner, or farmer—can scarcely comprehend each other's priorities, much less learn to trust one another.

But what if the punchline came through an unexpected twist? What if, instead of clashing, both sides found common ground in the messy middle between self-interest and science? What if over drinks the fisherman confessed to feeling powerless in the face of dangerous seasons and dwindling catches, while the environmentalist lamented the loss of childhood memories of reeling in big fish? What if these rivals put their heads together and somehow came up with a tough, pragmatic solution that was radically new—yet deeply rooted in human experience?

Though it may sound implausible, that bar exists. It sits on a narrow road in Galveston, Texas, not far from the docks on Wharf Road. That outcome is real, too. We'd advise you against trying to match Keith "Buddy" Guindon beer for beer in lengthy talks about rebuilding red snapper and grouper populations he'd fished to the brink in the Gulf of Mexico, but the conversation itself might change the way you think about environmentalism. In that bar, and others like it, difficult decisions from such brutally honest conversations are exactly what brought this book into existence.

Welcome to the hidden world of "catch shares." This revolutionary social contract with the sea has not only slowed, stopped, and in some cases reversed the devastating effects of overfishing

1

along our coasts, but the centrality of pragmatism and collaboration could help solve some of the thorniest and most urgent natural resource challenges we confront worldwide–including the climate crisis. Our story, with Buddy as the protagonist, takes you on a journey into the heart of one of the most remarkable yet least-known conservation successes of our time.

Catch shares at its core represents a powerful idea. By aligning nature's integrity with human incentives, these rights-based systems secure bottom-up collaboration because they create a community of guardians for the future. Collective stewardship, a simple yet transformative concept, has replenished some of our most depleted fisheries back into functioning ecosystems. It has empowered marginalized people, fostered innovation, improved compliance with scientific standards, and built resilience against a rapidly changing world. And the implications go well beyond our coastlines. America's quietly effective strategy to replenish the ocean offers a blueprint for other nations—and other natural resource challenges—to follow.

Rights-based systems emerge to fit a unique resource, place, and people. They adapt to change, never frozen in time. Yet the durable pattern of catch shares at sea, rebuilding life year after year like compound interest, means you can envision a future where forest loss stops after local communities are properly rewarded and compensated for keeping their trees standing. Where fertilizer runoff is reduced by farmers with incentives to use nutrients more efficiently. Where climate pollution falls once industries profit from slashing emissions. Where depleted water tables rise because well owners can trade unused acre-feet from their shared aquifer. Where biodiversity—from monarch butterflies to red-cockaded woodpeckers—again flourishes thanks to landowners financially motivated to protect its habitat. These outcomes are no longer naive dreams; they are tangible possibilities demonstrated most thoroughly at sea.

What's more, by tackling overfishing, catch shares generate ripple effects for closely linked crises like climate change, food security, and human health. While rights-based fishing alone can't reverse ocean warming or acidification, they do relieve such mis-

2

eries by reducing overexploitation, enabling flexibility, unlocking innovations, and curbing emissions from the global fishing fleet. More importantly, catch shares sustain the world's most nutrient-rich protein source for vulnerable billions who depend on seafood to live. Science has shown that healthy fish populations lead to healthier ecosystems, particularly coral reefs. By replenishing life offshore, catch shares help solve interconnected crises—to nourish, employ, and boost resilience in our increasingly hot, hungry, and unstable world.

Skeptical? We initially were, too. Yet rigorous bioeconomic models have demonstrated that exactly this upside scenario lies within reach—if we choose to grasp it. Both of us are ocean lovers, seafood eaters, and lifelong environmentalists, which is why we grew obsessed with understanding how to solve the overfishing problem. Reading all the bleak headlines about sickly seas, dying reefs, and collapsing fisheries suggested a world spinning its wheels against multiple impending threats. The sheer scale and complexity could easily leave us all numbed by bad news and bracing for the worst. No one denies the breadth of overfishing, but what can people do at the market, restaurant, or ballot box to turn the tide?

This book offers one answer. Though far from disinterested, our narrative relies on an abundance of empirical evidence—drawing from countless rights-based systems, distilling lessons from a library of global case studies, citing reports and design manuals—that show how catch shares have helped troubled fisheries in the Pacific and Atlantic, spreading contagiously on US shores and now overseas until today fishermen and governments have together forged more than two hundred social contracts with the sea, co-managing more than five hundred different species back to health across forty different nations, with potential to end overfishing worldwide. (We have chosen to use the traditional term "fisherman"—which is considered gender-neutral in the industry—rather than alternatives like "fisher" or "fisherfolk," and other terminology is accurate to the time when various events take place.)

It sounds ambitious. Yet at its heart, our story is about entrusting the sea's fate to those who most depend on it—fishing communities. Their role in this unfamiliar story of oceanic recovery wasn't, and for many still isn't, obvious. It's hard for Americans—whether fishermen or environmentalists like us—to resolve the paradox that smart, strategic extraction of wild sea creatures will help replenish the ocean. Growing up on the Pacific and Atlantic coasts, we saw harvesters with powerful gear depleting species one after another. As conditions worsened, nerves grew raw. There were times, reporting our scientific research to testy fishermen, when police stood by with hands on their holsters. Only by meeting people where they were, looking deeper at competing priorities, and trying to find a path in that messy middle could we begin to appreciate the perverse incentives that drove communities to plunder their own futures—and then work together for a virtuous spiral of healing.

We wrote this book not only to tell the story of catch shares, but also because it may inspire us to make progress on even greater environmental challenges, like climate change. For decades, ambitious solutions to global warming have been held back by ideological division. To be sure, climate denialism is more than just a misunderstanding–it is often fed by intentional misinformation designed to protect entrenched interests. But the result is an unnecessary divide over what should be a common project: building a safe, stable, and prosperous future.

Catch shares succeed by listening to the needs of people who are directly impacted by the overfishing crisis and its potential solutions—and substituting rhetoric with a focus on the science, economics, and the reality of people's lives. Using the same approach, we've started to make serious progress on climate change—enlisting farmers, businesses, and technology to take practical steps to reduce climate pollution. There are so many aspects of the climate question—from agriculture to alternative fuels—that can benefit from this kind of approach.

Four hundred years ago, William Shakespeare penned *The Tempest*, a drama of people transformed by the ocean's magic. To describe this altered state, he coined the phrase "sea change."

Today, that term has become overused and vague. But we embrace the Bard's original meaning: the profound conversion of confused, divided, and broken coastal communities who discover how to thrive, turning chaos into grace.

Sea Change introduces the unlikely partnerships and innovations that forged a quiet revolution. Perhaps it can provide insights that will help us deal with the difficult issues that we must face to heal our climate and protect our future.

Introduction

SETTING THE HOOK

O n the Japanese island of Okinawa, the native Ryūkyūan people live longer than anyone on earth. Their Blue Zone secret? Some credit anti-aging traits from an ancient gene pool, others a seafood-rich diet. On May 17, 2016, a discovery entwined both explanations. While sifting through floor layers of a remote limestone cave, archaeologists unearthed the world's oldest fishhooks.

The fishhook is one of our most singular and consequential inventions. News of this cultural first spread fast and altered our understanding of how we evolved. The relics confirmed that fishing technology had emerged sixteen thousand years earlier than believed, enabling humans' early migrations across open sea to inhabit offshore islands. The find supported anthropologists' theory that *Homo* got more *sapiens* by catching and eating more fish.

It also raised a troubling question. If wide open access to the ocean's natural bounty expands human potential, what happens to us today as wild fish disappear?

Seafood has long fueled growth of primates' larger, more complex brains. Fossil shell and bone "trash mounds," or middens, show that from 140,000 to 50,000 years ago our ancestors gleaned animals from coastal shallows. Seafood provided an evolutionary edge. From scouring estuaries, tide pools and surf zones this nutritious "perfect protein" helped humans inhabit and dominate every shore. Yet early beachcombers hit limits. Primates could only pry up mollusks, stab crustaceans, or scavenge dead fish tossed up by storms. They couldn't yet access all that protein swimming offshore, out of reach. Then one day, at least 23,000 years ago, survival instincts inspired our ancestral brains to experiment. At that turning point some Paleolithic innovator sat down in a cave, picked up a thick snail shell, carved a graceful and durable "J" with a fine hard point, lashed it to a fiber strand, impaled some bait on it, stepped to the water's edge and cast it into the unknown.

Over millennia fishhooks went viral. They became ubiquitous. The shape varied little: from the hollow eye where the line attached, a straight shank gave way to a curve, bending up past a barb and to a point. But each continent holds relics of hooks adapted to catch swimming prey. Early peoples carved fish hooks from bone, shell, wood, horn, antlers, even stone. Later civilizations hammered and bent them out of copper, bronze, tin, and iron. The dawn of the Industrial Age and mass production exploded technology all over again, affording everyone anywhere easy ways to catch many more fish in much less time. Second by second, factories stamped out hooks of high-carbon steel, honed for tensile strength, fast penetration, and tenacious grip. To boost efficiency further still, manufacturers began stringing those hooks along lines that spooled out for miles, allowing vessels to haul in not one fish per cast but dozens, hundreds, even thousands of fish every time they set their long lines.

Longline hooks played just one part in the progression of new technologies that exponentially increased the harvesting power of fishermen. Fossil fuels ushered in the modern age of fishing vessels. At one end of the spectrum, rickety fiberglass skiffs used petroleum-based fertilizer to dynamite tropical reefs and scoop up everything in the blast radius that died and floated to the surface. At the other, automated factory trawlers dragged enormous synthetic nets through miles of arctic seas to process the catch on board. Seafood harvesters repurposed wartime technologies—hydraulic winches, power refrigeration, spotter planes, global positioning systems (GPS), sound navigation and ranging (SONAR), long range navigation (LORAN) and radio detection and ranging (RADAR)—to blanket the entire ocean and target fish at unprecedented depths with pinpoint accuracy.

Over several decades, the number of vessels doubled. The number of fishermen spread out 37 million strong in four million vessels.

Across the seas, fleets that in 1950 had been harvesting less than 20 million tons a year were from 1990 through today removing 90 million metric tons of seafood—the equivalent weight of a quarter million fully loaded jumbo jets. One of Earth's first global economic enterprise keeps expanding, with fishermen today annually catching trillions of fish. Too many fish, it turns out, and too fast for the ocean to renew and heal itself: the definition of overfishing.

In a bleak global cascade, overfishing has shattered cod populations in the North Atlantic, crashed hake off southern Africa, and depleted reefs throughout Asia Pacific—diminishing the fish populations that had for millennia nourished humans, including Okinawans. In many parts, the overexploitation rate is accelerating; some authorities consider it unstoppable. Too often, overfishing flips formerly rich and complex marine habitats into degraded and simple ecosystems. Across much of the ocean its devastation continues to worsen. Though estimates vary, there is broad consensus that a significant number of the world's fisheries are in dire straits today, and recent analyses suggest that without radical management changes it may within decades be too late for wild healthy seas, and for the billions who depend on them for income and food, to recover.

Facing this uncertainty, some embrace abstinence. Consumers might voluntarily give up seafood; voters might forcibly ban fishing. Yet even those measures ignore whether landlocked sources of protein—via irrigated crops, urban hydroponics, or cellular cultivation—offer improvements. In an all of the above menu to close the looming global food gap, we need landowners to smartly intensify agriculture and fish breeders to expand mariculture. We even need labs to market new forms of artificial meat. It is necessary for coastal communities to work in concert with the wild beneath the waves, stewarding the sea back to its former integrity and productivity. Doing that involves hard individual and collective choices from boat to dock to plate. It means choosing to assign and accept clear responsibility over who, where and how to deploy the fishhook. That powerful tool once enabled our species' past. By redefining our social contract with the sea, the fishhook can once again ensure our future.

No one knows the existential stakes better than hook-wielding fishermen. Yet rather than stop or just ease off their oceanic harvest, these modern hunter-gatherers of the sea have had no choice but to speed it up. Keeping their family fed and sheltered compelled them to pour ever more time, energy and money into eroding the very source of their sustenance. Why? Too often fishermen answer this question with an existential sigh, "If I don't take the last fish, someone else will." They're trapped in a vicious cycle, a dead end in which everyone loses. This behavior is not unique to the sea. Wide open access to any shared natural resource like a meadow, forest, atmosphere, or river basin may encourage self-interest to exhaust or spoil the common pool. This "tragedy of the commons" has locked hungry people on every shore into a widespread systematic race to the bottom, against a ticking clock.

Yet behind so many noisy headlines of ecological catastrophe lies a quieter story of human agency over inertia, and of collaboration over polarization. These examples of responsive and responsible collective action offer new grounds for hope because they give coastal communities skin in the game that results in long-term resource stewardship.

The foundation of the approach is a social contract known broadly as fishing rights, or in the US as catch shares, in which a government sets science-based limits on an overall harvest, then clearly defines for fishermen and fishing communities a secure portion of various living fish populations—either in the form of percentile catch quotas or a share of traditional spatial fishing grounds—in exchange for their adhering to strict accountability. Fishing rights are assigned privileges that can often be purchased, leased or handed down to newcomers or family members, which gives holders enduring value. Well-designed social contracts combine fishing rights, rewards and responsibility so that fishermen are motivated to leave more fish in the water today and plan for a more abundant and valuable harvest tomorrow.

That's the essence. Despite their North American prominence, it is worth emphasizing here that no country or institution can claim to have invented this sustainable approach to fishing. It has countless precedents, some of which date back centuries. Nor are catch shares systems a panacea to be applied everywhere uniformly: a rigid policy hammer in search of nails. To the contrary, the defining characteristic of any social contract with the sea is its iterative and adaptive versatility. Drawing on available levels of science and governance capacity, communities have organized customary access rights, collaborating in a bottom-up process to enforce rules adapted to local contours, scale, and needs.

There is no single correct path. In one developing country, we witnessed codes of conduct emerging over a few months as a fragmented coastal village united over beer and handshakes to reach informal terms of agreement with local law enforcement. In Europe, we've seen licensed attorneys, university scientists, federal economists and trade associations all labor over several years to enshrine formal rights that can withstand legislative, regulatory, or judicial challenges. Coastal communities in Belize, Mexico, Chile, Indonesia, and the Philippines have begun asserting their power and designing their own recovery plans, showing what can be accomplished when unscripted fishermen, buyers, church groups, and waterfront mayors simply refuse to accept failure, and set out to secure a new social contract that stops the downward spiral on their own terms. Each case is unique. But they all shift progress along the spectrum from opaque and open competition toward more deliberate and transparent accountability under limited and rules-based access.

While recognizing the sea change has international dimensions, we've anchored this book in the US, which has so dramatically catalyzed the larger revolution. The legal framework that formalized secure fishing rights was redefined in America. We can even trace its bipartisan political DNA to an unlikely collaboration of two rival Founding Fathers. As national fishing pressure quadrupled while landings remained flat, America's social contracts began to transform some of the world's largest and smallest fisheries, in fresh and salty waters, motivating stewardship by commercial harvesters and for-hire fishing guides alike. Over a relatively short time, since 2000, state and federal alliances have reduced overfishing and rebuilt fifty formerly depleted fish stocks.

America's fishing dominion is vast and diverse. Our Exclusive Economic Zone (EEZ) extends two hundred nautical miles out from a thirteen-thousand-mile-long US coastline, splitting the difference where it bumps into a neighboring country's EEZ. In aggregate the nation's seas spread across nine time zones, from polar sea ice to the warm equator, nearly three and a half million square nautical miles. Those federal waters are larger than the landmass of the fifty states they surround and hold more ocean than any other country. As catch share fishermen rebuilt fifty stocks and recovered hundreds of species, they also measurably brought value to their communities on shore, transforming life and livelihoods from coast to coast to coast.

America's most pivotal and politicized coast runs along the warm Gulf of Mexico. (As noted, names and terminology used throughout this book are accurate to the times and events portrayed.) Each year, more than 1.5 million commercial and recreational fishermen in hundreds of thousands of fishing vessels boats ply those ecologically rich waters. Chasing dozens of species, their harvests rank second only to Alaska in productivity, and their landings have increased fastest in the country. Of all those Gulf fishermen, one of the most brutally successful and contentious figures is the protagonist of our story.

Keith "Buddy" Guindon fishes out of Galveston Island at the southern edge of Texas. For more than thirty-five years, he's unloaded his boats onto the docks along a dead-end strip of asphalt called Wharf Road. It's a place of humid air ripe with fish smells and diesel fumes, the creak of rope, scavenging pelicans and raucous profanity. Since arriving here in the late 1970s he has consistently outmuscled and outfoxed every other fisherman in the western Gulf. And through the first decade of the twenty-first century, he and others had nearly emptied the seas of the very reef fish on which this working waterfront was built.

A barrel of a man with amused eyes, a gruff voice and a Santa

Claus beard, Buddy is a Galveston legend, a hard-working seafood harvesting machine eager to catch more of whatever was out there and keep catching it until it is gone. He once owned a bar, and now owns a seafood market and adjacent restaurant. But for most of his career he and anyone else with a fishing permit have rented access to the federal grouper and red snapper fisheries off Galveston. In the years of wide-open free-for-all, they beat the Gulf like a piñata, competing to extract the most treasure from within it. The upsurge in market demand, combined with Buddy's lethal fish hooks, soon hollowed out supply. Verging on empty, Galveston's restaurants and stores began to resort to the unthinkable—selling farmed fish, often imported from overseas, and passing it off as locally wild caught. Wild seafood like red snapper or grouper had all but vanished from menus and display cases, a reflection of barren waters Buddy and others left in their wake.

Like so many other former fishery-dependent communities in America—Pier 39's salmon, Cannery Row's sardine, Baltimore Harbor's oysters, Fulton Fish Market's cod—Wharf Road risked becoming just another tourist trap, an outdoor museum of a bygone era. While Buddy's dominance of the fishery kept him in the game, other commercial fishermen went under, defeated by the strain of chasing elusive animals around in an increasingly empty sea. As competitors dropped out, Buddy hooked some of the snapper they left behind. Federal fishing regulators stepped in, enacting and enforcing rule after rule. But his *Falcon* found ways to haul in more fish no matter how the laws tried to hobble him. The broken system was worse than a failure. Instead of saving the red snapper, federal rules unintentionally accelerated its crash. At this rate regulators at the start of the twenty-first century would have had to close the fishery, taking Wharf Road—the beating heart of Galveston Island—down with it.

But they didn't. Something happened to reverse the downward spiral, and that something is what runs through the narrative spine of this book. It's an exemplary and infectious tale of how Buddy the destroyer became Buddy the restorer of one of America's most iconic fisheries.

What forces shaped Buddy's journey from anonymity to notoriety, from opposition to advocacy? How did a man who once embodied the very threats to our oceans become their unlikely champion? This book traces Buddy's transformation against the backdrop of a changing America, from the Cold War to the present day. We'll explore how personal struggles intertwine with national policy, as Buddy's story unfolds from the Great Lakes to Galveston, from pumping gas to piloting fishing boats. What drove him to become the hardest working fisherman in the craziest of times? And at what cost?

As catch shares enter the picture, we witness fierce opposition from unexpected allies. What arguments united liberals and conservatives against this new approach? And what ultimately led Buddy to admit he was wrong? The narrative expands beyond Galveston, taking us on a journey through technological innovation, climate change, and environmental catastrophe. How do catch share fisheries absorb unforeseen shocks? What role do they play in mitigating our dependence on fossil fuels? We'll see Buddy emerge as a national figure, forging unlikely alliances and confronting formidable opponents. How does a man who once resented government interference come to demand more accountability? What drives fishermen to welcome "Big Brother" monitoring devices aboard their vessels?

The story doesn't stop at America's border. How does Buddy's example ripple out to impact fisheries in Mexico, Belize, and even Cuba? What lessons does his transformation offer to fishermen around the world, from where America imports 79 percent of its seafood? Ultimately, this book tells a story about trust—lost, and then painfully regained. As Buddy's journey takes him from St. Paul to Tokyo, overcoming challenges both external and internal, what universal truths emerge about our relationship with the sea, with each other, and with our own past?

When archaeologists excavated the fish hooks on Okinawa, they broadened our recognition of human potential and of new possibilities from the sea. They also found other tools, a grindstone, beads, human remains, and evidence of charred fish that had been consumed, all indications that that the limestone cave was over the years seasonally occupied by small bands of people, who collaborated and traded both within and between communities. It's impossible to speculate across 230 centuries, but perhaps social contracts self-organized that early community in which someone chose to shape a hook from a shell and cast it into the unknown.

Back then, the cornerstone of human resilience required secure access to a sea teeming with life. It still does. And if that hook carver in prehistoric Okinawa was one of the world's first ocean fisherfolk, *Sea Change* reveals the hard choices of another one, off Texas, who decided that he damn well wasn't going to be the last.

Part I

PERSONAL

Chapter One
LANDLOCKED ORIGINS

If he packed tonight, Greg Guindon and his firstborn son could back out of their South St. Paul, Minnesota, driveway in the morning while it was pitch black, hurtle a few hours through the darkness, and be out on the water by sunrise. They'd have a lake all to themselves. Quiet bliss. Nothing but father and son on the surface with countless fish below. From an early age Buddy's tight bond with his father grew inseparable from fishing. His first memories are of floating on a nameless lake in the family's sixteen-foot AlumaCraft skiff: strapped into the car seat his dad had bolted into the bow, fists clenched around a fishing pole, eyes fixed on the point where the line vanishes into the water.

His father taught Buddy the quick spin-casting motion and release; how to knot and untangle lines; the need for patience and timing in setting the hook. He showed him where fish fed at the mouth of feeder streams or lurked in the deeper and cooler waters. Buddy learned when to use fluffy jigs, plastic grubs, spinners, spoons, and live minnows or nightcrawlers. By the age of two or three, he claimed, "I was already a fish-aholic. I couldn't get enough."

Father and son pursued every fish worth the effort, and each species left an imprint on Buddy. Rock bass, round and spiny, "had red eyes like the devil." White and black crappies provided nonstop action, especially when congregating to spawn. Big bluegill and other sunfish put up a mean fight. Beyond these fish that could fit in a frying pan, Buddy dreamed night and day of monster walleye and northern pike. In the bigger waters of the Great Lakes he discovered the ways and struggles and taste of perch, chub, lake trout, and lake whitefish. "You name it. If it was swimming in a lake or river, we caught it."

This was not catch and release. "We never let anything go," Buddy said, unless it was too small, and even then, reluctantly. "What we couldn't cook and eat ourselves, we gave to friends and neighbors and clients of my dad." Greg, an insurance salesman, found that sharing fish was both neighborly and good marketing; it helped him retain loyal customers and get new ones through word of mouth.

Buddy recalled fishing with his dad as a magical time of intimacy and security, "Fishing was like my dad's anchor, and I was the one he took along, for whatever the reason. He'd come to wake me at four o'clock in the morning, but I'd already be up and waiting because I didn't ever want to miss out." Buddy sensed that his father, a French Canadian, wasn't happy with his lot and station. At age twenty-three Greg had returned a war hero from service in Korea, awarded two Purple Heart medals for combat. He came home, got married, started a family, but never really settled down. To cover mortgage and groceries he took a job working for his own father's established St. Paul business, Guindon Insurance. But he felt restless, wanting more, and sought opportunities to get away from the daily grind or home stress. For Greg, getting out on the water was an escape from real life. For Buddy, fishing *was* life. "It was never just a sport or passing hobby like it is with most people. I just loved catching, and it didn't matter what kind of fish it was, as long as I could catch a lot of them."

His obsession with racking up numbers led Buddy to use any deadly tool at hand. Mostly that meant a baited hook and line. But sometimes he hunted fish with a bow and arrow or a hurled spear, a modified eight-pronged pitchfork with a barb welded into each point. At the confluence of the Mississippi and Minnesota Rivers, when seasonal heavy rains caused currents to swell, spilling over banks and levees, inundating entire landscapes, Buddy saw a fishing paradise. He would prowl the backwaters and washouts, stalking the pockets of water left behind by receding floodwaters. Wading knee or chest-deep, he'd survey the surface and close in on his quarry.

Buddy couldn't always see the big fish itself, but he saw the wet grasses parting, the water surface roiling at the point of disturbance, and went in for the kill.

That waterscape shaped his early reputation as a grim reaper of the aquatic world. He'd fill up a wheelbarrow with his harvest, push it back through the streets of South St. Paul, and offer fresh fish to neighbors and friends, just as his dad had—a display of his prowess for all the world to see. What fish remained he presented to his mother, Colleen, to cook for their family of seven. "She'd prepare any wild meat I brought home," he says, "as long as I cleaned it. Put it all in a big crock pot and have supper done, whether she was there or not to eat it."

Fish seemed endless in the early 1960s. "Back then," Buddy recalled, "everybody fished, but you mostly stuck to your own lakes. You could find a new place no one had been to, take the boat, drag it down creeks and drift in on private property, get into untouched lakes on big farms and, you know, get in there and whack 'em all day long."

If the action slowed on one exhausted lake, he says, there were (as the Minnesota license plate brags) ten thousand others to choose from. And if Buddy ever ran out of fish in the small lakes, he would always have those vast freshwater oceans just a day's drive north and east: Lake Superior and Lake Michigan. Surrounded by countless lakes filled with fish, Buddy couldn't imagine it possible to ever catch too much.

What he didn't know was that it had already happened: the Great Lakes commercial fisheries had just slid into one of the earliest and most spectacular crashes in North America. Those inland seas became among the first depleted waters on earth and the first to pioneer radical new legal tools and a remedial strategy that would later become central to Buddy's life.

HUMANS MAY HAVE begun pulling fish out of Lake Michigan even as it was still filling up. Unlike ancient oceans, the Great Lakes are geologically young, their fragile ecology evolving with the advance and retreat of two-mile-thick glaciers. They reached their current levels three thousand years ago, long after Paleo-Indians were gathering along the lakeshores. Some of what would become the Ojibwa people figured out how to mine and process copper into fishing gear, "leaf-shaped knives and spear-points, fish hooks, and harpoon points." From birch bark canoes at night they stabbed fish drawn to their torchlight, and in winter speared fish through the ice. Women made lines by stripping and twisting the fiber from nettles and hemp; men wove gill nets with cedar floats inspired, according to legend, by studying the web of a spider. Despite lethal tools and intensive harvesting effort, there is no evidence of overfishing by indigenous tribes. Why? Romantics may assume a noble form of self-restraint; that unlike Europeans, Native Americans had innate respect for wild fish cycles and reverence for the earth, and therefore removed only enough to subsist.

History offered a different thesis. Long before Columbus, tribal people engaged in vigorous and extensive commerce in fish. As late as 1820, observers reported how two native men in a single canoe could net hundreds of whitefish (*adikameg*) each hour, trading the surplus their families could not eat. As the cornerstone of this early commercial network, whitefish provided not only a staple food, but a kind of currency, bartered among and between inland Anishinaabe tribes, including the Ojibwa and Odawa. So, while Natives strived to harvest as much meat as fast as they could to maximize wealth, they ran up against two very real constraints.

The internal barrier was technological. On a vast body of water, there are only so many fish that muscle-powered vessels and homemade gear could catch. The external limit was political. Oral histories document that Indigenous communities feared retaliation for trespassing on a neighboring clan's foraging zones. The boundaries of those zones, and the codes prescribing their use—including exclusive access for the local clan—may not have been written down. But they were well known, clearly defined, and vigorously defended, at least among Native people.

By the 1800s, however, waves of Scandinavians began to overwhelm and displace those native traditions and codes. In Great Lakes fishing harbors names like Anderson, Ellefson, Ellison, Henricksen, Jensen, or Johnson still dominate. Starting two centuries ago their ancestors steadily built up, and then even more swiftly broke down, what were among the world's largest inland commercial fisheries.

EARLY IMMIGRANT GREAT Lakes fishermen faced no restraints. Capital and labor let them harvest as much as they wanted. Demand was booming across a hungry nation. Consumers in industrial cities like Chicago, Milwaukee, and Green Bay would pay top dollar for fresh, salted, cooked or smoked fish. With a few nets, a fisherman in 1900 could annually earn $4,000 (equivalent to $109,000 today). As fishermen climbed the ladder from row boats and muscle to sail power and winches, their landing and profits grew. They grew again with the arrival of steam vessels with the speed and power to go any-where on the lake, in any weather. Steam winches could hoist larger nets holding twice the weight from twice the depth. Steam saws cut enough ice blocks to chill fish during long-distance transport and lengthy storage. Steam railways opened markets from New York to San Francisco, an entire country hungry for native lake trout, yel-low perch, chubs, turbot, lake herring, and emerald shiner. Still the favorite, with its rich and delicate flavor, remained whitefish.

What cod was to New England, whitefish was to the Midwest. Starting in the 1830s, recorded harvests expanded 20 percent each year; by the 1880s, whitefish were central to the way of life in lake-side communities. At the fishery's peak, ten thousand people in 1,200 boats caught 150 million pounds a year, the annual equivalent in weight to a thousand space shuttles. Unlike cod, however, people began early to question whether enclosed lakes could support such massive harvests. On November 10, 1859, the *Green Bay Advocate* mused that "what effect this wholesale slaughter of fish will have on the supply, another season may tell."

By 1871, that musing had turned to alarm: Federal researchers warned about the "diminution of the food fisheries of the lakes," and predicted a crash that would reduce the catch 50 percent over the next two decades. Few fishermen listened. Then, as now, aggressive and savvy fishermen trusted their immediate experience on the water; despite scientific warnings, the best fishermen knew where to find fish, and still managed to fill nets. Each felt that if he could just get out on the water earlier, sail faster, work harder and longer each season, he could dominate rivals to win more of the prize—a classic zero-sum game known as the race for fish. Their individual skills blinded these leaders to overall scarcity. Each felt he could find and catch the last animal, much as someone with a straw can find water even as a puddle evaporates—right up to the last moment. Only when whitefish harvests flattened out did they take part in an urgent, ongoing global debate about the end of food.

IN 1798, THE Reverend Thomas Robert Malthus offered a bleak warning that would haunt the next two centuries. Unbridled "passion between the sexes" would boost human population until it collided with the finite capacity of natural resources to satisfy hunger, he warned, leading to massive die-offs due to famine, disease, war and collapse.

Industrial Age fisheries offered a burgeoning new food source that might test this gloomy hypothesis. In 1882, at London's global Fisheries Exhibition, Thomas H. Huxley assured those worrying that fisheries might be "extirpated by the agency of man" that, in fact, the sea offered "supplies of food of almost unlimited extent." The same spatial area that on land could produce fifty cattle or five hundred sheep a year, he argued, could yield seventeen tons of fish at sea in a single day. He concluded: "the cod fishery, the herring fishery, the pilchard fishery, the mackerel fishery, and probably all the great sea fisheries, are inexhaustible. Nothing we do seriously affects the number of the fish. And any attempt to regulate these fisheries seems consequently, from the nature of the case, to be useless."

The one exception, he warned, were freshwater rivers or lakes that were "shut in" by land. Those, Huxley allowed, could indeed be exhausted by "the destructive agency of man... the chief enemy," and thus merited government regulations and laws.

By the 1950s, the invisible collapse of "shut in" Great Lakes whitefish had become visible, and state officials responded with the kinds of regulations Huxley had recommended. Michigan dictated the type, character and size of mesh nets; required vessel registration; and imposed license fees. Wisconsin closed off sensitive deep waters to fish-trapping pound nets, compressed fishing seasons, restricted gear, and capped landing quantities. The fees paid by fishermen were used to hire inspectors to monitor catches and establish hatcheries to compensate for overfishing.

No fisherman ever felt *he* was the one overfishing. Blame invariably fell on others. It was newcomers; out of state vessels; newly enfranchised Native American tribal fishermen. It was those interloping weekend anglers like Buddy and his dad who drove up from St. Paul. If you simply got rid of *those* strangers and amateurs swarming our fishing grounds, Wisconsin officials routinely heard, there would be plenty of fish left for *us* regulars to harvest. The desire to push out and keep out others has both ancient and universal roots yet runs counter to the American Dream promising free and open access to whatever a rugged individual can claim. At issue was whether commercial fishermen merit exclusive control of the resource, and rights to co-manage it. In 1954, a Midwestern economist argued they did.

Economists tend to ignore a resource until it becomes scarce. When fish were abundant, they fell largely under the domain of natural scientists: experts in ichthyology, marine biology, chemistry, ecology, geology, oceanography and physics studied the life and competitive responses of the aquatic animal in its natural habitat. University of Indiana Professor H. Scott Gordon, by contrast, cared far more about what motivated the *people* who caught them. "On the whole," he pointed out, "biologists treat fishermen as an exogenous element" whose behavior has no place in their models. Gordon went beyond Malthus and Huxley to ask, if wild fish were renewable and theoretically inexhaustible and so valuable to coastal economies, why were fishermen so poor? And why would fishermen destroy the

25

precious assets on which their fortunes depend?

His answer was both simple and controversial. Unlike farms, Gordon observed, there were no "social controls" on access to fishing; unlike hens, roosters, and baby chickens, wild fish propagating in the ocean became a fisherman's valuable property only after he killed them. That motivation drove everything else. A living property that belonged to everybody, he argued, belonged to nobody. The sea's natural "wealth that is free for all is valued by none because he who is foolhardy enough to wait for its proper time of use will find that it has been taken by another." Free open access forced fishermen into a vicious spiral, chasing more of a shrinking supply to collapse and local extinction, first of the species, then of fishing communities who depend on it.

Gordon did not shy from the implications of his reasoning. It meant that even the best intended top-down external measures regulated the wrong thing, trying to control the private energy, technology, and self-interest of Huxley's enemy, human agency, instead of harnessing it to achieve public goals. In short, rather than obsess about fishing inputs, governments can set the desired outcome, then empower fishermen to negotiate with each other how to arrive there in the fairest, cleanest, most profitable way. Otherwise, he noted, human ingenuity would ensure that no matter how strenuously officials tried to restrict efforts, each new rule seemed only to backfire: shrink the lobster season, and people set more traps; cut the halibut season in half, and captains doubled their engine power. That old regulatory approach only encouraged fishermen to outspend each other, incur costs that ate into profit margins, and over-capitalize in ways that further overstretched the fish population. Forced regulatory gluts—the landing of all the fish at once, during the truncated season—lowered prices and earnings at the dock. "This is why fishermen are not wealthy," Gordon wrote, "despite the fact that the fishery resources of the sea are the richest and most indestructible available to man."

Gordon proposed an alternative that would allow fishing communities to earn more money and do so with less work: end competition for living natural resources. If governments quantified the overall catch limit, and limited access to a defined group of fishermen, he argued, the new system could then assign each vessel exclusive access to a defined percentage, or quota, of fish. Far from "radical," Gordon pointed out in 1954, such self-organized, rights-based institutions had long been the norm among traditional and Indigenous fishing communities: "stable primitive cultures appear to have discovered the danger of common property tenure and to have developed measures to protect their resources."

Fourteen years would pass before so-called modern cultures grew unstable or desperate enough to adopt this ancient approach in practice and adapt it under formal state law.

AS GORDON HAD predicted, the pile-up of regulations only accelerated the Great Lakes crash. Whitefish harvests had sunk from tens of millions of pounds at the turn of the century to just forty-nine thousand pounds by the late 1960s, raising the prospect of an outright ban on commercial fishing. Facing escalating tension and with nothing left to lose, Wisconsin leapt first: in 1968 the state's legislature voted to limit state fishing permits, cap the total amount of fish that could be caught, and define secure individual transferable quotas (ITQs) for wild lake trout, chub, perch and whitefish.

The first step for state officials charged with designing that first quota was figuring out who got access: they decided to limit rights to individuals or groups who already held state licenses and had kept fishing logs. "There was no huge arm twisting," said Pete Flaherty, a lawyer for the Wisconsin Department of Natural Resources who helped midwife the transition, "but you had to show you were an active commercial fisherman, lifting nets from the water thirty days a year. That was the bottom threshold, though there were exemptions like a busted boat, or a poverty level income."

The next step was dividing up the fish. After setting aside 10 percent of the fishery as a common property reserve for the public and future stakeholders, regulators assigned the remaining 90 percent to qualifying individuals based on their historic landings. If in the past decade a fisherman had averaged two percent of the white-fish catch, his share would be 2 percent of the future total allow-able catch. That first year, a 2 percent share of forty-nine thousand pounds (about twice the weight of a school bus) meant he could catch just 980 pounds. But if he helped rebuild the fishery all the way back to its peak harvest of twenty-four million pounds, his 2 percent share might translate into 480,000 pounds.

This led to the third piece the state built into the catch share design: transferability. If a fisherman decided that 980 pounds was just not worth the time, fuel, and effort on the water, he could lease or sell it to someone who felt it was, opening a way into the fishery for small boats and new captains. One such new fisherman was Charlie Henriksen, an ambitious young deckhand who had long dreamed of his own business. In the initial round of allocations, he hadn't qual-ified for a share, which was a sore spot. Back then, he recalled, "it was the whole idea of accepting limits on what you could do. You know fishermen—when the fish are there, you want to catch them." But he held his breath and bought in. In hindsight he didn't see any alternative to investment, not if he wanted to remain a professional harvester; and he felt doing so forced a discipline on fishermen that had been missing, a way to make business decisions. But mainly Henriksen had what some fishermen refer to as the curse, a near biological need to be out on the water setting and hauling nets each morning. "You have to feel pretty strong about doing this on the Lake, day after day," he said, sipping coffee and looking out from the wheelhouse, "not just to enter the fishery but to stay in, make it work out for you and your family. It really has to come from inside."

The transition to that original catch share system on the Great Lakes—Lake Superior first, then Lake Michigan—wasn't smooth, neat, or pretty. A smaller fleet of fifty-six vessels soon adjusted to the lower catches of renewable fish the Lake could support. Nailing down consensus over who got how many shares required marathon late night negotiations. The anxiety of decisions regretted can still be heard in the voices of men who sold their share in the fishery and now wished they hadn't (though re-entering the fishery is possible as long as there are fish to catch).

"It wasn't flawless," said Flaherty, looking back. "But it did what we set out to do, what we designed it for."

In some ways it has done more, building resilience in the face of new miseries. Four decades later, despite growing and unforeseen shocks to the fishery—habitat lost to development, rivers flushing in pollutants and setting off algal blooms, invasive sea lamprey, round goby, zebra mussel and quagga mussel, acid rain, and unregulated harvests by tens of thousands of recreational anglers—those first catch share fisheries continue to yield. Commercial harvest of lake trout and chub had doubled. Whitefish harvests, while still not back to nineteenth century levels, managed to recover more than thirtyfold since 1968 to 1.6 million pounds. Whitefish have recently shown up in Wisconsin rivers where they haven't been seen in a century, sometimes even eating those invasive fish and mussel species. "What we're seeing with the whitefish," said Henriksen, "they might be the most adaptable fish in nature. They're more adaptable than some people I know."

Out on the water one morning Henriksen and his crew lifted the vessel's trap nets and hauled in 3,500 pounds whitefish, rising dividends on an appreciating asset that Charlie can pass on to his grown son, Will—who was right there fishing alongside him, ready to take the helm and enjoy a long and profitable future in the fishery.

WHILE LIVING NEARBY, Buddy had no awareness of the fishing revolution launched on the Lakes. He simply wanted to keep fishing with his dad and bring home the bounty to his mother. Though she was tiny, Colleen Guindon dominated her kitchen and ran her home with the kind of ferocious discipline her son feared as a child and later emulated as a captain. "She always had a wooden spoon nearby," Buddy recalled, "and she used that wooden spoon to keep things under control. She was only four foot eight, but a very, very strong-willed woman. Pure Irish. I didn't get out of line with my mom, let's put it that way."

The family was boisterous and tight knit right up until the day it unraveled. It was 1968. Buddy was thirteen years old. His younger sister Kim was celebrating her birthday. And his father decided the time had come to leave. "He didn't pick that day to torture her," Buddy recalls, "He just had a ride heading south. He didn't tell me any of the reasons why. But they split up, and he went away, and I didn't see him again for a long time."

Buddy's gruff voice softens as he recounts that day. "It was a big emotional fucking ordeal. It was devastating for me. Just as it is with any kid. We had a relationship built on fishing, and then that was over."

Chapter Two

COLD WAR EXCLUSION

The void left by his father's departure fell to Buddy to fill. Colleen Guindon struggled just to cook for and clean up after her six "K" children, Keith (Buddy), Kimberly, Kristie, Karen, Kenny, and Kathleen, each with their own needs and demands. They shared a small house, the three girls all packed into one bedroom, the brothers in another. Overnight, fourteen-year-old Buddy became the man of the house, taking whatever work he could find after school to support his mom and siblings. He drove furniture delivery trucks though he didn't yet have a driver's license, slogged away in the tanning factory that processed hundreds of hides each day. "It was a horrible job that smelled like death, all those slaughtered cows, horses, and donkeys," Buddy said. "Still, it paid ten dollars an hour."

Now and then he might carve out a few hours to go fishing with friends, sometimes even bringing along his little brother. But it never again felt the same as those mornings with dad. And tough as his mom was, without a male authority figure, Buddy began to run wild. He discovered the joys of girls and drinking and—the inevitable outcome of mixing both—fighting. He remained close and devoted to his family, but also felt constrained, perhaps as his father had, from figuring out his own fate. By the time he graduated from high school, the Marine Corps looked like an easy escape. "It was the peak of the Cold War," he recalled, "and the Vietnam conflict was still going strong, and so I thought, 'Hell, that's what I should do.'" Sent to train at Camp Pendleton, on the Pacific coast north of San Diego and the Mexican border, Buddy did not fish for the duration of his enlisted service. Instead, he learned to box, which channeled his anger and competitive hunger and gave him an identity, apart from his family, that was all his own. "That's what they teach you to do in the Marine Corps, to fight. Fight with your hands, your feet, your rifle."

As Buddy shipped off to the Pacific, the US government was struggling with Soviet encroachment closer to home: off the coasts of Oregon, Washington and Alaska. Year after year, the vast and commercially lucrative fish in those Pacific Northwest waters were being scooped up by Soviet vessels—until America stepped up to claim them exclusively for itself. It wasn't just the US, of course; as fish grew scarce other nations also engaged in the practice of extending their borders hundreds of miles out to sea, laying a crucial staging ground for the next phase of the catch shares revolution.

ON 19 SEPTEMBER 1966, the ninety-three-foot wooden-hulled research vessel *John N. Cobb* was throttling three miles off Cape Elizabeth, on the coast of Washington, when its chief scientist Charles R. "Bob" Hitz witnessed at close range the foreign occupation of what were still not yet defined as America's waters. Awakened when the engine gears abruptly shifted into neutral and the boat started drifting, Hitz climbed out of his bunk, stepped onto the bridge and gazed out at the calm, glassy sea. What he saw shocked him: fifty ships, some of them the length of a football field, were trawling up and processing hake, also known as Pacific whiting, on a scale and in a place that he would describe as ominous, and even rather sinister.

To the east was the coast of Washington State, with the Olympic Mountains in the background and the sun starting to show above the horizon, reflecting off the ocean. Everywhere else there were ships, a huge fleet of Russian ships and as the sun rose the red hammer and sickle on the stacks seemed to glow from the reflection. It was a Russian city as close as three miles off the coast of Washington, unbelievable during the Cold War.

There had been rumors of such a fleet, but Hitz's eyewitness account, when relayed to Washington, helped catalyze the politics that would transform commercial fishing in the US. Hitz's description made its way to the desks of two powerful Senators: Warren G. Magnuson, a liberal New Deal Democrat from Washington, and Ted Stevens, a conservative Republican from Alaska. Up to then, the two had little in common and rarely collaborated on legislation. But both were World War II veterans who, after fighting in the Pacific theater to turn back fascism, now supported the policy of containment of the Soviet Union. Both felt outrage over the extent of these subsidized fleets cruising the continental shelf from the Bering Sea down past the Columbia River, in plain view of both their states, sucking up tons of valuable fish. America's fish. Fish, the Senators agreed, that should be harvested by voting constituents, not foreign communists. "Fisheries are one of the major battlefields in the Cold War," wrote Magnuson in an angry and widely circulated pamphlet that raised alarm along both coasts. The "prowling and ravenous fishing fleet" under Soviet (as well as Japanese and Spanish distant water fleets) control, he argued, was putting the nation's fish at risk.

However, those fish weren't the nation's fish. At least not yet.

For its first two centuries of existence, America's control of its waters extended just three to nine miles off its shores, shallow waters and saltwater tidelands that belonged to each coastal state. Beyond this demarcation was a no-man's-sea, in a state of anarchy, open to plunder by vessels from anywhere in the world.

Magnuson and Stevens set in motion a governance system that would change all that. They drafted legislation that would secure a far more expansive area by claiming, nationalizing and governing what would now be regarded as America's federal waters. Joined in the House by Alaska's (Republican) Don Young and Massachusetts' (Democrat) Gerry Studds, the Senators pushed for fishery conservation zones, or what nine years later under President Reagan became known as the US Exclusive Economic Zone (EEZ). It is hard to overstate the ambition and ultimate significance of these political efforts. Unless they're about the EEZs of another nation like Cuba, the US waters would extend two hundred nautical miles from the "territorial sea baseline," reaching not only off the continent's coasts but also off the nation's island states and territories: from Puerto

Rico and the US Virgin Islands in the Atlantic to the Marianas and Hawaiian Islands in the Pacific. Within those waters, the US asserted sovereign rights "for the purpose of exploring, exploiting, conserving and managing natural resources," both nonliving oil and minerals and living marine fisheries. The legislation also established governance to manage this vast jurisdiction: federal policy decided by eight regional fisheries management councils, composed of diverse representatives from each state in the region.

In 1976, Congress passed the Magnuson-Stevens Fishery Conservation and Management Act (aka Magnuson-Stevens, or MSA). Today people lump MSA in with that era's raft of progressive environmental laws, since it now includes amendments to stop overfishing and rebuild depleted fish stocks. But in the Cold War, the driving motivations were largely about commerce and geo-politics. Logistically, that brought a challenge of claiming, occupying, patrolling and defending 3.4 million square nautical miles, the world's largest slice of ocean. The prospect of having to board and expel foreign fleets raised the ever-present odds of conflict. "Enforcement of fisheries policy is a complex undertaking," wrote retired US Coast Guard Captain Jeffrey D. Hartman. "There is always the concern of impacting international relations. Back in the days when the Cold War was hot in Alaska, this could get interesting."

The law also opened a rift among America's Cold War architects with global repercussions. Some US leaders feared MSA might subordinate foreign policy to the demands of domestic fisheries. The State Department favored free trade and open seas, so MSA smacked of protectionism. The Defense Department sought to preserve America's ability to sail anywhere, wrote historian Carmel Finley, "unimpeded by regulations as seemingly far-fetched as where a boat could fish." If America kicked foreign fleets out of US waters, the Pentagon worried, other nations might reciprocate on the same grounds. Sure enough, by 1982 every country demanded its own 200-mile jurisdiction under the United Nations Convention on the Law of the Sea, an international treaty that the US is not formally party to but adopts for its own use.

A third practical challenge was economics. Even after passage of the 1976 law, the US North Pacific remained occupied by Japanese and Soviet interests. Those foreign fleets had over the years established dominant, vertically integrated seafood supply chains that linked hook and net to dock and supermarket. American vessels and processors lacked the capacity to take this over immediately so, to avoid supply disruptions, MSA allowed for a phase-out period. From 1978 to 1990, Soviet and Japanese ships could sell fish up the chain but had to buy it from American fishermen, who were quickly learning to catch, sell, and process themselves. Under these "joint venture fisheries" scrappy and ambitious US fleets began to take over more of the fishing role. At roughly that time, Buddy completed his tour of military duty in Asia and started looking around for what to do next.

IN THE US Marine Corps, Third Division, Buddy had been deployed from Camp Pendleton to Japan, Philippines, and Korea aboard the *USS Blue Ridge*. During his second year, while off in Vietnam, he played a small role as courier in the evacuation of the United States Embassy in Saigon. Buddy didn't share much about his time abroad, other than to describe those years as an adventure. "It was fun," he recalled, "It was a different world, a new experience, and it got me out of Minnesota to see the world." In 1977, Buddy was preparing to re-enlist for another round, but his company gunnery sergeant urged him to get the hell out. Buddy had grown too violent, too hard-living and rough even for the "Fightin' Third Division" of the Marines to handle. "You stay with us any longer," his sergeant warned him, "and you'll find yourself convicted and locked up in the slammer." Instead, he was honorably discharged and put on a plane back to the States.

Chapter Three
PARTING THE (SALT)WATERS

Buddy returned in the winter of 1978 to a more confused and divided country than the one he had left four years earlier. Vietnam, Watergate, spiking gas prices, Jim Jones, bell bottoms, long hair, the Bee Gees: he couldn't make sense of it. To make matters worse, Buddy discovered that his own family had moved on, with little space or need for him.

His mom, Colleen, had found a career running a nursing home, levering her little four-foot-eight-inch frame to lift old men without a fuss and keeping orderlies on the move. Buddy's four sisters were making their own decisions without looking to him for advice or approval. His brother Kenny had left Minnesota for Austin, Texas, where he had just enlisted with the US Air Force. As winter came, Buddy found precious little consistency between his old and new life in St. Paul.

He did have one familiar comfort: ice fishing. After years in Asia, and not a single chance to fish, Buddy welcomed the winter cold and winds whipping across the lake. When temperatures dropped, he'd round up a few old buddies, drag a hut out onto the frozen lake, fire up a propane heater to keep warm, carve out a thick hole in the ice, drop in a line and yank out pan-size fish hour after hour. "The best thing about it," he recalled, "is that you don't need extra ice to keep your beer cold. Just set it out there beside you."

Another familiar comfort was fast food. Among the first things Buddy did back on American soil was head to McDonald's to order his favorite sandwich, a Filet-o-Fish promoted by the chain's imaginary pirate character, Captain Crook. "I didn't then and still don't know what they put in it," he said decades later, which for a fisherman and owner of a fish market is quite a confession. "But it's a great-tasting, flaky, flavor-filled fried fish. And it's good."

In fact, the filet sold by McDonald's in the US comes from one of the world's most harvested fisheries, one that would have an early, indirect yet profound impact on Buddy's own future. Harvested in Alaskan waters, this mild white fish called pollock had been one of the prime drivers bringing Magnuson and Stevens together to expel Soviet and Japanese fleets. But it had also then opened deep domestic divisions—eventually pitting the two senators' constituents against each other as vessels from Washington and Alaska raced to compete for ever-shrinking numbers of this most versatile of fish. That fight and its resolution, would lay the next critical step in the reform of fisheries management and set federal policy on a course that Buddy would oppose and then, eventually, lead himself.

SIX YEARS AFTER, Ray Croc launched McDonald's out of Des Plaines, Illinois, his venture hit a snag. It was 1961, and Lou Groen, a franchisee in Cincinnati, Ohio, endured weekly and annual sales slumps as Catholic customers avoided meat on Fridays or Lent. Groen offered an inspired solution: the Filet-O-Fish sandwich, "the fish that catches people." Kroc hated the idea. He didn't want his "stores stunk up with the smell of fish." But Groen persisted, and in what may have been the first and only fast food cook-off contest, crushed Kroc's proposed alternative among customer demand and went on to win fame, fortune, and forty-three more franchises. Today, McDonald's restaurants in one hundred countries offer Filet-O-Fish sandwiches (with 279 million sold annually in the US alone), and demand still peaks during Lent.

McDonald's initially tried halibut, Atlantic cod, red cod and New Zealand hoki. But one by one, each of those fisheries got played out: declining in catch, losing economic viability and curtailed under regulatory sanctions. Even farmed fish proved undesirable and unreliable. The company needed a high-volume wild marine fishery, consistently harvested, cleanly landed, and efficiently handled in a global supply chain resilient to unexpected disruptions. It was a tall order, but in 1975 they found the species they were looking for. And by 2013 it became the only fish the US franchise would serve. The Alaska walleye pollock leads a dreadful but exciting life. It grows fast and dies young, but in between enjoys wild oceanic orgies. Though far from charismatic, what this humble species lacks in individual glamor it makes up for in aggregated volume. In late winter and early spring pollock mate in massive spawning aggregations in the southeastern Bering Sea. When summer storms stir an upwelling of plant nutrients, those hatchlings thrive; upon maturing, they migrate seasonally toward their polar feeding grounds, filling the water from just below the surface to 1,600 feet deep. Against the sandy sea floor, a juvenile pollock's speckled back helps conceal it from bigger and faster predators: cod, salmon, and sablefish; seabirds including murres, shearwater and Fulmar; sea lion, and orcas. But camouflage couldn't hide it from people.

Each year humans on two continents haul three and a half million tons of pollock from the sea. Beyond fast food sandwiches, pollock is the main source of supermarket fish sticks, valuable roe and the shredded surimi that goes into imitation crab. It is the source of most fish oil and of the meal used to feed farmed fish and other livestock raised as food. Once McDonald's began serving it, pollock grew into the world's largest fishery for human food and became America's most lucrative harvest, worth more than a billion dollars a year. But before that could happen, rival fishing vessel associations, led by the likes of Bob Dooley or Jim Gilmore, would first have to stop fishing it to the point of near collapse.

BY 1991, WITH the Soviet Union dissolving, the joint ventures phase had ended in the North Pacific; every aspect of pollock fishing was now 100 percent under the United States. But in bulking up to take over, America's pollock harvesting fleet overshot the mark, becoming twice as big as the fishery could bear: a top-heavy condition known as "overcapitalized." All that excess fishing capacity, explained University of Alaska fisheries economist Keith R. Criddle, brought on the cycle of shorter seasons, wasteful discards, and financial instability for the owners who couldn't earn enough to pay off loans. With catch dwindling and seasons shrinking, fishermen found themselves trapped in increasingly expensive and sloppy battles for fish, waged with vast trawl nets, enormous engines, and pricey lawyers filing lawsuits and lobbying Congress: "the pollock wars."

On one side were guys like Bob Dooley. A big guy with a soft voice, Dooley talks with his hands and his hands speak of fish. From the time he was a boy, living on California's Half Moon Bay, fish have been his family's life. For thirty-eight years his mom ran a seafood restaurant; his dad was a commercial fisherman; his uncle owned a charter boat fishing business. In his twenties, lured by the pollock gold rush, Dooley set out to the North Pacific to make it big. By his thirties he and his brother John owned the 149-foot *Pacific Prince* and 106-foot *Caitlin Ann*. Along with eighty other "catcher-boats" trawling in the Bering Sea, the Dooleys delivered a third of the annual pollock harvest to Alaska's ports.

Pitted against Dooley were sixteen much larger, Seattle-based "catcher-processor trawlers" dragging miles-long nets to haul in the rest of the annual catch. On those boats, fish were dumped into onboard machines that can behead, gut, and scale two and a half fish per second; other machines filet and stack nine hundred fish per minute. Even those ships were dwarfed by three gargantuan "motherships" that process without catching, manned by 140 people including ninety who work below-decks in shifts round the clock.

On top of that came an influx of new fishermen and processors. Soon, all sides were capturing too many pollock too fast. From a 1974 peak of nearly two million tons of pollock harvested by foreign vessels, Alaska's pollock catch had by 1991 fallen to just 1.25 million tons. At-sea processors began to fear for their future. Half the catcher-processors went bankrupt, selling off their boats. The Dooley brothers barely stayed afloat. The reduction in boats failed to relieve fishing pressure. So did political restraints. Predictably, after fishery managers decided to cut the season in half, the remaining vessels just doubled their efforts.

By 1996, federal officials blocked new entrants into the fishery. While that limited the increase, it did nothing to slow down the frenzy of all those men and machines already chewing up the sea. Finally, in 1998, the Alaska and Washington Congressional delegations came together again, to broker a truce and rationalize the fishery. The political compromise they hammered out became known as the "The Bering Sea Pollock Conservation Cooperative American Fisheries Act Program," or AFA.

The AFA divided the pollock harvest into four groups—the catcher/processors, the motherships, Dooley's inshore catcher boats, and native Alaskan coastal tribes. Partition into these sectors was designed to protect consumers, workers, and vulnerable people. The bigger vessels, more efficient in use of time, fuel, labor and capital, kept fish products including the Filet-O-Fish affordable. They'd built, claimed Jim Gilmore, the public affairs director of the Seattle-based At-Sea Processors Association: "a better mousetrap." Meanwhile Dooley's smaller boats, delivering to onshore processors, sustained local jobs and communities. And Indigenous tribes gained new levels of security through their "Community Development Quota."

Once the fish had been allocated, fishermen within each sector were then given a share of that catch, their individual quota: the law allowed them to buy or sell that quota to others within their sector, and to set up markets for voluntary quota transfers between sectors.

Granting secure shares of a fishery to a small number of companies raised questions about natural or benevolent monopolies. More than a century earlier, Congress had passed the 1890 Sherman Anti-Trust Act so that regulators could keep business activities competitive and investigate and pursue trusts that weren't. The American Fisheries Act avoided any risks of price-fixing or corporate collusion by forbidding fishermen to coordinate their processing, marketing, or sales activities. Vessels among Dooley's co-ops, Gilmore's association, and native tribes would no longer fight each other over the supply *of* living pollock. But they would continue to compete fiercely over the market demand *for* pollock once caught.

Both catcher boats and at-sea processors were initially hesitant and suspicious. "At first we were going, well, I don't know if this is going to work'," said Dooley. "It was pretty tough. It was fear of the unknown. We didn't know what to expect. We didn't know how the quotas were going to work." Soon enough, though, they figured out how to compete in ways that transformed Alaska's waters into America's new frontier for transferable fishing rights—between vessels and among sectors—within America's federal waters. Where the old, truncated seasons had long forced a frenetic race for fish in ways that ruined habitat, fish, jobs and people, the pollock fleets now deliberately slowed to a crawl. Each shareholder could set a unique and more unhurried pace to catch his quota. Vessels dropped trawl nets into the sea less often and more selectively, with fewer "tows" per day. Waste from having to throw back both regulatory discards (fish that are marketable but illegal to keep) and accidental bycatch (species with no market value) plummeted. Fishermen began to insist on and provide credible data, sharing information on how much they caught where and at what time just as soon as it was available.

As the fishery stabilized, so did the market. Catcher boat owners like Dooley gained new bargaining power with buyers on shore. Instead of all the fish coming in at once and deflating prices, he could now negotiate when and how much and at what price a processor would buy and get a share of the revenue in advance. "We worked with our processor cooperatively," he said, "learned about what it took to bring better fish to the plant—not just any fish, but what the plant needed." When processors asked for roe fish during certain times of year, or larger fish when the market prized filets, Dooley could deliver. As shareholders sought to squeeze maximum value out of each ounce of flesh, vessels and processors also diversified uses: selling not only whole fish, filets, fish sticks, surimi and fishmeal but also pollock mince, heads and guts, roe sacs, stomachs and bladders. "All that had been lost before," said Dooley, "but now we can time our work, and fishing, and direction, and effort to make every little bit count."

On Gilmore's side, slower fishing in the water meant slower processing inside. Trawl captains not only eased back the throttle, but they also began answering managers below deck, deferring fishing decisions about pace to the factory. "Back in the race-for-fish-days," explained Gilmore, "the guy who read the Fishfinder won by plugging the hold with as much fish as they could to process as fast as they could. And that led to a lot of waste getting dumped over the side rather than slowing things down."

Waste was another word for dead fish, fish that could have been sold (thus hurting the industry), eaten (thus depriving hungry populations), or left to spawn and generate new life (thus depriving a healthy, resilient ocean). But after the formation of the cooperatives, with a fixed cap on volume, the whole fishing process was paced to extract maximum value of the final product. By handling the fish more carefully, keeping them on-board no more than an optimal three hours before going into the machine, bringing them to market year-round rather than in a flood a few months a year, and marketing every bit of the fish they caught from nose to tail, fishermen saw pollock prices double from $200 per ton to $400.

Guts were now carefully segmented, packaged, labeled and prepared for shipping out to a booming Asian market: roe sacs, favored in Japan; stomachs, a delicacy in Korea; gallbladder, to China; fish meal, to aquaculture and farms. As part of 100 percent utilization, even the fish oil was used to power the on-board fish processing machines. "For us, we can follow the fish where they lead us, and take the plant to them," said Gilmore. He described the new care and concern by fishermen. They now discussed optimal ocean temperatures for seasonal harvests. They fretted over the pH balance of the sea's chemistry. They followed nutrient cycles, found ways to avoid harming marine birds and mammals, and anticipated the seasonal break up of sea ice. "It all almost sounds like we're involved in winemaking," he laughed. "But rather than production, we really have started to think of the fishery in terms of resource husbandry."

Alaska pollock was not just the first federal fishery in a catch share; it was also the world's single largest harvested source of seafood eaten by humans. So, the stakes of getting it right were high. After ten thousand years of humans not even bothering to catch this fast swimmer, followed by a four-decade onslaught that pushed pollock to collapse, government officials and private industry had finally found a way to come together and pull back from the brink. They haggled bitterly over initial share allocations, since each fisherman had initially to accept a right to harvest fewer fish under catch shares than under open access. Yet as they began to negotiate under a stable and predictable system, fishermen quickly realized potential gains from quota trades. "You can't play a quality game if everyone else is doing quantity," said Dooley. "But once you mandate the amount of fish each of us gets, then you know it's not how many pounds but how much value you can extract from that fish that matters."

THE POLLOCK FISHERY was a world away from Buddy's immediate reality, home from the war. He ate his Filet-O-Fish sandwiches, caring not one whit about where it came from or how it was caught. And he went ice fishing not to extract economic value out of the walleye, but to enjoy the chase; whack as many as he could, and bring home meat for the family crock pot, even if there wasn't much of a family left to eat it. Still, as he sat out there in a hut on a frozen lake, drinking beer with his friends and waiting for a bite, he often recalled his last time out fishing with his dad—not there in Minnesota but down where his father had landed in Galveston, Texas, on the Gulf of Mexico.

Eight years earlier, when he got the invitation to visit, Buddy had hesitated. It was a long way away. He'd missed his dad terribly. He also resented the hell out of him for ditching them all without explanation. But ultimately, he could no longer resist his dad's promises that they'd catch fish like he'd never seen. Arriving in Texas after twenty-eight lonely hours on a Greyhound, he'd barely climbed down from the bus when his dad piled him into a borrowed boat and took him out on the Gulf. A new universe yawned open. Compared to his little Minnesota lakes, those seas felt endless to

Buddy. The warm, salty bath was a far cry from the frigid waters he was used to. And the animals he hooked—red snapper—bent the rod 180 degrees after he set the hook.

The old father-son fishing magic pulled Buddy in, but there was something else he discovered. A bonus. After a day on the water reeling in big crimson twenty-pounders, Buddy watched as his father lifted their catch out of the ice chest, wrapped newspaper around the massive fish with their still glimmering scales, and walked into the kitchen of Phil's Restaurant, just near the docks. When he came out, he had another piece of newspaper, this time wrapped around a wad of dollar bills. It was a stunning revelation: you could earn cash by doing exactly what you love most. "That was incredible to me, and hit me like lightning," he said. "Turn fishing into money? I couldn't believe it. You can get paid for this shit? It seemed too good to be true."

Now up in Minnesota, shivering through a day of ice fishing, that old memory lingered in the back of his mind. It haunted him, pulled him in two directions. Sure, it felt good to be home from Vietnam, wearing civilian clothes, seeing old friends and family. But restlessness had also returned. He was running out of money. He needed a job. And while his body was living, eating, drinking and sleeping in Minnesota, his dreams kept wandering 1,300 miles further south.

Then one night, the phone rang. It was his father, who he hadn't seen since that fishing trip, calling long distance from Galveston. Things were really shaking down there on the Gulf, the salesman told his son, lots happening all at once. He operated a supply boat. He had a bait camp. Now he'd just bought an Exxon gas station and couldn't keep up with the brisk trade. Would Buddy come to help him run it, the two of them, side by side?

Part II

LOCAL

Chapter Four
BECOMING THE HIGHLINER

Buddy was no longer a kid. He could more than hold his own against any adult male, including his father. He could tell his dad no, stay near his mom and sisters. He sure didn't owe Greg Guindon anything. There was no point in overanalyzing but maybe he had something to prove, or still longed for some way to heal, to reconnect. In any case, he needed cash, and that memory of fishing red snapper in the Gulf kept working away on him. So, after some of the usual tense banter that seemed the only kind of conversation he and his dad could have, Buddy agreed to help out. He packed up what few clothes he owned and headed to Galveston, Texas, to seek his fortune.

Some father-son enterprises blossom and thrive, passing the torch of responsibility from one generation to the next. Pumping gas was not, at least for the Guindons, one of them. "I love my dad," said Buddy, "but he was a very difficult and demanding person to work with." It wasn't long before Greg began taking off for weeks on end, leaving his son to run the station. Even so, he refused Buddy an ownership stake in the venture. "We do better together when duck hunting or fishing," Buddy concluded. "Something that doesn't have a master-slave relationship."

Being left to his own devices taught Buddy how to run a business. He learned how to keep accounts of invoices and inventory, interact with customers, deal with inspections, oversee staff, and repair engines. At the time, it all felt like a distraction from what had really lured him to Galveston. His father's true legacy, instilled in those long-ago mornings on misty lakes in Minnesota, was waiting for him just offshore. He would earn enough money, he calculated, to make a life chasing those big fish in that big sea. Of course, doing so would require a big boat, meaning that he had to find other ways to make bank.

A door opened six months after his arrival. The owner of a nearby dive bar, called Streater's Place, had gotten underwater with creditors and asked Greg Guindon if he might want to buy the place. Greg wanted nothing to do with it, but Buddy did. A few days later, he walked into the bar and haggled down the price to just $2,000 cash, plus assumption of outstanding debts. It was a gamble but Buddy figured he could live in the bar, never leave work, and use his savings and his own hands to fix the place up and secure a liquor license under his own name. Other than groceries, he'd have no expenses, not even the beer bill that had been his biggest outlay. "I drank for free," he said. "It was not good for me, but that's how you end up with your own bar."

Streater's was the kind of place with a wall celebrating the annual cockroach race. While never fancy, Buddy kept it lively, attracting customers whose conversations opened his world further still. Working the bar, Buddy overheard marine biology students from Texas A&M talking about how the ocean was going to hell, with fish populations declining. He overheard businessmen discuss the pros and cons of various investment opportunities. He overheard women assessing the guys who were hitting on them. When the opportunity arose, he approached the prettiest of those women and asked her out on a date. Most laughed, some fled. One just smiled, stuck around while getting to know him better, and eventually took him up on it.

Her name was Katie Nesbitt, a Texan so bursting with youth and energy that Buddy was surprised to learn that she had two grade-school sons—Nick and Ricky—by a previous marriage. He was captivated and nervous; not intimidated by her poise, which attracted him, but still cautious. Buddy was used to getting turned down, and had his heart broken a few times. It was easy for him to joke with women, but hard for him to trust. Less than a year earlier he'd come off a long-term love affair with a woman he'd imagined settling down with and raising kids, until he discovered she'd been involved for much of it with another guy. Katie felt different. Just her presence in the bar calmed him, as much as anyone could. So, one night he told his new five-foot-tall, big-eyed, dark-haired friend that he wanted to take her out somewhere classy, only he had nothing to wear but his usual old t-shirts. When she showed up and gave him a nice new shirt with a collar and buttons, he took that as a good sign.

Trouble was, he wasn't the only guy with eyes for Katie, and Streater's brought out the belligerent side of men. Buddy never worried about keeping order in his own bar; he doubled as the bouncer, breaking up disputes with relish. A sign above the bar read: "If you fight, you fight me."

His reputation spread, drawing brawlers from afar, and that night of his first date with Katie an ox of a man called "Limousine Johnny" decided to test his mettle. Johnny drank enough to hit on Katie, then started taunting the guy who'd already won her over and was wearing her shirt. "Reached across the bar and slapped me," Buddy recalled, chuckling. Katie, who herself managed a bar and restaurant at the Ramada Inn and had dealt with her own share of quarrelsome drunks, rose to Buddy's defense, stretching up her full five-foot frame to shield all 250 pounds of him. He didn't need the help, but in her presence felt unusually calm. He asked a few friends to distract Katie in conversation and then, in a relaxed voice, told the big man to get out of the bar before someone got hurt. Johnny refused. He would only leave, he bellowed, if it was to step out back with Buddy.

Once outside, with Buddy's brother watching from the door, Buddy played Limousine Johnny like a matador plays a bull, stepping quickly aside as the big man lunged, turned, grew winded, and made a fatal mistake: he grabbed and ripped a tear in that cherished new shirt. Years later, Limousine Johnny was still boasting of the night he'd been knocked out cold by the famous Buddy Guindon. "I've always loved to fight," Buddy acknowledged, swinging a clenched fist in a slow-motion roundhouse. "Whether in the military, or behind the bar, or on the dock; I never fought for no good reason, but I never shied away. And I'm good at it, too. I'm a beautiful fighter."

KNOWING BEFORE AND after that first date exactly what she was getting herself into, Katie stuck around. And the more time she and her sons spent with Buddy, the more his combativeness seemed to subside. She never met a man, she says, who was more driven, more of a workhorse. And she accepted that—as part of the package deal—he'd always have an equally wild and aggressive side. "Buddy's going to go out and do what he has to," she said one afternoon in her living room, her voice even, without a trace of a sigh or self-pity. "And there's only so much I can change, or even want to change. I've learned to trust his instincts and how to choose my battles."

Married June 30, 1990, Katie patiently set about redirecting Buddy's fighting spirit against the more worthy adversary he'd dreamed of: the sea. He'd already laid out the cash to buy a fishing permit. But those were lean years. Unable to afford a car he had to commute back and forth from bar to dock on a bicycle. Once there, he had only enough time and his own small skiff to get a few miles out into the Gulf, not into the deep waters and offshore reefs where he knew the biggest and most abundant fish congregated. Even shallow waters were open to him only under calm seas. The boats he could borrow or rent were small, narrow, cheap, and unstable—the kind that capsize quickly when a squall whips up out of nowhere. Galveston had been transformed by legendary storms, especially the catastrophic hurricane—documented by Erik Larson in *Isaac's Storm*—that on September 8, 1900, arose from the Gulf over a matter of hours, leveled the entire town and killed over six thousand people. To afford a boat that could handle even ordinary storms he did what he could in his spare hours: fishing like a madman close to shore and selling whatever snapper he caught at any price he could get. It never amounted to enough. Up to the late 1980s, unrestricted access to any and all who wanted to be a fisherman made for a perpetual buyer's market, keeping fish prices flat and low.

Then things got worse.

NORTHERN RED SNAPPER is an iconic animal. A large reef fish species native to the Gulf of Mexico—it has a sloping forehead, compact body, and large pinkish-red scales. It lives long, matures late and congregates in social clusters so that catching one usually means catching more. Its nut-flavored flesh makes it a favorite at Texas supermarkets, restaurants and backyard barbecues. Too popular for its own good, red snapper cascaded from the 1960s through 1980s into steep decline: from 1981 to 1987 alone, landings had shrunk from 16.9 million to 5.1 million pounds. More troubling was how red snapper's naturally high reproductive capacity was also cratering. Some can live one hundred years, and the older they get, the more fertile. Huge red snapper "sows" in their prime—ten to fifty years old—spawn thirty-three times more prodigiously than three-year-olds. Still, those Big Old Fat and Fertile (or Fecund) Female Fish (BOFFFFs) are also, by sheer virtue of their weight, the most valuable at market, worth more to fishermen like Buddy as that day's meat than as potential mothers of future harvests.

Fish in national waters are—like America's rivers, air, parks and wildlife—owned by every American, a public resource that required federal management and protection. After turning a blind eye for years to the snapper's decline, regulators at the National Marine Fisheries Service and its regional Gulf Council finally felt enough pressure from the public and environmental groups to do something, *anything*, to bring back snapper. So, with the best of intentions of overseeing a politically charged resource, they began to experiment.

First, they dispatched scientists to assess the situation offshore. To estimate the amount of red snapper still swimming and spawning, fish biologists collected randomized samples. They looked at gender ratios and fertility rates. From ear bones, which revealed age from growth, they found patterns of distribution among old and young fish. By 1990, a series of these stock assessments had laid bare how several decades of overfishing had not only pounded snapper numbers overall but had also slashed spawning potential—that complex but critical metric of fertility over time—from 45 percent in 1950 down to 2.6 percent. At that precariously low level, the northern red snapper fishery was rapidly heading toward a point from which it might never recover. As with New England cod, Lake Michigan whitefish and Alaska pollock, too many Buddies had been taking out too many snappers too rapidly for the fish to catch its breath and recover.

Rather than abruptly end all fishing, the National Marine Fisheries Service sought ways to dial back pressure. They asked their scientists to determine how many snappers could be caught while still leaving enough in the water to reproduce, then set that as the "total allowable catch." They announced that starting January 1, fishermen would be allowed to harvest until that fixed amount was gone; the fishery would then close.

For someone like Buddy with a boat too small to go out in the rough winter months, a season that began in winter and ended in spring would be a disaster. He'd be too small and slow to hit the prime time hard and hit the densest schools with the biggest fish. By the time he could get out, most of that quota would be gone. So, in 1991, Buddy sat down with Katie, by then several months pregnant with their first son: "I had to make a decision whether I was going to be in the fishing business or not. And if I was, I had to have a bigger boat."

Buddy had one in mind: the *Falcon,* a forty-foot fishing vessel. She was, at the time, a floating money pit and an eyesore, with a cabin burnt and blackened by diesel exhaust. But its owner remained attached to her nonetheless, as fishermen often are to even the most raggedy boats. Only after burning another $80,000 on her did the man finally surrender title to Buddy, who after borrowing from the bank and his father, got it for $35,000.

Buddy spent the next few months pouring sweat into her. He also retrofitted her gear with six bandits—hydraulic winches that vertically lift weighted fishing gear from the depths at high speed, preferably loaded with red snapper. When he had her seaworthy, he pulled together a ragtag team of three deckhands, none of them experienced out on the rough Gulf waters. That maiden voyage did not go well. "We caught fourteen thousand pounds in four days, which was a lot of fish," Buddy recalled, before mentioning how pressure, fatigue and injuries took a toll. "On our return, one guy went to the ER and stayed. Another went to the ER and was discharged after being treated for a bad infection in his hands. And I don't remember what the other guy's problem was." None of that crew would ship out with Buddy again.

THE JOINT ARRIVAL of the new baby, Hans, and the seaworthy *Falcon* filled the Guindons with hope. It also drained their joint bank account. "I was still so poor then," Buddy recalled, "I had to decide whether to feed my kids or buy new clips for the longline gear that I needed to get into grouper fishing." He'd buy the gear, figuring he could earn enough with it to fill the fridge sometime down the road. While he'd often skip sharing that reasoning with Katie, she always somehow understood, and made do. For three years, Katie raised three boys in two rooms above a bar that crashed with the noise of drunks and music and fights until 2:00 a.m. every night. She got them to daycare or to school every morning and made it to her own job, while Buddy went off to sea for weeks at a time. "It wasn't an easy period," Katie said of those first years of marriage. "And we hated to be apart. But he was working so hard, and I knew he was doing everything he was doing for us. Sometimes I'd rush over and try to meet him for an hour or so on the dock before he had to turn around and head back out."

Buddy took the helm of the *Falcon* just as the new federal regulations set loose the Gulf-wide race for fish that would be known as the Derby. That first year, having sold the bar, he was at sea every single day of the week for months on end, no matter the weather, sinking and lifting lines until August, when the commercial fleet hit its catch limit and regulators shut them down. The following year, somewhat wiser, he and other fishermen raced harder and hit their limit far sooner. In the reactive arms race, instead of giving them eight months to earn their living, regulators closed red snapper fishing after less than eight weeks.

Federal rules proliferated nationwide. Starting from just fourteen initial regulations in 1980, there were 417 in the first three quarters of 1994 and they kept growing. In the Gulf, some rules created mini derbies, limiting fishing to the first ten days of each month. Others set minimum size limits. Still more capped at one ton of fish, the amount each vessel could bring in per voyage, hoping to slow and spread out the harvest. But none of those early attempts to control fishing effort worked; each seemed to bring a new unanticipated and unintended consequence. "They tried to hold us to two thousand-pound trip limits, and thought that could last all year," Buddy offered by way of example. "Only nobody thought about how you could just make three trips per day and catch six thousand pounds." Minimum size limits motivated fishermen to toss fish under thirteen or fourteen inches overboard. Conversely, trip limits compelled them to "high grade" or keep only the largest and most valuable for sale as meat, including more of those precious and declining numbers of BOFFFFs. Buddy hated throwing away five fish for every one he kept, especially since two thirds of his discards were too traumatized from being pulled up fast from the depths to survive the return voyage. That is, for every fish he landed, three others died. "You're killing next year's crop of fish and that was stupid," said Buddy. "But I had three kids to feed, and I had taken all of our life's savings and put it into this boat, so I felt very responsible to make sure it worked day by day."

Federal fishery managers weren't picking on Buddy or red snapper harvesters. His experience fit a universal pattern. Regulators introduced rules to hamstring fishermen. Boxed in, fishermen got creative and caught more than expected, leading the feds to ratchet down still tighter with something new. Wash, rinse, repeat. In this regulatory whack-a-mole, legal mallets smashed down on each new burst of fishing energy: attempting to rein in vessel numbers, trip length, boat size, or hours logged.

Rather than see his business fail, Buddy found ways around

the strangling regulations. He caught on the sly, dodged enforcement, and sold fish on the black market. "Most everyone took a few shots at illegally bringing in fish after the season closed. Until Dean Blanchard went to jail," he recalled—referring to a colorful and charismatic Cajun shrimp broker from Grand Isle, Louisiana, who served eighteen months in prison for transporting snapper across state lines. "When he got busted, we all pretty much cut it out."

Over the next several years, Buddy and his brother Kenny, who was by then also fishing commercially, diversified their business. They began buying and selling fish, and in 1996 launched a wholesale and retail fish house that Buddy named after the love of his life. Katie's Seafood Market wasn't much of an investment: just a corrugated aluminum dockside shack with a refrigeration unit and ice machine, and an upstairs office so small you could almost touch all four walls at once. Since a fishing boat might show up at any hour to be unloaded, Kenny slept on that cramped office floor.

For the Guindons, it was a savvy first move to capture more value from hook to plate: a buffer against volatility. Other than the *Falcon* and his gear, it was also the only tangible piece of fishing Buddy could own and bequeath. "I wanted it to be more than just a place to buy fish, and sell fish," said Buddy. "I wanted something to pass down to my sons."

Still, even as the snapper dwindled and his own options narrowed, Buddy hung in with fishing, loving a fight he'd discovered he could generally win. With skills honed over his lifetime plus uncanny instincts, he could generally find whatever schools of snapper remained to be caught. He still carried around in his head a three-dimensional map he began drawing at Streater's. Back then he spent his days wiping the bar and listening to fishermen: the losing ones muttered into beers about the places and depths they'd come up empty-handed; the winners bragged (after a drink or two on the house) about which rocky reef, or what depths of a particular oil well platform or mud lump, had delivered their biggest haul. "Over on Wall Street I guess you'd call what I did market research or due diligence," he chortled one night over beers. "But it gave me a pretty damn good sense of what was out there, who I was up against, and what it would take to catch more fish and make more money than any other long-liner or snapper fisherman out there. To become what's known as the highliner. And west of the mouth of the Mississippi, year after year, there was just one highliner. And you're looking at him."

BUDDY HAD MADE a reputation for himself. And it should have felt good fighting savvy captains, tough regulators and stormy seas, and coming out—against all of them—on top. But even the high-liner couldn't ignore the fact that red snapper and the communities they supported were both still on the skids. It was a vicious down-ward spiral: by squeezing the fishermen, officials just pushed them to go out farther and fish harder and faster. The quality and value of the fish plummeted. Rather than take time to pack their keepers carefully in ice—the constantly rushed fishermen bruised some fish, tossed overboard more, and let others dry out, losing color, and then had to accept a lower price. With all boats unloading their catch at the same time, the glut further crippled prices. Fishing rules locked these harvesters in a demolition derby that sacrificed food, caused accidents, damaged equipment, and destroyed wealth.

Had it rescued the fish, the regulatory system might have been worth it. But it didn't. Despite vigorous enforcement of increasingly stringent regulations, the snapper's future continued to slide toward a vanishing point. It wasn't just that the combined catch had fallen in half over two decades; or that snapper's age and size kept shrink-ing; or that consequently the spawning potential kept falling. The broken system even defied the basic rule of Economics 101: as the supply of wild fish fell, so did prices.

Even as a highliner, Buddy saw his life and family suffering. "My life was a disaster," he said. "I didn't go to my kids' baseball games; I didn't go to church. I didn't do all the things that normal people do." For his 40th birthday Katie drove hours to surprise him on the docks at Matagorda, only to have a five-minute celebration and kiss before he headed back out. She and a few other beleaguered wives tried to restore some normalcy: organizing shared holidays, starting with Easter. In the morning, Buddy and the other fishermen's kids would hunt chocolate eggs and marshmallow chickens. Then the families would all gather for supper, the fishermen warily watching each other, hoping no one slipped out to get an early jump at sea. The truce never lasted. They were trapped in a "You win, I lose" paradigm.

Friendly rivalry was exciting. But sometimes the derby wasn't a game, and some losses would prove irreversible.

Chapter Five
RECALCULATED RISKS

One thing that both inspired and infuriated Katie about her husband was his inability to say no. It's like the word was missing from his vocabulary, she said. With infinite demands, and only so many minutes each day, and so many days each month to catch fish, Buddy lacked the ability or desire to ration his time. Instead, in each twenty-four hours he tried to cram it all in—support three meetings, fix an engine, explore a business prospect, relocate a vessel, answer twenty phone calls and thirty texts, unload plywood, and land a few thousand pounds of snapper. That left little time to eat or sleep, let alone spend time with her or their sons. Katie made her peace with raising the boys alone while he was at sea. Still, her voice had an edge when the topic turned to the dangers Buddy faced offshore. She felt his constant rush against the clock led him to take chances and suffer injuries—a popped knee ligament, a torn rotator cuff, and the time, as we'll see, when he lost part of his face—that could have been avoided.

Buddy didn't see health and safety in the same light. In his mind, he did prioritize. Number One was to provide for his family and so accept calculated risks that came with doing so. (He couldn't recall a Number Two.) As a serial brawler and veteran, Buddy lived by the creed that what-doesn't-kill-you-makes-you-stronger, and kept his focus on all the strengths he brought to the fight. He never even drank coffee to keep alert at the wheel, viewing that as a bad-tasting crutch for weaker souls. He claimed to need just four hours of sleep, leaving more time for pressing needs. He also believed you never volunteer stories about pain, suffering or panic. If most fishermen were prone to exaggerate the size of the ones that got away, Buddy tended to downplay near misses he got away with. When that happened, Katie would lean in to jog his memory. Or Kenny, admiring his big brother's spirit, shared stories Buddy was reluctant to tell.

IN 1992, THE third year under months that allowed just ten-days of fishing for red snapper, Buddy was in his usual state of perpetual motion, pushing himself to the edge of endurance. He hated keeping idle the latter twenty days each month, especially with a good boat bobbing quietly on the dock. So, when the red snapper derby ended, Buddy and Kenny decided one day to continue filling their hull— this time with other commercial species: yellowedge and Warsaw grouper.

Usually when fishermen targeted new fish, with new gear, under new conditions, they did research to ease into it. That wasn't Buddy's style. Besides, there wasn't time. The grouper's own derby brought the brothers a day's journey offshore—and quite literally out of their depth. They hired a greenhorn to steer the boat while they retrofitted a used longline spool onto the work deck, trying out a new system that neither Buddy nor Kenny had even begun to figure out.

The work was almost the exact opposite of what they were used to. Snapper had a dazzling color; grouper was dull brown. Schools of snapper clustered in the water column; grouper were found on continental shelf reefs, ambushing prey at 200 to 1,500 feet down. Snapper fishing emphasized the vertical; grouper required horizontal thinking with lines five miles long. Snapper rewarded fast and frequent baiting of hooks on lines, dropping them over the sides then lifting with the mechanical bandit winch; grouper dragged out over fewer and less frequent sets of a wire leader connected to a longline loaded with hooks that would unwind from a spool, or drum, then out over the stern. You had to strike the right balance of weights and buoys to ensure the longline set stretched out on the seafloor or at the desired depth—assuming you even knew what depth was desirable.

A hundred miles off Galveston, Buddy was working the starboard rail, reeling back in the jerry-rigged contraption with the line guided through copper crimps so it wouldn't slide off in the wrong direction. Buddy knew exactly when and how to respond to snapper on a bandit rig, but the longline felt different. There was swiftly increasing tension. At first, he couldn't gauge whether the source of pressure came from hundreds of grouper, or if the line had just gotten snagged on a reef. He turned the boat, and while he should have eased off, slowed down, or at least shut off the reel and stepped back, he instead leaned out over the rail to see if he could figure out what was going on. Just then, the monofilament line broke, whipped back at what seemed like ninety miles an hour and tore down through his mouth from the right side of Buddy's nose, opening both lips and the left side of his cheek. Buddy grabbed at his face as blood began spilling, spattering the deck, the fish, the gear. The two-man crew, in horror, could see both rows of Buddy's teeth from the outside. Still spewing blood, Buddy ran inside for a mirror, wondering what he had left to salvage. Knowing they had seventeen hours back to dock, he stuffed his jaw full of paper towels and tried to hold the wad in place wrapping duct tape around his head.

With no doctors on board, the crew wasn't sure he'd make it, but they cut the gear loose—$3,000' worth—then wheeled the boat around and throttled toward port. An hour later Buddy stomped out on deck, clearly furious. Buddy wanted to yell but couldn't talk through that torn mouth, so he wrote it out on a pad.

"Turn around."

"What?"

"Head back out. Get that gear."

Caught between watching Buddy bleed out or facing Buddy's rage over sacrificed fishing equipment, the first mate began to turn the boat back out to sea.

Buddy couldn't smile, but his eyes twinkled. "Just kidding," he wrote. "Just want you to know I'm still tough."

The doctors who stitched Buddy up had to work around whole missing pieces, leaving a big bad jagged shiny scar. Only then did Buddy go to retrieve the longline gear. He lived, of course. But to keep people from staring at the scar he grew out his beard, sometimes to epic proportions spilling down to his chest. It was an exemplary lesson in stoicism for the other fishermen. "Yeah, he's bulletproof," said Kenny, watching his brother limp home after beers late one evening. "Pound for pound the meanest sonofabitch in Galveston."

Katie, who'd also seen his vulnerable moments, had a different take. While she loved Buddy, facial scars and all, she wondered whether such ordeals could have been avoided if her husband wasn't so caught up in the adrenaline rush and unprepared. When she heard Buddy, now sixty-nine, still boasting about his endless supply of energy, Katie smiled and gently shook her head. "Oh, he gets tired," she says. "Believe me. And you know, people make mistakes when they're tired."

THE OCEAN RARELY forgives mistakes. After the US government started keeping records in the late twentieth century, commercial fishing consistently ranked as the year's most dangerous occupation, with injury and fatality rates higher than loggers, miners, farmers, steelworkers and bush pilots. Even those statistics might have understated the danger, ignoring all the near misses and nonfatal maiming—like Buddy's face-slashing—that no self-respecting fisherman would bother to report.

To reverse these grim odds, federal officials drafted safety rules. Some set the proper age, condition, and maintenance of fishing gear and vessels. Others specified the appropriate level of crew competence, or weather conditions to avoid. There were guidelines for new and often expensive training programs, life rafts, personal flotation devices (PFDs), fire extinguishers, engine upgrades, deck retrofits, compliance inspections and search-and-rescue teams. Many such measures—the maritime equivalents of on-land driving lessons, seat belts, air bags, speed bumps and disk brakes—undoubtedly saved lives at sea. There was no question, for instance, that a PFD demonstrably improved the odds of survival for anyone who fell overboard. Yet there was no equivalent at sea to a fish-harvesting speed limit. To the contrary, as regulatory mandates forced fishermen into rushed and reckless behavior, safety gains from technical approaches were often overwhelmed by the race for fish. The derby encouraged Buddy to cut corners, defer maintenance, work in the fog of exhaustion, and sail out even amidst gathering Gulf storms. One night, after back-to-back non-stop eight-hour shifts at the helm, Buddy could fight the exhaustion no longer and let himself fall asleep. Unfortunately, while Buddy napped, so did his equally exhausted lookout at the helm, leaving the boat to drive itself three hours through the Gulf's oil fields; by some miracle it didn't crash. "We got lucky," Buddy conceded.

Katie saw the injuries from hasty decisions pile up. She understood what was going on beneath the surface. As rivalries intensified over a finite resource, the primary focus on the scarcity of time and fish reduced decision-making capacities, and left less room for seemingly secondary concerns, like safety. "Buddy would go out for long periods even when the boat was not in working order, exactly," Katie recalled. "When there were problems, he just patched it quickly and went out. He went out no matter whether he was sick, or should have been in bed, or was tired. In all kinds of weather, it was extremely scary, but when the officials told you that you had to fish, that's just the way it was."

Another time his brother Kenny went fishing alone, exhausted, when a line fouled the propeller during a rough mid-winter mini season. Diving under the boat to untangle it, he cut his hand on torn metal. He spent several hours in the water, too fatigued to hoist himself back in until a high wave finally flipped him up and back on board. Back on shore, doctors stitched up the cut tendons of his hands. Kenny allowed that he got lucky, too.

Still, there's only so much luck to go around. Buddy claimed not to remember any time he felt personally in any danger from rough seas. Katie sure did. "That's his fisherman's memory," she said, rolling her eyes. "He totaled a boat one time. Totaled it. Had the Coast Guard searching. There was a write-up in the newspaper about it because they couldn't find him for two days."

That at least had happened before their marriage, and sons.

Years later, Buddy decided to give a taste of fishing to his boys, teenage Hans and grade school Chris. When the Coast Guard issued a storm warning Katie, at home, heard it. But for hours, no one could reach the *Falcon*. The boat had been caught by that rapid storm front. Tossed by heavy seas, with thick, wet, salty winds whipping across the deck, Buddy described how he lost a crew member overboard and, in the desperate minutes it took to pull him back in, the vessel had begun taking on water. Usually, as waves hammered and swamped the boat, a signal alarm would go off. But this one didn't. The wiring had failed, shorted out. Looking out at the empty sea with no vessels in sight, wondering what on earth got him into this fix and how he might get out of it, even Buddy admitted, ten years later, that "yeah, it was a bad situation." Bundling up his sons, he settled them into a still-tethered life raft, ready to launch if need be. They spent the night enduring the storm, aimlessly drifting, radio fried, his boys white-knuckled, clenching teeth, and Buddy trying everything he could to keep them afloat. Finally, someone passing in a Coast Guard vessel noticed a blinking light in the middle of the night, and brought them in. Buddy normalized the whole ordeal as the kind of risk he considered part of the game but knew his wife would never fully accept. "It was scary, very scary," said Katie, shaking her head. "It was two days of hell."

UNTIL FISHERIES REFORM began in earnest in the 1990s, such escalating dangers confronted every fisherman still caught in archaic, overly prescriptive regulatory nets. But nowhere were those dangers greater than in Alaska. While ordinary people recognized derby fishing there as a recipe for personal tragedy, a few saw the makings of a reality TV series, a *Hunger Games* set on the waves. Weather-resistant cameras, fitted aboard crab fishing vessels at any angle, could capture in real-time any mayhem that occurred on board, or overboard. After Jeff Conroy pitched the drama to Discovery Channel—the last great cowboy story, Marlboro Men against the sea—*Deadliest Catch* broke the mold. The lucrative low-cost show soon gained four million viewers, complete with spinoff books and branded video games.

Risk may be a complex force. But it can be assessed. Fishermen forced to compete for a shrinking supply of crab in a short winter season had to endure Bering Sea storms. Between 1989 and 2005, these waters claimed eighty-five lives: lost overboard, killed or taken down in ten crab boats that sank in pursuit of the valuable crustacean. In the first twenty-four hours of the first season of *Deadliest Catch* alone, six fishermen died. And ratings soared.

As the dangers of fishing derbies mounted, one Alaskan with a particularly intimate experience of that lethal harvest began asking the same questions Katie did. Rather than quietly tolerate or buffer losses, he wondered, why can't fisheries somehow reduce the need for exposure to risk in the first place? As a bridge between dying fishermen and those left behind, this ex-crab fisherman set out to construct an escape route, with ripple effects across America's seas.

ARNI THOMSON WROTE true accounts of brave men lost in cold waters. He never got paid for his writing but became a beloved and respected author whose audience was irrevocably moved, perhaps even saved, by his words. He wrote for the siblings, the parents, the children of those lost at sea. He wrote for the widows. Such writing wasn't his first choice; he'd been a crabber himself for years and aspired to become a novelist. But he rose to the occasion when in 1981 the writing of obituaries chose him. "A crab boat went down, and I knew almost all of them who were on board," he recalled. "Some of the guys asked me if I would write a few words, and I said okay and sat down. That turned out to be the first of many memorials I would do."

The Bering Sea in winter has never welcomed visitors. For millennia, native Inuit, Aleut and Inupiat fishers and hunters kept their boats hard to shore during those dark months. Newcomers weren't so prudent. Going out was relatively simple: a guy could pick up a cheap offshore supply boat or an *Exxon Valdez* oil spill cleanup leftover, retrofit it for pulling crabs off the seafloor, and start to make big money. But then one day the sea might violently heave and claim a thumb, crushed by the gear. A surge might sever an arm caught between steel cable and winch. A seventy-foot rogue wave might knock over the vessel and swallow it within minutes.

For nearly a decade Thomson wrote about lost lives as if they were inevitable. In some years Alaska crabbers faced a death rate at least forty times that of the average US worker. Then one Sunday in 1989, four hundred people gathered in Seattle's First Lutheran Church to honor six fishermen who had been seventy miles off Kodiak Island trapping Alaska crab when their ship, the *Vestfjord*, disappeared. Thomson knew a few of the orphans. Yet somehow, looking out at the stricken faces of those children, he found both the right words and a new determination to slow this march of funerals and grief. He described how the new captain of the *Vestfjord*, Dick LeGary, had fallen in love with Dody Woodside and become like a father to her four children, advising her son to finish school before taking up fishing. He spoke of Kevin Melnick, whose widow Julie sat in the pews holding their seven-month-old son, who would never get to know his dad. He shared how, the night before the sinking, when Kevin's mother Mary, "put a candle in the window on a piece of paper with the word *Vestfjord* written on it, she could not have known. It was just something she always did." He then asked for a moment of silence, knowing that up in Alaska, crews were at that same moment cutting their engines and falling silent themselves. In the next moment, those men would resume their frenzied race, pitted against all others.

Around that time, Thomson began to put the deadly pieces together.

He saw how the desperate cycle that threatened lives was linked to the decline of the crab fishery. At its peak, in 1980, fishermen had hauled in 200 million tons of king crab a year, yanking thousands of heavy traps holding millions of dog-sized crustaceans up off the shallow bottoms. But within just three years, the harvest had crashed by 90 percent, putting dozens of crews out of operation. Owners had walked away from boats that banks then foreclosed upon. Survivors squeezed over to harvest different species, including the initially more abundant but less valuable bairdi or opilio snow crab—an economic shift in fishing effort known as leakage. Alarmed regulators reacted predictably: closing seasons sooner and thus speeding up the reckless race. That sped the downward spiral: degrading catch quality, depressing prices, destroying oceanic wealth until vessels could barely catch enough crab to cover bait, fuel, ice, repairs, groceries and (maybe) wages. And amping up the risks and their grievous consequences, which Thomson was now left to eulogize.

The frenzy of the race had driven the *Vestfjord's* owner to operate a bigger and faster but top-heavy boat. It had driven the skipper to take his crew out into 70-knot winds, thirty-foot seas, temperatures (with wind chill) at minus 40 degrees and the severest icing conditions ever recorded in the Northeast Pacific. Out there, blasts of frozen air could flash-freeze everything so thick that the sheer weight of the ice on deck could capsize a ninety-seven-foot boat. The crew sent out a mayday from the waters off Trinity Island at 12:05 a.m. Alaska Standard Time. Then nothing.

Over the next sixteen years, Thomson would memorialize many of the crews from seventy-three more crab vessels, including the *Northern Belle, Big Valley, Northwest Mariner, Katmai, Lin J, Alaska Ranger* and *Ocean Challenger*, all scattered on the Bering Sea floor. "I went to a lot of funerals," Thomson said. "And I started keeping records of all the boats that were lost and the men that were lost on them. I kept a log from 1981 through 2004. I also started writing letters."

Thomson wrote personal letters to the families. He also wrote to the editors of *The Seattle Times* and *Post-Intelligencer*. To the Chairman of the North Pacific Fishery Management Council in Anchorage. To the Safety Coordinator of the Seventeenth Coast Guard District in Juneau. To Alaska Senator Ted Stevens in Washington, DC. He wrote to draw attention to what he saw as the systemic problem causing the early needless deaths of his typically uninsured, and often uninsurable, friends. He laid out how the race for crab was not just bad for fishermen's health but also for the region's small businesses, wrecking their capacity for long-term planning. Congress made policy based on two-year election cycles; investors sought quarterly returns. But the season length for crab vessel owners was at best seven days for snow crab and ninety-six hours for king crab. You can't plan an entire year's business on just a few days of activity, explained Thomson.

By 1999, as even the once abundant snow crab crashed from 190 million to 25 million pounds, Alaskan crabbers had enough. Thomson, who had been doing his homework year after year, now showed both fishermen and regulators how other catastrophic Alaskan fisheries had managed to rescue both fish and men. Halibut fishermen in the early 1990s often had to harvest an entire year's catch in just a few twenty-four-hour derbies (launched, literally, by a starting gun). In that madness, the Coast Guard often was called on search and rescue missions thirty-three times in a brief season, putting still more lives in danger. Since 1995, however, the year halibut transitioned to catch shares, that fishery became biologically healthier, seasons grew longer, earnings rose higher, and gear losses—leading to ghost fishing that once annually destroyed two million pounds of fish—became "inconsequential." Beyond the fishery's recovery, despite much longer seasons over the next decade, catch shares cut seasonal Search and Rescue missions from one every hour to one or two each *year*.

Thomson's letters earned a growing audience. His numbers got the attention of fishing vessel owners, wholesalers, processors, shippers, and seafood dealers. His highlights of fewer Search and Rescue missions helped forge an alliance with Christopher J. Woodley of the Coast Guard, as well as Karen Olsen, who would testify how she "lost two cherished friends who have fished in the open access fisheries, Bob Denison and George Lunstrum, and to me [graduation to catch shares] is not complicated." Mary Crowley, a three-generation fishing family matriarch, heard other "mothers that testified that their sons went overboard and never came back again." By 2005, his advocacy and the voices of widows thawed resistance. They ushered in changes for crabbing that would establish a powerful new precedent for all America's fisheries.

A buyout program—getting fishermen to retire early—didn't fully work. So officials then ascertained the sustainable catch, setting it far lower (at seventeen million pounds) than the harvest in peak open-access years, giving both crabs and their bottom habitat a chance to recover. They allocated 92 percent of that total allowable catch to the remaining 250 vessels, based on the catch histories each had reported to federal managers. Those vessels were required over time to pay back the buyouts, through a tax on their landings. The outcome sparked doubters and counter-arguments (whose voices appear in the next chapter), but upon setting a clear limit of what could be sustainably harvested, matched by flexibility in how to catch it, the number of active crabbers settled around 169 vessels. Both the small and large operators who remained knew exactly how much they could harvest before leaving the dock. Each could negotiate prices and delivery time accordingly. As the pollock and halibut fishermen had, crabbers too became far more prudent. Now free to fish twenty-six days or more in the winter, captains became "fair-weather fishermen," waiting out or heading back to avoid the worst storms.

The combination of time, incentives and flexibility improved safety in other ways. Vessels became more stable, as captains cut by 40 percent the number of heavy crab traps they carried on board and let them "soak" on the bottom longer. That ensured better weight distribution, lower centers of gravity, even keels and greater buoyancy and control—greatly reducing the odds of capsizing. The dangers of being injured by a crab pot also diminished, as captains cut by two-thirds the number of pots they lowered and lifted each day. Fewer drops, longer soaks and steadier haul-backs also meant less exposure for the crew to icy decks, big waves, and powerful machinery. Finally, rebuilt crab stocks, revenues, and millions of dollars in profits gave owners the funds and motive to invest in safety measures they'd often had to defer.

It wasn't just Alaskan crabbers who reduced their exposure to risk. In fifteen major US and Canadian fisheries, the shift to catch shares has improved safety—including injuries, Search and Rescue

71

missions, and lost vessels and lives—by 260 percent. In the West Coast sablefish fishery, with seasons lengthened by the switch to catch shares from nine days to seven months, the average annual fishing trips on high wind days had dropped by 79 percent from the open access derby era, "a revolution in risk-taking behavior by fishermen due," according to researchers, to the change in economic incentives provided by catch shares.

More than 85 percent of Alaska halibut fishermen told researchers in 1999 that fishing was far safer without the race. During 2015, the Coast Guard documented the safest year in Alaska's known history, with zero work-related fishing fatalities. "I believe catch shares have saved lives in Alaska because crabbing deaths are much less common now," said Scott Campbell, Jr., captain of the *Seabrooke* and a former star of *Deadliest Catch*. "Crabbing before and after catch shares is like night and day. There's no way I'd choose to go back to the old derby days."

BUDDY LACKED TIME to watch much TV, reality or otherwise. But he'd heard about and caught brief glimpses of Campbell on that show in bars. In the first two seasons, in 2005 and 2006, crab fishing remained lethal under the ongoing derby. That reinforced his sense that fishing was dangerous, but what could you do?

By 2005, the Guindons had four sons who needed more food and clothing each year. Looking down the road, Buddy knew they'd each need school, and good paying jobs, and the kind of security and future opportunities his own dad could never provide the family. He felt he had no choice but to take chances for his family, even if Katie wasn't convinced such risks were entirely necessary. And if he sometimes made dumb mistakes out of exhaustion, so be it; Buddy still believed fishing was a game he could win. He felt bad whenever rival fishermen got injured or quit or went bankrupt or all the above; he thrived on camaraderie and friendly competition. But he was a fighter, a survivor. So, while there may be fewer fish in the sea each year, Buddy could work harder, devote more time out on the water, take on debt to buy a second vessel, increase his slim margins with a fish house of his own, and capture a slightly bigger portion of what snapper remained in the Gulf.

Of course, all that assumed a consistent future. But at any moment, officials could shut down the fishery. Prices might crater. Disaster might shock the Gulf. Collapse would leave Buddy still as a highliner, yet standing at the peak of an empty sea, unable to fish. Caught between his dream and nightmare scenario, Buddy fought on in purgatory, running out of reliable choices. Not only was he unable to say no, he couldn't even say yes. "I love fishing, but I saw no future in it for my sons, or even for me," he said of that time, one night over beers. "I just wanted to scrape out enough for us to get ahead before it was all gone."

Chapter Six

THE NATURE OF DISSENT

Round-the-clock fishing left Buddy little time for politics. But politics would find time for him. At the dawn of the twenty-first century a few commercial fishermen and environmental advocates had begun forging a new and (to some) unholy alliance to bring about yet another wave of regulatory reforms to Gulf reef fisheries. Buddy understood the former group, guys like him worried about how to feed their families. Those environmentalists were another kettle of fish. The urban busybodies often seemed more worried about protecting nature than people; some pushed the government to prevent seafood from being caught and eaten. He thought his fellow fishermen were foolish to have joined these types in an "ad hoc red snapper IFQ panel." The group met under the oversight of the Gulf Council to figure out what to do with snapper in an area covering roughly a quarter million square miles offshore from the Mexican border to the Florida Keys. By 2005, one of those fishermen, with two of those environmentalists, were driving to Galveston in hopes of persuading Buddy to join their club.

Felix Cox had been catching snapper for twenty years out of Aransas Pass, Texas, about two hundred miles southeast of Galveston. He came calling on Buddy on behalf of a small batch of fishermen who'd already overcome their own doubts about catch shares. These included Wayne Werner, who fished out of Galliano, Louisiana, and who had led the fight *against* catch shares when they were first floated in the Gulf—winning a moratorium blocking them from 1996 to 2002—but had come around after the derby cost him his uninsured fishing vessel and nearly his life. Several other allies included David Walker, fishing the *June Sue* out of Andalusia, Alabama; Donnie Waters, third-generation waterman who operated the *Hustler* out of Pensacola; and Russell Underwood, sailing out of Leeville, Louisiana, at the wheel of his *Norman B*. David Krebs, a long-line fisherman and owner of Ariel's seafood market in Destin, Florida, had also opposed catch share programs throughout the 1990s but after years of painful derby fishing and poor market conditions, he and these other fishermen went to New Zealand to understand how, through catch shares, the industry improved the science, value and marketing of fish. They returned converts.

Felix didn't go to New Zealand, however, and for this meeting with Buddy he brought two non-fishermen, Pete Emerson, a resource economist, and Pam Baker, a marine biologist with whom Felix had begun collaborating since 1998 about this "new animal," catch shares. Both worked for Environmental Defense Fund (EDF), an NGO founded by scientists in 1967 when it was a small, litigious advocate for wildlife and public health. But the group had evolved into economic pragmatists, with a "reverence for the marketplace," and a recognition that "capitalism is a powerful thing," which set it apart (and in some cases brought criticisms) from other environmental groups. Working with private businesses—including such corporate giants as McDonald's, FedEx, Walmart and Duke Energy—EDF began designing market incentives aimed at achieving environmental goals in what they believed to be a more flexible and thus effective manner. It pioneered water markets in California that rewarded farmers for cleaner and more efficient irrigation. It developed incentives for landowners to host endangered wildlife in private habitats. And, most prominently, in 1990, it helped design a cap-and-trade system that rewarded power companies for reducing the sulfur dioxide pollution that caused acid rain—a flexible new system that has slashed emissions by 96 percent, with benefits about 40 times the cost—cleaner, faster, and cheaper than anyone imagined possible.

Building on progress with a healthier sky, a few EDF employees wanted to address that other global commons and planetary life support system closer to home: the sea. Early work included coastal conservation, endangered species, coral reef protection and water pollution. Spread thin by chasing so many worthy but daunting challenges, the small staff quickly felt like it was winning local battles—a slightly improved estuary here, a cleaned-up pig farm there—yet losing the larger struggle for ocean health.

By 1996, in the lead-up to reauthorization of the Magnuson-Stevens Fishery Management and Conservation Act, team members began to step back and consider their efforts to halt pollution and degradation. Bad as all these negative impacts were, not one could hold a candle to the relentless devastation inflicted by fishermen, like Buddy, to cause an increasingly barren sea. Once they agreed the single biggest threat to ocean biodiversity and ecosystem health was, by far, overfishing, EDF began investigating how to end it. They began to focus the group's strengths in science and incentives, and the team's economist Pete Emerson made his case of how, based on lessons thus far, he believed the very individuals most responsible for the problem of overfishing could be enlisted to reverse the trend. "The concept of aligning industry economic incentives with conservation objectives seemed like it could scale in ways consistent with the extent of the problem," said marine biologist Rod Fujita, who co-authored a paper in the 1990s on catch shares. Still, not everyone agreed. And in any case the timing was less than ideal; two years later Congress put a spending moratorium and other restrictions on this political hot potato.

In the Gulf, Pam Baker hoped to shift motion back from pause to play. After earning a master's degree in marine affairs at the University of Rhode Island, she worked as an on-board observer of fishing activity. Her concern was always around how fishermen's economic incentives would align with conservation so that the marine ecosystem and the fishing communities would each benefit. She brought this outlook to her early work in Belize and Micronesia, before coming to EDF. There, she learned from her mentor, Pete Emerson, about the quiet power of economic incentives; she later read work from, then followed up with a month-long fellowship at a Bozeman, Montana, think tank called the Property and Environment Research Center. PERC economist Don Leal was promoting a "free-market environmentalism" approach that leveraged Nobel laureate Friedrich Hayek's work showing how simple prices communicate complex information, and Austrian economist Ludwig von Mises' studies of human choice and action, then applied these ideas to resource conservation in papers like "Homesteading the Ocean" and "Fencing the Fishery." These theorists, along with other bio-economic thought leaders like Nobel laureate Elinor Ostrom were asking in their own way the question Pam wanted to answer about conservation of the ocean in ways that helped people prosper: *What if rather than top-down rules governing when and how fishermen could work, each was given sole responsibility for his or her clearly defined share of the living sea?*

Though many of those thinkers developed a theory from historical examples of how "rights-based" systems helped narrow local interests sustainably manage their shared natural resources, few had turned theory into formal practice at the large and complex scale of the Gulf of Mexico. Pam, initially following the lead of Pete, set out to do just that. She began to spend more time on fishing docks and found harvesters to be knowledgeable about fisheries in ways that far outweighed scientists and government, brutally honest, and often stubborn because their livelihoods were in peril. Pam discovered Felix lived just down the street from her home, and they soon joined forces as a potent team.

Felix helped Pam appreciate a fisherman's suspicion of unfamiliar theories developed in universities and think tanks. The abstract logic of a model—showing aggregated cost curves against revenues or describing how quotas shift effort to maximize economic yield—was unlikely to persuade fishermen. It required a face-to-face approach, and the two initiated quiet conversations with Krebs, Werner, Underwood and Walker, offshore rivals who nonetheless came together in an informal coalition. On November 12, 2003, EDF and its partners briefed the Gulf Council on the potential benefits of catch shares. Shortly after, fishermen persuaded Senators Trent Lott and Ted Stevens to amend the moratorium to give the new approach a try. So the door was open, but the alliance still needed broader support among fishermen, especially the guy who caught more snapper than anyone. Pam and Felix drove to Galveston to make the case to Buddy.

For Pam it was a trip back in time. She recalled having first met Buddy while studying marine biology a decade earlier. From the Galveston campus of Texas A&M, she and fellow students would hit Streater's for two-dollar pitchers of beer.

Buddy agreed to meet out of respect for Cox. "Some of the other fishermen were much more knowledgeable than I," he allowed. But he didn't expect to be convinced. "We had our work keeping us busy and I was going all right." He didn't want another sudden, irreversible reform. He certainly didn't welcome schemes hatched by "ologists" who had never run a seafood business, never had to meet a payroll, came from a donor-funded environmental advocacy group, and claimed that fishermen could spend less time at sea, harvest less fish and still earn more money. Buddy appraised Pam, Pete and Felix from beneath his baseball cap, his eyes narrowing.

Almost as soon as Felix began to make his logical case, Pam sensed it would likely go down in flames. Here's how it works, they began to explain to Buddy: rather than control your fishing effort with prescriptive ten-day monthly seasons or two thousand-pound limits, a catch share system sets a scientific target, then lets you reach it however you want—making decisions like when to fish and how much to land. Buddy saw where this was going; "scientific targets" always meant one thing: catch less. And yes, they conceded, we might *initially* need to reduce each fisherman's catch (as it later turned out, by as much as a third in the beginning) to ensure rapid recovery and higher catch limits several years down the road. That sounded fine to those who only caught seven tons of snapper each year, groused Buddy. They'd only had to scale back three or five thousand pounds. But as a highliner, he caught that much each week. Giving it up involved a huge sacrifice now, for shaky and hypothetical future gains. Pam made the business case for how, right off the bat, Buddy could time the harvest and selling of fish that could help him get better prices.

She could tell when Buddy tensed up. His arms crossed. His body language closed his visitors off. The conversation got complicated when they explained to him how quota would initially be allocated among several hundred fishermen through a complex formula based on catch histories. Fishing logs that lowballed past landings would be penalized with a smaller share.

Buddy wasn't impressed by examples they could offer up about how well quotas worked elsewhere, from Alaska to New Zealand to Iceland. In those cold waters a few dozen massive ships trawled single species at large scale. His waters were warm, his boats small, cramped and competing with hundreds of others, spread across many ports, using not nets but hooks and lines to catch a diversity of reef fish. Baker seemed nice enough, Buddy concluded, but like most environmentalists had no clue about the realities of fishing offshore. And while Cox, who was struggling on the margins, might believe he'd benefit, Buddy was still hitting the fishery hard and couldn't see an upside to risking the loss of control, or sacrificing now for some intangible gains down the road. "You can't ever enforce it," he told Pam, trying to end the conversation. "You just can't. It simply won't work."

Buddy embodied opposition to catch shares for red snapper. He was not out front on the political scene. But the personal fears and doubts he expressed were felt deeply and widely, not only in the Gulf but in fisheries considering similar reforms around the nation. The opposition born in the Great Lakes had only grown more ferocious as catch shares spread globally over time. In four defined categories, critics rejected catch shares as: ideologically confused, politically dangerous, ecologically impotent, and socially inequitable. Their arguments all merited a thoughtful response.

IDEOLOGICALLY, TRANSFERABLE QUOTA systems—much like any previous constraint on size, licenses, vessel, permits, gear, allocation and so forth—fell into a no-man's-land: The fish were no longer a free public good open to one and all, but neither were they a pure form of private property. Fishing rights encompassed a sea of gray. A fisherman with an exclusive and renewable catch share might still have access that was temporary, revocable, and have restraints on its transferability. In this, they were like airwaves licensed out for television or radio stations to make their exclusive broadcasts, or a long-term grazing permit that granted a rancher yearly access to grass on federal lands rather than permanent title to that grassland. America remained the ultimate owner of the marine resources within the nation's exclusive economic zone, with the power to grant (or deny) provisional rights to those able to harvest fish resources.

This in-between status had for some long been a source of deep discomfort. Early on at the Department of Marine Affairs at the University of Rhode Island, Seth Macinko warned that "people are being scared into accepting" quota programs, which encouraged "ocean grabbing" by elite interests, and concluded that "fisheries resources already have an owner. The American public. If fisheries are poorly managed, it is due to poor management, not a lack of ownership." University of Wisconsin professor Daniel W. Bromley had also denounced catch shares as a "legally incoherent" abdication of political responsibility. He, too, mocked the "utopian claims" of catch share advocates and vigorously disputed the "ownership fetish" at the heart of Gordon's thesis—arguing that holding equity to a living resource hardly transforms commercial fishermen from malignant exploiters into benevolent stewards of the sea. "This spurious and misguided embrace of individual transferable quotas," he concluded, "can only compound the tragedies of past malfeasance by the dangerous endorsement of this bundle of confusions, contrivances, and deceits." Similar critiques about social equity had been reiterated over the years as the basis of investigative articles, videos, and full-length books.

If some on the left disliked catch shares because they saw them as privatizing public wealth, some conservatives thought the access privileges they grant to the resource don't go nearly far enough. "Unfortunately," lamented PERC's Don Leal, "individual quotas in the Alaskan halibut program are not secure property rights...

and can be taken away without compensation at any time." The late Ralph Townsend, of New Zealand's fisheries ministry, felt the co-management systems linking government and fisherman under catch shares to be inferior to formal fishermen corporations, which would by necessity be self-enforcing. Competitive Enterprise Institute's founder Fred L. Smith derided the system as a kind of creeping "eco-socialism" that left ownership vague, long-term incentives in doubt, and a government with no reason to compensate fishermen if it "takes" back the resource. More broadly, the supportive scholar Jonathan H. Adler bemoaned how conservatives routinely ignored or rejected catch shares as part of what he saw as the political right's "reflexive—almost reactionary—opposition to anything green. Environmental policies are suspect because they threaten industrial activity and growth, and environmental concern may even be a stalking horse for a more sinister ideology."

Such ideological polarization was latent already in 1968, when the neo-Malthusian ecological philosopher Garrett Hardin laid out his famous warning against overpopulation, deploying the parable of a medieval pasture exposed to livestock owners. On land or sea, each producer may know the natural resource to be limited and vulnerable to overexploitation, yet any patch of grass (or reef) conserved out of altruism would simply be captured by a rival driving the shared system to irreversible collapse. "Ruin is the destination toward which all men rush, each pursuing his own best interest in a society that believes in the freedom of the commons," Hardin wrote. *"Freedom in a commons brings ruin to all."*

Given such existential stakes, Hardin urged society to abandon its naïve belief in freedom of the commons in favor of political coercion. In doing so he fueled the rise of two mutually exclusive approaches to any wild commons, including ocean fisheries. The left favored rigid, top-down environmental regulation, in which taxpayer-funded authorities fenced off and guarded natural reserves from private theft. The right favored strict, top-down environmental privatization, in which taxpayer-funded authorities fenced off and guarded natural property from public theft. Neither allowed for a flexible, bottom-up, self-organizing, cooperative messy middle ground, in which, the late Nobel Prize winner Elinor Ostrom, demonstrated the oldest and most durable governance solutions that took shape and flourished.

Never comfortable with ideology, Ostrom favored common sense. She countered the models and assumptions of coercion-minded doomsayers like Hardin with historical case studies and data from hundreds of cultures around the world where societies self-regulated the work taking place within their overlapping shared resources, which ranged from forest to meadow to farmland to lagoon. She showed that where conflicts emerged, the communities that achieved a lasting resolution were those whose tenure systems included each community member within responsible limits established for all. That is, people found ways to manage their own commons by managing themselves.

Ostrom and her colleagues directly challenged the example on which Hardin stood. The actual medieval commons, they showed, was never a free-for-all but rather jointly owned. Each had its own complex and intricate webs of customary but clearly defined resource access privileges to, for example, graze animals, dig turf, cut firewood, remove stones and gravel...or catch fish. Indeed, Ostrom's ever-expanding body of empirical evidence documented how exclusive dominion over or co-management of fisheries had long been the norm for many native, traditional and informal fishing areas in the US and overseas.

IDEOLOGY COULD REMAIN simple and pristine in isolation. Reality embraced life's inherent mess. The challenge was how to adapt the past's real successes to modern complex pressures. Those informal customary systems had often evolved over long periods of time among small, tribal, local waters. How could dispersed strangers formalize fishing rights to intensively regulated commercial industries at federal scale amidst factious national politics?

The core challenge was determining exactly "who" writes the rules. As the political proverb goes, if you're not at the table, you're on the menu. Yet as we have seen, when any small group with narrow goals tried to manage participants—basically, every regulatory system prior to catch shares—the governance system tended to backfire, triggered unintended consequences, and became self-defeating. By contrast, the design of catch share programs grew more and more democratically inclusive over time. The resulting performance largely reflected the extent to which the design process diversified participation beyond elected officials or fishery managers to include vessel owners, captains, native tribes, deckhands, wholesalers, retailers, processors, coastal communities, recreational anglers; and even people who had never caught fish in the past but might one day wish to do so.

Much as all species respond to natural selection pressures, and form follows function, fishing rights also adapted, evolved, diversified and improved to thrive in their respective niche over time. For early pioneers like New Zealand, the limited scientific information available in 1986 led to a program that overestimated how fast the fish called orange roughy reproduce. As a result, fishermen complied with catch limits, but their quotas, set too high, still hurt fish populations. Meanwhile, since officials had defined quota in absolute weight, rather than percentage, they had to pay for tighter restrictions in a cumbersome and needlessly expensive process. Two decades later, Pacific fishermen absorbed these practical lessons to design what was among the most comprehensive catch share programs on earth. Political inclusion took more time, deliberation, and trade-offs between competing interests—much like democracy itself—but also had the potential to deliver faster recovery of depleted species, more flexible access, and a broader range of benefits.

The most embittering debates centered on "consolidation" of the fishing fleets—too often at the expense of new entrants seeking room to join in the recovering fishery to become second generation catch share seafood harvesters themselves. Concentration of capital and power was an emphatically appropriate sorry—if one looked at the full picture. Yet all too often, catch shares were blamed for mayhem that preceded them, or that came from unrelated economic forces. The reality was that under open access fishing, fleets had grown many times bigger than the fish populations could bear, leading both to crash, and shrinkage, long before catch shares were even considered.

For example, in the late 1980s, a new race developed in the Southeast for wreckfish—a large, tasty, long-lived and slow-growing deep-water species. A recipe for overfishing. In 1992, managers allocated quotas to ninety eligible vessels. Three years later the market dwindled. Trading stopped for the next thirteen years. By 2010, the fleet had consolidated 88 percent, to fewer than two dozen boats. The reality was more subtle. Wreckfish still offered economic value, but the return on investment simply no longer merits a large-scale commercial effort. Tastes changed. Economies were dynamic. Today only five vessels bothered dropping lines in those ultra-deep waters. Fishermen voluntarily stopped going out, chose to go after more profitable fish closer to shore, or left to pursue greener pastures on land. Of course, before 1992, regulatory officials had little reason to track exactly how many fishermen came and went where, doing what, and anyone who left or went bankrupt did so anonymously and silently without any claims or benefits. Only after catch shares registered all vessels did each fisherman have a name and defined value.

Proponents found it tempting to say catch shares offer a silver bullet, but context was paramount. Robust political processes and implementation mattered more than ideological beliefs. Any catch share was only as democratic as the participatory effort put into its design. Paradoxically, secure and exclusive designs could often emerge from the most diverse and inclusive groups of stakeholders. These stakeholders might include a shore-based processor who invested millions into fishing assets, or a community of Indigenous peoples who'd never fished deep waters in their lives, or both. All these stakeholders were implicitly bound by and anchored to the same natural resource. By explicitly bringing them to the table, a catch share could breathe, anticipate change, or accommodate the desires of latecomers. Fishermen and managers can choose at the start to restrict certain transfers, anchor quota to communities or places, or vessel types or sizes, and cap ownership accumulation so that no single entity, local or distant, could wield excessive power over others. Incentives encouraged stewardship by tapping an individual fisherman's self-interest. Yet this long-term self-interest also led fishermen as a group to take preventive measures against monopoly power, speculative disruption, and social inequity.

Catch share designs would become more innovative in response to mounting criticisms that they can "lock out" new entrants struggling to join in and benefit from a recovering fishery. How to resolve this impasse? The Cape Cod Fisheries Trust was a community-based solution; it bought fishing permits and quota, then leased them out to local fishermen at affordable rates, allowing younger or financially constrained fishermen to ease into the fishery—without having to take out a second mortgage. By managing shares for the community, the Trust ensured that local, small-scale fishermen had access to, and through their diversity and numbers enhanced the value of, sustainable fisheries.

Similarly, the Gulf Reef Fish Shareholders' Alliance launched its "Next Generation Fishermen Program." Under this initiative, established quota holders donated portions of their shares to a similarly structured trust, which leases them to younger fishermen at reduced costs—a strategic way to pass on shares, balancing economic opportunity with conservation goals.

On the West Coast, local fishermen, scientists, and business leaders oversee the Morro Bay Community Quota Fund, set up to ensure local groundfish harvesters could own and manage catch shares. Initiated by The Nature Conservancy, the Fund ensured access for future generations, balanced economic needs with conservation, and kept community fishing infrastructure intact. Further north up the Pacific coastline, Linda Behnken's Alaska Longline Fishermen's Association had also set aside catch shares under their own community trust for halibut and sablefish, quota which were then leased to members at affordable rates, allowing new entrants and a younger generation to remain active, and competitive, in a consolidated industry.

While imperfect and still evolving, these early-stage programs all sought to maintain a vibrant fishing economy and protect against consolidation. By keeping shares in the hands of local fishermen and small-scale businesses, these trusts and funds helped preserve the diverse character of fishing communities and more broadly distributed the benefits of a recovering and increasingly valuable resource.

EVEN SO, ADVOCATES who lunged deeper into catch share waters remained largely isolated. The bulk of environmental groups and conservation scientists remained openly hostile to tradeable and proportional quotas. When you "treat a public resource (i.e. fish) like an investment that can be bought and sold for personal profit," claimed Food and Water Watch founder Wenonah Hauter, "the results are often disastrous—for the environment, the economy and the consumer." Many believed overfishing was just the result of under-regulating. They felt as suspicious of fishermen holding and trading harvest rights as they did of factories holding and trading pollution rights. In a panic about putting wily foxes in charge of the ocean henhouse, some understandably feared that bad actors might empty the ocean, liquidate the marine assets, "high-grade" the largest, most valuable individual fish and then discard the rest. Still others objected on practical grounds, that the multi-years transition to catch shares might cost too much money and take too much time. Finally, powerful voices including Michael Pollan, Sylvia Earle, and E. O. Wilson warned that as commercial fishing undermined the ocean's natural integrity, the best way to restore marine ecosystems was to fence off the sea, curtail seafood harvesting, and adopt a largely plant-based diet.

But that would miss the fact that fish are astonishingly compact deliverers of the most crucial nutrients all humans need. For example, a four-ounce wild pollock filet is not only low in fat, cholesterol, and carbohydrates, but also provides 537 milligrams of nutritious omega-3 fatty acids, essential to healthy brains, cell membranes, retina and sperm as well as to reduced inflammation, blood clots and blood pressure.

The most heated and still politically potent critique of catch shares focused on their social distributional consequences. *Which people benefit more than others, and how much should they get?* This was, ironically, Buddy's main source of confusion and dissent: he knew how derbies wasted food, destroyed biodiversity, distorted markets, eroded profits, and forced men like him to risk death by fishing during tempests. But he thrived on the rush, made it work, and couldn't let go of the winner-take-all notion that as more fishermen dropped out, his portion might grow. What he feared was losing his competitive advantage. He'd worked hard. He was winning. So why risk losing the bulk of his gains now for the mere promise of a potentially better life emerging in some vague and possibly distant future?

Many opponents shared what was then Buddy's palpable sense of social insecurity. All people rightly fear experiencing loss—of a job, of social status, of control, of tradition, of a sense of self-worth. These criticisms cut to the quick and deserved deeper consideration, for fisheries reform revealed a microcosm of larger concerns in twenty-first century America about the concentration and distribution of wealth, growing economic inequality, and ensuring fair opportunities for those who never had a seat at the table when fishery shares were allocated. Why, critics reasonably wondered, should someone like Buddy—who did as much as anyone to grind red snapper populations down to almost nothing—be awarded 4.7 percent of the total allowable catch? Why did he deserve more than someone who did less damage in the first place? Shouldn't he pay for all his past damage instead?

Such questions have often kept many of us up late, staring at the ceiling, wrestling not only with fairness but also with trade-offs between ecological, social, and economic outcomes. But this approach worked because managing fish really means managing people, and people most effectively managed themselves through responsibilities and rewards. To replenish the sea by rebuilding fish populations, a fisherman's exposure to risk had to be linked with commensurate benefits. Buddy had paid for his share day after day as he invested several decades of blood and sweat, labor and capital, missed weddings and funerals and time with his family into catching the most red snapper, as the highliner. He may have had the most in terms of money and self-worth to gain if a new catch shares system could rebuild red snapper populations, but he also had the biggest investments to lose if it couldn't.

That initial allocation of quota formed the crux of every catch share program. It impacted economic, ecological and social performance, and emerged only through negotiation among stakeholders. Felix Cox and other advocates recognized the need to address this issue early on and transparently, which is why they agreed that a red snapper catch share program would cap or constrain fishermen to hold no more than 6 percent of the fishery. Others allocated quota to communities or residents in territorial waters. Taking these steps inhibited economic efficiency, but helped democratically ensure no single port, state, sector, vessel, or individual, including Buddy, would be able to dominate others. University of British Columbia's Rashid Sumaila, a catch shares skeptic, noted that concentration limits were "already a feature of many existing quota systems... [ensuring] the economic efficiency benefits of ITQs may be captured while minimizing their negative social impacts."

That said, social equity entailed unintended outcomes and costs of its own. Fear and resentment of "slipper skippers" or "sea lords"– quota owners who leased out shares to "modern day serfs" but didn't fish themselves—became a standard denigration of catch shares. Yet recent studies found that knee-jerk blanket restrictions on ownership and transactions might make inequity worse for the most vulnerable, as "allocation markets shrink, lease prices increase, discards increase—and negative impacts can be particularly strong for smaller-scale fishers who own no quota and are entirely lease-dependent."

The root of the concern was that workers without quota get screwed. The truth was that fish value chains had long been constricting globally, with or without catch shares. More importantly, researchers found that under catch shares both wages and job security improved. When Alaska crab fishermen in 2005 converted to catch shares, "a larger number of short derby fishery jobs have been replaced by a smaller number of longer, safer, more stable and often more lucrative positions," lifting overall crew wages. Laborers who once competed for jobs that might last four days could now land gigs that lasted four weeks; greenhorns in the 2007 season of *Deadliest Catch* worked fewer hours each day, slept more hours at night, and were paid 12 percent more per day than those initial crews who made their 2005 debut. That stable, steady, upward trajectory allowed fishermen at every level to reinvest their gains, employing and diversifying their coastal communities.

Curiously, the debate over social equity could ramp up only after catch shares put an end to an era when *every* fisherman was dirt poor, risking their lives, and depleting the sea. As derby years crashed fish populations, sank boats and dissipated profits, even the best fishermen, like Buddy, were still just one bad harvest from bankruptcy and one bad storm from something worse. Commercial fishing had always involved physical work, and some might romanticize the hardship days when all seafood harvesters were equally strung out, battling fierce weather, and in debt. As fisheries recovered, some fishermen began to climb out of tenuous poverty, stirring resentment among those who didn't, against blue-collar entrepreneurs, like Buddy, as "one of the true kingpins of the Gulf."

Peer envy is instinctive. It's a natural human condition. Even in Alaska, Indigenous people busily reinvesting their substantial royalties from catch share fisheries had come under fire, with social activists objecting to how community fish quotas had enriched coastal villages more than those further inland, creating divisions within larger tribes. Ideological, political, ecological and social struggle between haves and have nots over land and property predated Karl Marx and Thomas Malthus. Now, in a few decades, the same questions were being raised offshore, as secure assets, self-interest, incentives and inclusive markets generated new levels of natural capital and economic wealth at sea—providing all parties with a growing pie worth fighting over.

All this swirling debate around him just deepened Buddy's resistance. "As the first referendum vote approached, I started reading more about quotas but still thought: 'What the hell are they trying to pull now, and where am I going to be in this deal?' I didn't like it. Didn't like them changing shit around." Ideologically, he knew that since his shares weren't property the government could take them away at any time for any reason. Politically, they could take the quota he had invested in and give it away to better connected interests, competing sectors with bigger voting blocs. Ecologically, he felt uncertainty: regulatory strings and confusion would only further worsen the health of red snapper populations. Socially, he knew the old rules were broken and "eventually we'd run out of fish to catch. But I was still winning. I felt like I was at the top of my game. So, any change that might come through new regulations might take that away from me. And the way things were going, the new system could take our fishery away from us to other interests." He walked out of the meeting with Baker and Cox unmoved, dead set against their agenda.

While Buddy's fighting instincts served him well under the derby's anarchy, Felix Cox was one of many who couldn't withstand it. Before he could see his fishery take root and recover under catch shares, he sold his boat, permit and shares, worn down physically and mentally by the political ordeal. On shore he became a real estate broker and turned to woodworking and gardening until his death on February 17, 2014. Cox was an upbeat character; he sang and played guitar. He never complained, never impugned the motives of Buddy or anyone else for their opposition. He just wished a new system could have been adopted soon enough for him to continue doing what he loved at sea.

Chapter Seven
THE RENAISSANCE BEGINS

The 2005 Galveston meeting with Buddy was a speed bump. But Pam Baker never gave up on developing a system that helped people and communities. She met with state and federal officials and kept talking, writing and calling up guys in every fishing community from Brownville, Texas, to Sarasota, Florida. She commiserated with seafood harvesters like Cox who faced the challenges of making ends meet; sat with worried dock owners and restaurants whose own businesses depended on viable commercial fishermen. With nothing left to lose, in a fishery on the verge of collapse or government shutdown or both, those men in turn listened longer and closer than Buddy had as she described how catch shares could save their businesses. Slowly, more and more came around.

Buddy dug in harder. When on January 17, 2006, fishermen were invited to vote on the first referendum—on whether to consider a catch share in principle—he voted no. When the second rolled around two months later—on the Gulf Council design that Felix and Pam and the ad hoc red snapper IFQ advisory panel had developed—he voted no again. He gave his all to defeating the reform, delivering an earful to every fisherman who unloaded seafood at Katie's on why both the idea of catch shares and the allocation were not just flawed and stupid, but dangerous. When despite all that both votes passed, winning support from 80 percent of the fishermen, Buddy braced for the worst.

Red snapper catch shares went live on January 1, 2007. For Baker it felt like the first lunar mission, with a dramatic countdown. "Everyone was holding their breath," she recalled, "wondering, 'What's going to happen now?' It was eerily quiet." Days went by, then weeks. Finally, someone called her up and said, "You know, it's working. People are just out fishing."

Unaccustomed to losing, Buddy felt angry at how the votes shook out; he was sure everyone else had been duped. Regardless of the vote, fishermen would have faced a painful regulatory cut in how much fish they could catch; it was an essential measure to slow or stop overharvesting. Well, Buddy thought, good luck with that. If they wanted to court disaster, reduce their catch, and give up the competition, they could go ahead, but he wouldn't join them on their voyage to doom. "I'm facing this crazy implementation of catch shares, and it meant taking a reduction of my potential catch by 50 percent. So I decided," his voice turns sarcastic, "out of the goodness of my heart, of course, that I'd get off my boat and let others catch the small amount of fish available to us all that first year. I didn't know where it was going, but didn't feel good about it. So I sold one of my two fish houses to reduce my debt load, and did all the things you do to tighten your belt preparing for tough times."

As the months rolled by, however, Buddy couldn't deny what he began seeing on and off the water. He noticed that the fishermen bringing him snapper had managed to fill their boats on shorter trips, saving time, labor and other operating costs while keeping fish fresh. He also saw that because the fish weren't coming in all at once, and were in far better shape, the market offered much more per pound. "Prices on snapper skyrocketed," he said, "to where the market was paying boats $4.50 to $4.85 per pound. In that first short period of time guys were getting twice as much money for the same fish, while expenses dropped to less than a quarter."

It wasn't just Buddy, or Katie's Seafood market. The catch share system began transforming an entire way of life for red snapper fishermen throughout the Gulf. Captains were selecting when, where, and how to fish. The commercial season, once squeezed into a few days a month, or a few months each year, now stretched over 365 days. Working together, the captains found ways to transform waste into the food that it was. By counting and tracking all quota they could keep what they caught: any excess accidentally hooked, any undesired fish, could be leased or traded with other fishermen who hadn't, rewarding and reinforcing efforts to fish clean.

Through a slower pace, and the need to count each fish against their individual allocation, the fishermen no longer went over the commercial sector's quota. In fact, for the first time they came in *under* the Total Allowable Catch that year, and every year thereafter. This was unheard of, but made sense as a collective risk-reduction and wealth augmentation strategy: it's easier for all fishermen to slow down and forgo a bit of this year's harvest, knowing their share will increase in size and be available to them next year. With individual security, the high levels of distrust and antagonism among Wharf Road neighbors over the available supply came to an end. At joint Easter parties, fishermen no longer ducked out to gain a few hours' competitive advantage.

For the first time in memory, it became a seller's market, favoring harvesters over buyers. Buddy quickly realized that both sides would gain as fishermen learned to space out their landings over the course of the year or sell their catch in advance. "Convincing fishermen to hold back was tough at first," he recalled. Harvesters were of the mind that buyers and wholesalers (like him) were just trying to get more money from retail consumers. That was part of it. But Buddy made the case that by spreading out fish harvests longer rather than catching the entire quota in the first few trips, the fishermen could also earn more while letting the fish recover back toward historic levels. "It sounded crazy, I know, but we could all catch less fish and yet make more money."

Deep in his gut, Buddy was realizing how profoundly he'd been wrong. Cox and Baker's crazy strategy wasn't a disaster but a godsend, a gift that could secure the fishery's, and thus his family's future. When Wayne and others invited Buddy to attend a catch shares meeting with Pam in Florida, they didn't have to ask twice. Suddenly he was eager to find out more from her and others about how catch shares had worked in the past and whether he could apply the reform process not just to snapper but to all the other fish he caught and sold.

BY THEN, BAKER was already scoping out exactly that possibility for two other potential mainstays of Buddy's fishing prowess in the Gulf reef ecosystem: grouper and tilefish.

Grouper fish present unique challenges. These reef species are not only slow to reproduce like snapper, but many are also "protogynous hermaphrodites," meaning that as juveniles all are female but as they mature some change sex to become male. By harvesting the biggest fish, Buddy and hundreds of other longline fishermen had been taking out not only the most prolific female breeders in their prime but much of the male population, further crippling reproductive capacity and speeding overfishing throughout the Gulf. Groupers also aggregate to spawn, making them especially vulnerable to overfishing.

Golden tilefish exhibit gold and blue on their back and gold and silver on their belly. Like its less glamorous relative, Blueline tilefish, they can grow to reach a meter in length or more, live four decades, and fall for longlines or hand lines in cool deep waters dangled over clay, mud or sand sea floors. Like grouper, they taste delicious, with a fine flake meat that some chefs liken to crab or lobster, fueling market demand. As a result, like red snapper, tilefish were caught in a tailspin of overexploitation, resulting in the same "race for fish" derby.

Gulf red snapper had proved that it was possible to turn the tide on a big commercial fishery and prevent collapse. But that was one species, and even so, the route to reform had taken a decade. Looking ahead, catch share programs could involve multiple species of grouper and tilefish, a fisheries complex that was highly vulnerable to being overexploited by harvesters, who in turn were fast running out of fuel, cash, time and fish. Seeing the potential for recovery not just for red snapper, but for fisheries around the country, EDF doubled down on the risky proposition to establish and leverage strategic partnerships that would unleash a "blue economy" anchored by fishermen. Catch shares were viewed with suspicion and even hostility not only by many academics and fishermen but even more so by environmentalists (including some at EDF), who even after red snapper successes still couldn't see the logic of entrusting the perpetrators of overfishing with more control.

AS BUDDY AND the others settled into the new system, they continued to find new ways to make it work for both fish and fishermen. They were finally able to wait out squalls, make repairs, and "harvest to price"—a practice of selectively fishing only when dockside demand for snapper had climbed to a more profitable peak. Over the next two years, Buddy saw a 39 percent increase in the volume of fish he could catch and a 40 percent increase in the price paid for each fish he brought to the dock. He also saw red snapper discards plummet and spawning rise to levels not seen since the 1970s. As revenues doubled, Wharf Road enjoyed lower risks to safety, higher profits, less waste, and more full-time jobs landing bigger, pricier red snapper. "Catch shares improved the stability of fishing employment," concluded a 2009 Gulf fishery review. "They allowed vessel owners the opportunity to provide full time jobs to qualified captains and deckhands, without the variability that results from short seasons."

Armed with new intelligence about the past and potential of catch shares, Buddy started buying up more shares from fishermen looking to get out or downsize, expanding his stake in the game until he held 4.77 percent of the red snapper quota—more than any other fisherman. "A few more years of this," Buddy thought, and "I'd soon be in a position to sell my shares, sit back with a glass of wine and watch sunsets with my wife."

Buddy often spoke of retirement. No one believed him. Not for nothing did deckhands nickname him Captain Bligh, after the despot whose tyranny, obsession, intolerance and harsh tongue-lashing finally drove the *HMS Bounty* to engage in the world's most famous mutiny. Buddy didn't dispute the comparisons, nor would any friend, deckhand or son—no matter how ill-treated or resentful—ever suggest prematurely taking over. After ranking as a highliner for decades, Buddy was just not one to ease off the throttle.

The unexpected promise of catch shares left him, if anything, more energized than ever. He spoke often how he felt "grateful for this opportunity," like he "owed the world something and wanted to give back more than I got." Soon he was eager to help others see fishing the way he had begun to.

Cynics dismissed his lofty words as a thin veil over naked self-interest. "No matter what Buddy tells you about caring for habitat and the transformative power of catch shares," scoffed fellow Galveston fisherman and friend Billy Wright, "for him, for me, for any of us fishermen, it's all about the money." Buddy never tried to hide his economic self-interest; if anything, he spoke bluntly, even crudely about making more money by catching less fish. "The bastards, they tricked me," he deadpanned about Baker and Cox and the 80 percent of commercial fishermen who had voted for catch shares. "They forced me to get into this new system. They made me build a life where I'd have to figure out what to do with the money I earned. It was an amazing problem to have, to pry open your eyes to a new world and say, 'Thank *God* that I lost that vote'!"

All his energies were quickly redeployed. After decades spent fighting each day *against* rivals, *against* regulations, *against* ever scarcer fish, he could now start to fight *for* Galveston fishermen and *for* the Gulf's recovery. He would no longer see his private gains as a thing separate or distinct from the health of red snapper and by extension the entire reef ecosystem. He was now ready to throw in with Baker and other EDF staff in their effort to convert more of the similarly overfished populations he caught—deep-water groupers, shallow-water groupers and above all, tilefish—and meet them and other reef fishermen at a hotel on the Florida to organize advocacy around catch share programs for these other reef species. When Billy Wright called him about joining that first planning meeting, Buddy's only question was "how fast can we get there?"

He expected to meet the man or woman who called the shots. Upon arrival, however, he discovered that designing a healthy, regional catch share program from the bottom up means no one person was ever in charge. There's no owner to negotiate terms, no lone official making rules, no captain to bark out orders, no chain of command. Everything—from wording goals and defining the resource to identifying participants and setting the allocation formula—was up for negotiation among many diverse stakeholders. That was both the democratic beauty and the messy infuriating challenge of this new evolving system. Toward the end of that first long night of talk, Buddy saw momentum waning. He and the other fishermen were used to working autonomously. Few had experience or appetite for political organizing. True, no one got up from the table or left the meeting, but that was mostly to avoid getting roped in. "Fishermen don't volunteer for anything," said Buddy. "The last guy standing gets to make the calls, and if you step out of the room you get appointed." Finally, Jerry Anderson, a fisherman out of Panama City, Florida, stood up and broke the logjam. "He said the only way to go is for us to put our money where our mouth is, and he wrote out a five-hundred-dollar check and put it on the table as seed money to form a new coalition. That created a kind of rush to match him and join in." The race to harvest fish had mutated into a competition to restore it and gave birth that night to the Gulf of Mexico Reef Fish Shareholders' Alliance, dedicated to "resource stewardship, environmental protection, targeted advocacy, reduced discards of vulnerable species, safety at sea, and enhancing the economic value of the fishing industry."

Buddy, who all his life had jeered at "activists," went all in. First, he joined the board of directors. Then he volunteered to be treasurer. "I'm going to be raising money from my group in Texas," he told them. "So, if the Alliance doesn't do the right thing, I'll take my money back." Finally, he recruited the one executive, a woman named Tj Tate, who could run day-to-day operations, spend wisely, make priorities, and deal with a hundred cantankerous men who had never collaborated.

By 2009, the Alliance had transitioned grouper and tilefish into a second catch share, while Buddy began proselytizing their wonders to the other Wharf Roads around America. "My whole endeavor was to figure out ways to preserve this new strategy, and not to let the naysayers win the day."

He found the best way to do that was through fishermen exchanges that took him to California, where trawlers were preparing to design a catch share program for dozens of groundfish—a category that includes cod, flounder, halibut, rockfish and sole—so-called because these species live on, in, or near the bottom of the sea they inhabit. In Florida he sat down for beers with other reef fishermen who fished exclusively for grouper. He even flew to Baltimore and met with crab fishermen in Chesapeake Bay. In each place he encountered the same initially suspicious reaction: Sure, catch shares may have worked for *you* with red snapper, but it will never work for *us*. "The only way to get past that was for me getting out on a boat with them and going out fishing," said Buddy, "and telling my story about a prior-service Marine who believes in repaying his debts. I talked about how I owed all the people who worked so hard to bring about this new management system. Then, once on their boat offshore, it was just a few fishermen comparing notes, talking about what worked so well in one place, and might also turn things around here."

The fish story got better with time, backed by economic and scientific data. The transformation from fragmented crash to healthy resurgence applied to both the fish and the fisherman. Teaming up with his brother Kenny and bringing his four sons into the business, Buddy might eventually secure the Guindon family a small fortune—*if* the various species they fished could be restored to historic levels. Their future fates were more interwoven than ever. Rather than haul up entire schools today, Buddy could now see the advantages of letting the young ones escape to grow bigger for harvest several years down the road. Rather than see every fish as merely meat, he now had reasons to leave behind those BOFFFFs, so they could spawn in vast quantities, even though many of their babies might not be caught until Buddy's youngest son came of age. With this long view, the value of a live fish's fecundity potential outweighed its price per pound today.

Heading out to sea, commercial fishermen had every incentive to rebuild with care and deliberation the same Gulf fisheries they had once so rapidly depleted. The initial sharp rebound of red snapper would start to flatten out, especially on Florida's east coast, and new entrants would struggle to participate in the natural wealth as it grew offshore. But at the time, with Buddy right there at the center, it felt like the wind was at fishermen's backs and that nothing could stop the Gulf renaissance underway. Few seemed to anticipate how certain dark ocean forces lay beyond the power of Buddy, or any human, to control.

Part III

REGIONAL

Chapter Eight
SPARKING INNOVATION

L ooming over the low-slung aluminum shed housing Katie's Seafood Market is the Ocean Star Offshore Drilling Rig and Museum. Housed inside the retired jackup rig—a buoyant platform with movable legs that can raise the hull above the sea's surface—three floors of interactive displays on seismic technology and drilling history provide a wildly popular tourist attraction and educational monument to the Gulf's most lucrative and politically powerful offshore economy: petroleum. The Ocean Star dwarfs the commercial and recreational fishing vessels along Wharf Road, yet many fishermen heavily rely on the rigs it celebrates.

When Buddy's after red snapper he often headed for a few of the thousands of abandoned oil and gas rigs reportedly scattered across a quarter-million square miles of the Northern Gulf. He appreciated how the steel rigs could serve as a kind of artificial reef. The flat metal surfaces anchored and built an additional red snapper habitat for shellfish, squid, and crabs. This provides nutrients and energy for all the animals—shellfish, squid, crabs, shrimps, barnacles and crayfish, worms, starfish, and sea urchins—that the voracious carnivore likes to eat. A rig's vertical structure, in the middle of otherwise open water, also provided snapper a place to hide and rest from larger predators. Knowing snapper congregated around the structures, Buddy and the other fishermen—including recreational anglers—had long ago learned which rigs to fish hard, when, and at what depths. With catch shares, each rig remained an asset long after the wells beneath the seafloor played out. "We need to leave these reefs in place," he said. "The rate of removal has been so accelerated that fertile fishing areas surrounding a rig might be there one week, and the rig and the fish gone the next. When the food source provided by the infrastructure of the rig is gone, the fish will leave the area."

Those benevolent rigs could also, however, devastate fish and fishermen, as Buddy discovered on April 20, 2010, when the Gulf fishing world blew up offshore.

At 9:45 p.m. a nine-year-old rig drilling an exploratory well for British Petroleum a mile deep and forty-one miles off Louisiana—in a reservoir known as the Macondo Prospect—warped under heat when high-pressure methane gas rose up the riser, ignited, exploded, swallowed the platform, and blew away eleven workers whose bodies were never found. After thirty-six hours, just as America prepared to celebrate Earth Day, the entire flaming platform collapsed onto the Gulf seafloor, unleashing an oil gusher that over the next eighty-seven days would discharge 4.9 million barrels of crude into what had been one of the world's fastest-recovering fisheries.

Watching the news, Buddy reeled. He witnessed the worst man-made environmental disaster in American history, as oil began killing marine life at an unimaginable scale. A small sampling of the death toll included: nine hundred bottlenose dolphins, a hundred thousand juvenile sea turtles, a million birds from loons to brown pelicans, billions of small unseen plants and animals that form the base of ocean food webs, two trillion larvae of fish that breed in the Gulf.

Those initial obvious oil impacts were horrific enough. But scientists feared the hidden and persistent impacts even more, from stillborn mammals, to suffocated deep-water corals, to persistent volatile compounds. "Nearly fifty million gallons of very toxic organic chemicals like benzene, toluene and xylene" evaporated from the surface. Decomposing organics sucked oxygen out of the water, exacerbating the Gulf's dead zone. "The pathways taken by all the oil—and their footprints in time and space—were altered by the use of chemical dispersants in ways that have not yet been fully analyzed." Even BP's decision to spray and inject two million gallons of the dispersant Corexit into the oil gusher and onto surface oil compounded oil's toxicity fifty-fold, spread it out through a far wider area and deeper water column, and left unresolved questions about long term effects, including on animal DNA.

Concerned about seafood contamination, federal officials began to shut down fishing, but in rapidly shifting ways that caused growing uncertainty. The government closures started small, based on observed and predicted oil plumes, but grew every few days through the summer of that year until in July reaching 84,000 square miles of offshore waters—37 percent of the Gulf from Atchafalaya Bay, Louisiana, to Panama City, Florida, all the way to Cuban waters. That fall, the closed areas began to decline, but some oiled areas of the Louisiana coastline remained closed two years later. On paper, that meant Buddy's fishing grounds off Texas had been deemed safe, while closing down the waters of his Gulf Reef Fish allies, like Wayne Werner, right next door in Louisiana. Frightened consumers watching the unending footage of gushing oil, demonic flames and towers of black smoke didn't draw any distinction; they turned their back on all Gulf fish, devastating business at Katie's. "People would call us up at the market and say, 'is there oil on your fish?' and we'd assure them there wasn't, but you could hear the doubt in their voices," said Buddy. Callers hung up quietly. And they wouldn't come in.

Federal seafood safety officials collected samples from oiled and non-oiled areas, put them through a rapid olfactory assessment (aka sniff test), and sent a subset to the lab, putting top priority on nearshore sedentary species like shrimp, crab, and oyster. Removed from even this low threshold were grouper or snapper, dismissed as a health concern since for many months officials hadn't even developed a method to test for dispersants. "All this contributed to the public's skepticism," said Tim Fitzgerald, a seafood expert. "The government tried to reassure consumers that they had it all under control, and even if scientifically that may have been true, the message was totally detached from the reality on TV screens." For four months, as people watched that plume camera and cut to the oil mats on barrier islands and oil-soaked brown pelicans gasping for air, "they knew there was no way everything was okay, and said 'I don't care how much testing you do; I don't believe you.' The way the government communicated perpetuated the level of distrust."

The long-running disaster depressed seafood consumption not only in the Gulf but throughout America, and during the very months when the red snapper market was usually at its hottest. Amid attempts at gallows humor, Buddy and other fishermen began to ask if he should have retired earlier and sold out shares before the disaster hit. Now he and his fishing buddies worried whether they would soon even be able to give quota away, or if there would even *be* snapper, grouper, or tilefish left to catch in the decade to come. To save their livelihoods, Buddy and the Reef Shareholders' Alliance would have to make a leap unlike any they'd made before.

These guys were innovators by necessity. Offshore, they had to be jack-of-all-trades, improvising fixes to breakdowns or other calamities. If Buddy ran out of bait, he chopped up mud eels or cut fingertips off rubber gloves to use as makeshift lures. He hired those who could bolt, weld, chicken-wire or duct-tape a quick solution. But if rugged individuals were resourceful in a pinch, fishermen as a group had yet to unlock their collective potential. Many still practiced the every-man-for-himself habits they'd developed in response to the here-and-now pressures of the derby: use only existing tools; avoid long-term risk, business plans, or marketing schemes. Catch shares offered new potential to experiment. But it took a catastrophe—like a federal emergency in the Pacific, or the oil spill in the Gulf—to break the old customs and inertia and expose fishermen to a whole world of new research, technology, transparency, and financing models emerging around the globe.

PIONEERING CAME NATURALLY to Sara Skamser. In her twenties she'd worked as a welder on Sturgeon Bay ships and Midwest boxcars and for weeks at a time on tugboats on the Columbia River. Despite all that, she couldn't break into Alaska trawlers. Captains looked her over and explained that while they'd like to hire her, "our wives would feel threatened" if they brought an attractive hippie chick like her out to sea on a small boat for days or weeks at a time. (Years later, after Skamser met their wives, she learned from their rolling eyes exactly which half of the marriage felt most threatened by a taller, stronger, harder-working female on board.) But her greatest passion and prowess was in making and setting trawl nets. In Sara's deft hands, the warp and weft could be made to respond like a living thing to different ocean currents, wind speeds and engine torque. She could balance the horizontal pressure exerted by the "door" wings that pull a trawl net open against the vertical force of floats and weights, adapting bridle and pulleys to the needs of each boat, target species and captain. She could make or repair strong, beautiful nets. "Nets that performed," she said, "the way nets were born to work."

So, one day in the late 1980s, while recuperating from the latest rejection in a Kodiak, Alaska, bar, she drank up enough courage to enter and triumph the crab festival women's arm-wrestling contest, beating out a massive backwoods' trapper named Shirley to take home a prize of $1,000. She invested those winnings in a Newport, Oregon, fishing net-building shop called Foulweather Trawl, where she would custom-make trawl nets for fishing families. She would still catch lots of fish, she joked, but indirectly through her craft. "So, I still work with all those captains and owners who wouldn't hire me in the first place," she said, laughing. "My revenge is that now I get to invoice them."

For more than ten thousand years, a fishing net's function was to catch the most meat, in the shortest time, with the least effort. Trawl nets, first deployed by fishing vessels in the seventeenth century, proved the most effective at killing everything in a vessel's path, but indiscriminately. Targeting adult shrimp, cod, groundfish, pollock, squid, or whitefish, trawlers also caught vast quantities of unmarketable stuff: seaweed, driftwood, baby fish, trash fish, jellyfish, birds, mammals, tires. Sorting out all this caught stuff was expensive to fishermen, costing labor, time, fuel, and space in a net that could otherwise be filled with money fish. It also generated controversy for harming the ecosystem. Environmental advocates say that when trawl doors and nets are dragged along sea floors, "everything in their path is disturbed or destroyed, including seagrasses, coral reefs or rock gardens where fish hide from predators."

Trawl fishermen caught in the race for fish had little time, patience, money or skill to design or adapt nets to be more selective. To the contrary: chasing volume over value, many began to source ever-bigger nets from automated, capital-intensive global chains and Sara saw her new business withering.

That began to change as Pacific trawl fisheries crashed. In 2000, groundfish were declared a federal disaster, a slow-motion emergency that—unlike sudden quakes, wildfires, tornadoes or floods—had been years in the making. In response, trawlers going after whiting, cod, sole and dozens of other groundfish species along the Pacific coast prepared to convert to catch shares. By 2011, from the Mexican border to the Bering Sea, groundfish harvesters would be rewarded for slowing down and more selectively catching defined quantities of specific kinds of fishes. They would be held responsible not only for the fish they wanted and landed, but also for all other species caught on nets and hooks, target and non-target, dead or alive.

Done right, trawlers could reduce waste, save time, earn more profits, and secure the future. But doing so introduced a complex set of risks. Since different species share similar habitat, even the most careful targeting of a single abundant species like pollock or hake may still accidentally kill more than your allotted annual quota of overfished species like yelloweye rockfish, an event known to trawlers as a "disaster tow"—which can immediately shut you down for the year. Hence the desire for a more selective net, capable, at blind depths, of capturing the target species, of the right age and gender, and letting others swim free. It was a challenge Skamser would readily rise to. Listening to fishermen articulate these seemingly impossible new demands, she pulled out a sheet of graph paper and pen and set out to make their customized net. "There's clearly something in the air these days," she said. "There's growing demand for the kind of work we do. It keeps me busy, shaping everything we do. And it's exciting."

If mass-market trawl nets made it too easy to catch everything, how could they be made to *un-catch* certain species? To answer that question in the 1970s, Sinkey Boone and Noah Saunders had developed hardware for shrimp boats to insert into their trawl nets, allowing accidentally scooped-up turtles to escape, called turtle excluder devices. In colder waters, Scandanavians developed a similar device, the Nordmore grate, to help shrimpers avoid large fish. In the Gulf, anglers had sued shrimpers to make them install "bycatch reduction devices" that tried, with mixed results, to cap or limit the unintentional killing of juvenile snapper. The problem was that federally imposed technology was often distrusted as a gaping, profit-swallowing hole just asking to be ignored or cheated on. Even the best gear innovations were hard to push into the market, or develop by force. You needed incentives, showing clean-caught fish will eventually earn more per pound.

Government research efforts brought another effort at selective fishing. Across the continent, in St John's, Newfoundland, the complete collapse in cod stocks pushed Canada's federal Fisheries and Marine Institute to construct the world's biggest flume tank, offering trawlers what a wind tunnel offered pilots. The massive transparent tank revealed how a net design behaved and performed underwater: something that previously had been pure conjecture. Bob Dooley, the Alaska pollock fisherman, came here to see firsthand how new net designs might help him catch mature whiting—and almost nothing else. The flume shows skeptics how, for example, a simple step like rotating the fabric of a trawl net by 45 degrees could open up the mesh, reduce drag, and release small or younger fish unharmed. For fishermen who target or exclude a single species, or even sex, the net could be designed based on what is known of the animal's behavior in the wild. It turned out no two species evade predators (including humans wielding nets) in exactly the same way. For species that bolt vertically, or hunker down, the mouth of the net could be redesigned to capture or avoid them; later, the net could sort by size or shape as fish move within it. Still, the flume tank couldn't compete with nature; its smooth flat walls lacked crosscurrents, mud, kelp, rocks, or relief. Its waters lacked the density, thermoclines (temperature layers), corrosion or buoyancy of the sea. They were also empty: 1.7 million liters without a single fish.

Catch shares helped unleash innovation by converting the old, blunt government push into a flexible and nimble market pull. In that dynamic, it was hard to compete with the real deal. To better visualize performance of trawl nets in the living ocean, Skamser in 2015 turned to a Silicon Valley startup, SmartCatch, founded by veteran tech entrepreneur Rob Terry. The problem with fishing, Terry saw, wasn't the net and it wasn't the fishermen. It was the challenge of working blind. No matter how conscientious the fisherman, "the contents of their nets largely remain a mystery until the catch is brought up onto the deck." To eliminate guesswork about what happened at the murky depths, they mounted video camera eyes inside the mouths of fishing nets, so that fishermen in the wheelhouse could see every fish their trawl swallows. In conjunction with this system, DigiCatch, Terry developed SmartNet, so that if trawlers saw that they're catching the wrong species, fish by fish, or enmeshing rockfish when they're seeking sole, they could throttle back, go into reverse, change course, or perform the trawler equivalent of the Heimlich maneuver: opening or closing diverters to immediately release the bycatch, at the place and depth it was caught. As Terry described the system: "It gives fishermen both eyes and hands inside their nets" to "dynamically manage the content of their harvest." Though still too expensive for most fishermen, the user-friendly technology could be a game-changer if economies of scale brought down the price. Terry was working with Skamser to "position the company as a leader on the cusp of a revolutionary era of commercial fishing—the era of Precision Fishing."

Yet while Skamser's customized nets, Canada's flume tank, and Terry's camera systems could help reduce waste and maximize future value, they would get nowhere without early adopters. And most fishermen often operate on the knife edge of solvency, unable to invest in new technology that ensures higher accountability. An innovation-minded family fisherman, like any startup entrepreneur, needed a link to buyers seeking a premium product, a financial bridge to get him through the "valley of death" transition. Where's a catch share capitalist when you need one?

LARRY BAND GRADUATED from Stanford and Harvard Business School and spent seventeen years as an investment banker on Wall Street, but his first love was biology. He became interested in economic problems of overfishing. He studied the evolution of catch shares, watched them take hold and unlock the future value of wild resources, and realized how much untapped wealth fishermen could realize, given half a chance. He knew traditional banks wouldn't lend even to fishermen holding catch shares because they didn't have clear title equity to offer as collateral; the banks didn't recognize them as financially convertible assets. But Band did. Working closely with a savvy young "enviropreneur" at EDF named Kate Bonzon, he helped establish a new kind of financial bridging tool, a revolving loan fund known as the California Fisheries Fund. Within a few years it had a diversified portfolio of eleven borrowers.

One of those borrowers was Geoff Bettencourt, the fourth generation of a Half Moon Bay fishing family, who for two decades had sailed the *F/V Moriah Lee* as a catch-all groundfish trawler. Following the transition to catch shares, he borrowed from the California Fisheries Fund to invest in more selective traps that would help him target black cod, which he believed could fetch top price at nearby upscale markets, like Whole Foods. To get ahead under catch shares, Bettencourt retrofitted his boat to drop traps rather than drag nets, installed extra cameras to verify compliance with catch share restrictions on unintended bycatch, and even equipped his trap-identifying marker buoys with electronic signals. With the new gear he didn't just reduce excess bycatch of overfished species; he eliminated it entirely. Then he paid off the loan with higher earnings and would expand his business model to adapt to the ever-changing nature of fishing.

There were other CFF loan recipients. Bill Blue borrowed funds to upgrade his century-old boat to fish clean. The Fund enabled Roger Cullen to experiment with more-selective nearshore fish trap designs and longline gear. Central Coast Seafood and Morro Bay Fish Company borrowed funds to develop a marketing platform and distribution network for eco-friendly, high-quality products that linked catch share fishermen with retailers and restaurants in California and abroad. Community quota banks helped protect diverse communities. The Fund was deliberately kept small and narrowly focused, as Band and Bonzon had not set it up to make money. But the Fund went on to lend nearly $4.8 million helping dozens of fishermen, ports, and seafood businesses improve operations, winning awards, offering training courses, and becoming a model for ocean entrepreneurs exploring new possibilities for market segmentation or future trading.

WITH BUSINESS BOOMING, Buddy had felt no need to tie cameras to his lines or trade red snapper futures. In 2010, he had eighteen employees, dozens of wholesale and retail clients and thousands of individual customers. But after the Macondo explosion, he and the other commercial fishermen desperately needed a way through the catastrophe. How, he wondered, could the Gulf Reef Fish Shareholders' Alliance restore market confidence? Was there a way they could prove that any given red snapper had been harvested from safe, oil-free waters? At the same time, could they turn back a growing epidemic of seafood fraud?

In 2004, University of North Carolina scientists had discovered through DNA sequencing that 60 percent of fish sold as red snapper...weren't. As its value rose, a later study found that 93 percent of fish labeled "red snapper" was not *Lutjanus campechanus* but rather one of twenty-eight other species, and quite often farm-raised freshwater tilapia. Buddy's wild "grouper" faced the same market problem, often substituted with Vietnamese catfish.

To convincingly demonstrate to distant customers not only where in the Gulf their fish came from but that it was sustainably caught and was, in fact, red snapper, Buddy and his Gulf partners began imagining a brand-new kind of value chain, one with unprecedented transparency from hook to dock to plate.

Buddy saw that he and David Krebs were well placed to foster innovation. Not only had they been friendly rivals and regional highliners, but each also ran their own Gulf "fish house" markets that bought and sold the harvest of other fishermen. Together they set to work, starting with the point of capture. To prove that a fish did not contain harmful levels of oil-spill residues, they'd have first to understand, and go beyond, what the FDA and NOAA deemed food safety. They enlisted the help of nationally recognized toxicologists at the University of Alabama at Birmingham, who scrutinized federal protocols and compared them to those used after other oil spills around the world. They concluded that more-stringent safety-testing was advisable and partnered with an independent international analytical laboratory in New Orleans, Eurofins, to put those new standards into practice, with EDF's scientific support. Their sampling program tested snapper, grouper and tilefish from Texas to Florida. Within a day of fish hitting the dock, they were shipped overnight to Eurofins where they would be analyzed for oil-based contaminants including PAHs, heavy metals, and dispersants. With consumers still shunning Gulf seafood, establishing the safety of the fish was top priority. "At the start the focus of innovation wasn't about proving the sustainability of their fishery to their customers," said Tim Fitzgerald, "but simply whether it was going to make them sick."

Winning a clean bill of health would only benefit Buddy if he could convey that status to all the freaked-out strangers on the receiving end of his supply chain. He had to show, on a map, where each fish came from, and prove it was nowhere near areas off-limits to fishing. Existing fish traceability efforts, for tuna and salmon, offered little guidance: most focused either on industrial-scale hauls that went into cans or got wrapped in frozen steaks. Red snapper is a small-scale, high-value specialty item that moved through the market fresh as a whole animal or skin-on filets. It required a visible mark, prominently stuck to the fish itself. Again, most food handling technologies and data entry systems, like TraceRegister, only helped manage inventory, not this kind of challenge. But in digging around, snapper fishermen developed a synthesis. They combined Trace-Register's hardware with an obscure Fishtrax software to initiate a traceable supply chain. They would tag each fish with a sequentially numbered code and time stamp showing precisely where, when and by whom each fish had been caught.

Tagging a fish is harder than, say, labeling a banana. The tags had to be attached to the head, right behind the eye, through something called the gill plate which is made of bone. Fish are slippery, making such an effort hard enough with a dead fish on land. Buddy had to persuade crew members swaying aboard a small vessel on the high seas, to grab a wriggling fish in one hand and fire a plastic tag gun with the other, stamping each snapper before putting it quickly on ice.

It was a tough sell. How could Buddy convince his and other captains to learn, test, develop and implement a marketing assurance innovation for a commercial harvest that may not even survive the year? In an open access fishery, a rational person would've taken a government and BP payout then packed it in. But the situation now felt different to Buddy. Today, facing this catastrophe, Wharf Road fishermen had a real stake in the red snapper's future. It was in their long-term interest to save it. To rebuild customer confidence and the market value that would follow, Buddy was prepared to share the investment risk with others. With their combined market muscle, he and Krebs felt sure they would be able to sell tagged fish at a premium, and so offered their captains extra cash per pound if they made the extra effort. To further incentivize captains, they simplified the process. "Initially we tagged the fish right on the boat," said Buddy, but over time they refined the process to tag on the dock, reducing the burden of painstaking data entry, while still highlighting the date when, and ten-square mile block where, each red snapper was caught. By early 2011, with 15 percent of the snapper fleet now "going through tags like they're water," as Buddy put it, the Gulf Reef Fish Shareholders' Alliance hired a seafood industry marketing expert to trademark a compelling brand name. The transparency innovation became known as Gulf Wild.

It took a year for consumers to overcome the after-effects of the spill that depressed Gulf fish orders and prices. But by June 2011, Gulf Wild had begun to make headlines and win converts. The tech magazine *Fast Company*, usually devoted to Silicon Valley, profiled the system right after its launch, already "with one million tags, thirty-eight high-production commercial fishing boats, and one hundred fishermen."

Since Gulf Wild covered nineteen species, including red snapper and grouper, it soon caught the attention of Jim Gossin, head of Louisiana Foods, who called and asked what these tags on the fish were for. Buddy explained the system, Gossin sent his sustainability person down to check out the program, and soon offered to buy all the fish he could afford. His ninety-five-employee company, now part of Sysco, sold Gulf seafood to restaurants and retailers throughout the lower Mississippi region. Gossin had long been bothered by questions about seafood fraud and skittish customers and was relieved to be able at last to provide a tracking system that allowed any buyer to "find my fish." Each snapper's catch information got uploaded to the web and made public as soon as the vessel reached shore. From that point on, anyone, anywhere in the value chain—from, say, Alliance member Bubba Cochrane's vessel, to the dock landing at Katie's in Galveston, to Louisiana Foods warehouse, to a chef behind the kitchen at Landry's Seafood restaurant on the Riverwalk in San Antonio—could tap or scan the tag number into their smartphone and confirm not just the species but where it was caught and landed, as well as the story of its vessel and captain. By 2012, H.E.B. Grocery Stores, the San-Antonio-based supermarket giant with 350 outlets in Texas alone, was advertising: "Fresh, locally caught American Red Snapper; Part of the Gulf Wild program that promotes seafood sustainability in the Gulf. Customers can scan a tag to see where the fish was caught."

Gulf Wild snapper, grouper and tilefish soon won favor among consumers concerned not only with food safety but also with their impact on marine environments. Born of disaster, "to prove our fish didn't come out of oily water," said Jason DeLaCruz, a Reef Fish Alliance member and friend of Buddy, the new "focus is to make this a fisherman-driven program, to make sure he's getting a premium price for his product."

There was nothing like it anywhere on earth. While some food sector companies sought opacity over their value chain, fishermen were celebrating, and voluntarily self-regulating, the entire transparent process of harvesting seafood from hook to dock to plate.

The Shareholders' Alliance had pulled together the many strands of innovation kicked off by the transition to catch shares. They had sought new research to deepen visibility into the fishery, pioneered new technology and devised new market strategies to capture more of the value of the fishery for themselves and consumers.

A new breed of tech developer had begun disrupting the oldest offshore economy, unleashing powerful consumer interfaces, online platforms, market aggregators and systems thinking. Once they secured a clearly defined share of a future wild asset, commercial fisheries innovated in ways few could have predicted. This is no longer the same fishery that Buddy's father taught him to harvest. From Galveston to Gloucester to Newport and even Kodiak, catch shares had begun elevating the sea's capacity to absorb and recover from sudden explosive shocks like the Deepwater Horizon. More importantly, the system began building the ocean's resilience in the face of man-made catastrophes that were unfolding slowly but posed still-more devastating risks to Buddy's way of life.

Chapter Nine
AT SEA ADAPTATION

Two hundred fifty-two million years ago, the earth released prodigious amounts of carbon skyward. Scientists remain uncertain about what caused this event, but they know what followed. Over the next two hundred thousand years, the oceans warmed eighteen degrees and became more acidic. Dissolved oxygen levels plunged, reefs collapsed, and marine organisms starved and suffocated, wiping out 90 percent of life.

Similar changes are underway. Only now there is no mystery about the source, and the disaster for life is unfolding at an even faster pace. Since the dawn of the industrial revolution, humans' burning of fossil fuels pushed 2,000 gigatonnes of excess carbon dioxide into the atmosphere. Half of those emissions remained up there, but 30 percent of that excess carbon sank into the sea. The resulting changes from that ocean uptake are becoming visible in salinity, sea level, currents, acidity, oxygen, light penetration and even noise.

Buddy's fishing grounds lie at the heart of this vulnerability. Over the past fifty years, surface temperatures in the Gulf of Mexico had heated up nearly twice as fast as the global ocean. August through October contributed to prolonged periods of "abnormally warm" water conditions. And summer surface water temperatures that now reached as high as 90°F were linked to stronger hurricanes, a frightening prospect for the city flattened 120 years ago in America's single deadliest weather event.

But warmer waters also affect fish in myriad ways. Species like snapper and grouper need temperate water; they can swim deeper or move northward, but only until they hit the continental shelf.

Warmer water also expands. Sea level at Galveston was soon rising a foot above its 1963 level, higher than any other US coastal city. Combined with rising tides, those encroaching seas were slowly drowning the coastal wetland and estuarine nurseries vital for ocean life. Federal scientists warned that the Gulf was also a hot spot for ocean acidification, which weakened the ability of sea snails, oysters, corals, shrimp, barnacles, crabs, and other tiny organisms at the base of the red snapper food web to build their calcium-based bodies, shells, and homes. These impacts fell on top of the nutrient pollution flowing into and down through the Mississippi River watershed, made worse by a global heating that swung extreme weather from storm to drought to flood, increasing erosion and run-off. That excess nitrogen and phosphorus stimulated massive algal growth, depleting the oxygen required to sustain red snapper habitat, impacting primary food sources such as shrimp, forcing adult fish to move out of the dead zone, and reducing their ability to spawn the next generation.

Globalization added yet more volatility to Buddy's operations. Worldwide recessions inhibited local demand at shops like Katie's. Oil geopolitics set the international price of his diesel. Multiple compounding outside threats to red snapper meant people like Buddy had to learn to adapt. But how? Catch shares catalyzed the innovation that helped Buddy and the Shareholders' Alliance weather the BP oil spill. The new system also helped fish and fishermen build resilience, buffers and shock absorbers to global risks that may be less sudden or immediately obvious yet were far more destabilizing and growing worse by the day.

THE FIRST BUFFER that catch shares afforded fishermen was financial. Derbies had become a black hole at the bank. The race forced Buddy to keep over-capitalizing, bulking up boats, gear, engines and gas in a quest for speed and size. After 2007, reduced costs and higher revenues let him deposit savings and gain liquidity. He could also more strategically invest profits in safer diversified onshore assets like ice houses and fueling stations, adding long term equity to a more flexible business that he can sell or leverage as needed. Another buffer was knowledge. Under a catch share, the market price to lease or buy red snapper shares sent important signals about a fish population's current health, abundance, regulatory politics, and future potential. The new system nudged fishing families like Buddy's to cultivate soft skills: logistics, accounting, finance, modeling, branding, even supply chain management and website development. Diverse knowledge work made harvesters marketable in the twenty-first century service economy, growing their business or exploring a new career.

A third buffer was time. By expanding operations from ten-day spurts to a yearlong season, Buddy could now patiently wait out events beyond his control—market downturns, closures, delays, illness—or special events like his eldest son Nick's wedding. When a federal government shutdown hit in October 2013, king crab harvesters could outwait the political tempest.

Temporal flexibility extended geographically. If for some reason brother Kenny, son Hans or Buddy couldn't fish in the waters off Texas—due to a hurricane or toxic red tide bloom—they could lease quota to other shareholders, anywhere else in the Gulf. That's exactly what Buddy's Reef Shareholders' Alliance colleagues did when the BP oil spill shut down some of their prime fishing grounds. If the closure had come during a derby, it would have wiped out their year's earnings. Instead, fishermen continued to have livelihoods even when they weren't fishing, and consumers suffered no interruption in their access to fish. With risk spread across the calendar and the map, the whole fishery grew more resilient than the sum of its several hundred individual parts.

A fifth new shock absorber came through political coordination. In open access seas, commercial harvesters worked hard, but in competitive seclusion. Their fragmented state of existence isolated their views, muted their voices, and stunted their bargaining muscle. Since 2007, Buddy had more time and stronger interest to tighten regional cooperation among shareholders. Former rivals gained aggregated clout in the face of legal, regulatory, market or environmental upheavals. Snapper, grouper and tilefish harvesters could collectively sue those responsible for the Deepwater Horizon explosion for negligence and liability. And because the Gulf Alliance could readily document losses through well-defined catch shares and accurate valuations, they got more equitable compensation and punitive damages, paid out faster than those made to other fishermen.

The ultimate buffer was ecological. While the Deepwater spill was the most sudden and visibly horrific event putting Gulf seafood at risk, it was far from the worst slow-motion disaster. Climate change impact continued to fisheries by altering the biology, chemistry and physical dynamics of their habitat: hotter, more turbulent and acidic seas, bleached reefs, raised sea levels, flooded nurseries, and altered migration routes and mating patterns by adult fish forced to seek colder water and scarcer food. All of this called for building resilience—through more accurate science, faster governance feedback loops, and the ability to manage fish on the move—which catch shares made more possible.

Yet it also turned out that the strongest roots of resilience may come from recovery of the red snapper itself. That's where Buddy, through catch shares, was playing a symbiotic role. By rebuilding the numbers and spawning capacity of reef fish, he was ensuring a more robust and diverse gene pool and a broader range of age classes across distinct Gulf niches. He was also rebalancing energy flows throughout the entire reef ecosystem. By allowing more big predators like grouper and snapper to resume their hungry work, and keep prey species in check, Buddy was in turn protecting corals from the damage that an overabundance of those little herbivores did. By restoring the upper layers of the food pyramid, fishermen helped ensure the fundamental health and integrity of those below.

Fishermen did more than replenish life from within. They were also better equipped, and motivated, to resist external threats to their secure assets from without. In the Great Lakes, whitefish harvesters organized energy against invasive parasitic sea lamprey, round gobi and quagga and zebra mussel species. In the Arctic, after melting ice cover exposed waters already more acidic and more stratified by temperature, pollock fishermen self-imposed a moratorium in a 200,000 square mile zone until scientists could find a sound basis for harvest. Alaska fishermen invested in scientific laboratories to discover which and how crab species could better respond and adapt to the ravages of a more acidic sea. Back in the Gulf, snapper fishermen began warning Congress about climate change. Donnie Waters, Buddy's colleague in the Alliance, testified to the Senate Subcommittee on Oceans, Atmosphere, Fisheries and Coast Guard how commercial fishermen "in the Gulf states have no idea what we're up against with ocean acidification. If this is affecting coral, we need to know. We need healthy reefs to have a healthy reef fishery."

Against compound threats, catch shares empowered fishermen to be responsive, savvy and influential stewards, building buffers so that they—and the ecosystems they depend on—could together absorb random shocks. Still, adaptation was only half of the resilience equation. Each of Buddy's fishing vessels were complicit in putting oceans at risk. After all, to ply their trade, the world's fishing fleets consumed millions of gallons of diesel every hour. That vicious cycle can be broken only if millions of fishermen like Buddy discovered some way to decouple carbon emissions from productivity. With catch shares, they may have found some help.

Chapter Ten
MARITIME MITIGATION

Under open access fishing, each ton of captured seafood burns, on average, half a ton of fuel.

Prior to 2007, Buddy and other Gulf fishermen burned even more. Having fished out the waters near shore, they had to push their engines harder and longer to find the remnant snapper, grouper and tilefish left in ever deeper and more distant waters. Forced to come back to dock under each "trip limit" of two thousand pounds, they made multiple excursions. As a result, they'd combust, Buddy estimates, five times as much fuel per snapper as they needed to. As diesel costs rose from fifty cents a gallon in the late 1970s to three dollars by 2006, the numbers didn't always pencil out. Before each trip to sea, a Galveston fisherman weighed whether the fish he might land in the next forty-eight hours would cover the fuel he'd need to catch them. "I didn't much like it, but what the hell are you going to do," said Buddy. "It was either fill the tank or don't fish."

That same calculation weighed on nearly every fisherman in US waters, as the combination of dwindling stocks and burdensome rules forced them to consume more and more fuel. From 1968 to 1988, for instance, New England harvesters' consumption of diesel per pound of fish landed grew six-fold. And North America's fishermen were far more fuel-efficient than most: over the past four decades, fleets elsewhere in the ocean burned fifteen times as much fuel per fish. Fossil-fueled harvests dated back to nineteenth century coal-powered steam engines, like those in the Great Lakes. But the last half century brought a destructive feedback loop: cheaper diesel and larger internal combustion engines sped overfishing, which left fewer, smaller and scattered fish, which then drove demand for still more diesel and more power. "The wide application of fuel that has allowed fleets to expand," argued Peter H. Tydemers, a natural resources professor at Dalhousie University in Canada, "has underpinned much of the overfishing of stocks and deterioration of aquatic ecosystems."

For some, these rising emissions made a case for a return to small, artisanal fishing. Bottom trawlers, critics noted, consumed seven times as much diesel per unit of fish as traps, and the world's smaller harvesters would often catch four times as much fish-per unit of fuel as larger, more powerful fleets. But looking only at vessel size ignored what subtle incentives drove fishermen to chase species that could not be harvested in any other way. Artisanal fleets would fare poorly in the North Pacific with crab or pollock. It also ignored the correlation between fuel consumption and the value of targeted fish. The average herring boat burned just 3.5 gallons to catch a ton; long-liners or purse-seiners or deep-sea trawlers needed 528 gallons to catch the same ton of tuna or swordfish. Yet the latter earned forty times more at market. In both cases, and all those in between, the open-access competition for ever-more scattered and scarce fish meant fuel's share of all costs would often determine who could afford to stay in the race. In 2001, diesel expenses represented just a fifth of fishing revenues worldwide; by 2008, as oil nearly tripled from twenty-three dollars to sixty-four dollars a barrel, they ate up half. As the biggest and least negotiable expense, the global price of diesel had become the hidden hand in seafood harvesting: It sped the race to the bottom, and culled local fishing economies of those who couldn't afford to fill up at the pump.

Fuel had been almost universally politicized. As diesel costs mounted, governments in Africa, Asia, Europe and Latin America stepped in, introducing policies to ensure fishermen had full tanks. In small-scale fisheries, where an engine turned a subsistence fisherman into a business, governments subsidized fuel. Elsewhere, as "industrial fleets" dominated harvests, governments began awarding loans or grants to give fleets flying their flag the capability to travel farther—investing more fuel to catch more-valuable fish. Fuel subsidies became the single biggest driver of the expansion of "distant water fleets" moving into foreign waters. In aggregate, China's fuel subsidies to its long-distance fishing fleet rose tenfold from $30 million in 2006 to $300 million in 2011; since then, Oceana estimated $3.5 billion in harmful fishing subsidies. Diesel impacted more than the bottom line. For example, a 2021 study estimated that bottom trawling globally released around 1 gigaton (1 billion tons) of CO_2 annually, a massive sum nearly as large as the entire aviation industry. These carbon emissions slowly, invisibly devastated ocean life. While Buddy's personal carbon footprint may seem paltry in the grand scheme, each ton he harvested generated on average 1.7 tons of carbon emissions. That added up. In 2005 researchers found that in the twenty countries (including the US) that catch 80 percent of all seafood, fishermen burned thirteen billion gallons of fuel, or 25,000 gallons per minute. If fishing were a country, represented in climate negotiations, the commercial seafood harvesting sector would rank as the world's eighteenth-worst polluter, alongside the Netherlands. Add in small-scale and emerging economy vessels and the global fishing fleet would rank higher still—and a hundred more coastal fishing nations are racing to catch up. Commercial fishing, observed Daniel Pauly, "is the only major industry in the world that is getting more and more energy-inefficient."

WAS NOT JUST industrialized nations. The cause of that fuel-fish-emissions spiral was universal, as exemplified in Tanzania's capital. Each day, by 7:00 a.m., the Mzizimi fish market in Dar es Salaam grew crowded with thousands of people haggling over fish that are devoured within hours of harvest. With no wharf or dock, men would wade up to their necks to stand boat-side, reach up and grab buckets and baskets and strings of parrotfish, rabbitfish, catfish and swordfish, then wade back to bring them ashore. On poured concrete tables, knives flashed as young men gut msusa (barracuda), cut off the tentacles of pweza (octopus), scaled chewa (grouper), divvied up piles of mkizi (mullet), or sliced up kolekole (pompano). Swiped on pants, knives slipped back into knee-high rubber boots. A man sharpend knives and machetes by pedaling an upside-down bike, its back wheel converted to a spinning grindstone that sent sparks flying from the blade edge. Six suitcase-sized stingrays are heaped on a cart. A severed sailfish head peered skyward. A boy practicing his English boasted how hauling and gutting fish earned him five dollars a day. Women in Islamic garb scold camera-toting tourists who found the colorful market irresistibly raw and authentic, filled with countless sounds, sights and smells except one—diesel exhaust.

Fuel is often a luxury for fishermen in emerging economies. Even in this most modernized of Tanzania's 257 landing ports, only a fraction of boats—with western-yearning names like *Peace Boys* and *Homeboys*—had motors. Most of the country's thirty-seven thousand fishermen—one for each 100 yards of the nation's long coastline—still relied on wind or their own sweat to power their small dhows, canoes, dinghies, and outriggers. Despite those ancient methods, however, as Tanzania's human population has risen, its seafood populations have fallen. Between 2000 and 2023 the country added thirty million people, while landings of finfish, prawns, crabs, sea cucumbers, and mollusks plummeted by more than two thirds. Each boat now harvested a third as much per day as it did two decades ago, and each fish caught is half as big as before, further driving fishing families into poverty and spreading malnutrition among those who depend on their dwindling catches. Fishermen correctly blamed two forces: local overharvesting and global warming. As a remedy, Tanzanian policies doubled down on both.

Borrowing World Bank funds, Tanzania subsidized larger engines to help fishermen go farther offshore and compete with foreign vessels, like China's. The idea was to provide more protein for local communities and increase earnings that fishermen could reinvest in still-more powerful boats. Instead, those bulked-up boats exhausted nearshore fisheries and overpowered subsistence fishermen. Supply gluts deflated fish prices. More fishermen grew more dependent on more fuel, which spiked emissions per fish.

The fuel/depletion/emissions spiral would spread fast as countries subsidized fuel for fishing. In Mexico, fuel subsidies undercut government efforts to eliminate 130,000 metric tons of carbon when the government offered fishermen 15,000 cleaner-burning four-stroke motors: the dirty old two-strokes were merely passed on to other boats. Globally, some $22 billion in fuel subsidies have spurred short-term booms in fishing, often inflating gross revenues by $4.2 billion a year, while inflicting long-term damage. The World Bank belatedly woke up to acknowledge how fuel subsidies "create perverse incentives for continued fishing in the face of declining catches," a triple whammy, as emissions themselves further degrade ocean habitats.

One World Bank study found that—without the overfishing accelerated in large part by fuel subsidies—the current global harvest could be caught with nearly half the effort, saving nearly half the fuel, thus slashing emissions per fish by 44 percent. The circular logic here tempts advocates to demand tighter compliance with emission rules, stronger engine efficiency standards, high penalties for infractions, and an end to cheap subsidized diesel. "The elimination of fuel subsidies and the reintroduction of market signals into the operational and investment decisions of vessel owners," argued the environmental advocacy group Oceana, in its report *Fueling Overfishing*, "are key to creating a more fuel-efficient fishing industry and reducing its carbon footprint."

Treating symptoms, however, rarely cure the underlying disease. Once introduced, fishing fuel subsidies proved nearly impossible to end. In 2009, twenty leading countries pledged to phase out financial support for fossil fuel; many years later, all have stalled on or even increased subsidies. Making fuel more expensive might reduce fleet emissions. But it, too, exacts an inequitable toll. After 2004, the doubling of oil prices made it too costly to pursue distant and dwindling fish populations, lowering emissions and letting overfished species briefly recover. "As painful as it is to the fishing industry," explained economist Ragnar Arnason, "fuel price increase may actually contribute to a healthier fishery in the longer run, and by increasing sustainable catches also benefit consumers of fish." But it was as risky to count on global oil price spikes to save local fisheries by default, as it was brutal to hope for the least affluent fishermen and consumers to suffer the toll. Rather than a top-down approach, catch shares helped harvesters escape the trap, and reduce fossil fuel emissions, almost as an afterthought.

With a secure share, Buddy could, for the first time, ease off the throttle: snapper would still be waiting for him an hour, day or month later. Catch shares also shortened his commute to work. As snapper stocks kept rebuilding, he could reliably harvest his share a hundred miles closer to shore. Freed from trip limits, he could land full loads of snapper and grouper every time. "We used to burn 100 gallons a day to go out and come back with a single two thousand-pound haul. Now we catch ten thousand pounds a trip on the same tank. We're not going out any farther, or running around in a hurry, looking for fish." Instead, in what Buddy described as "a very relaxed, planned atmosphere," his crews started the engines only when necessary. They took time and care filling up the hold with snapper or grouper. The result, said Buddy, was that he and every other commercial vessel in the Gulf fishery were burning 80 percent less fuel and thus producing 80 percent fewer emissions than they did before 2007.

Put this another way: thanks to catch shares, Wharf Road went far beyond the cuts agreed to by signatories to the Paris Accord, overnight, and voluntarily.

No doubt Wharf Road was just one locality making progress on climate pollution. But it offered a scalable precedent for other fishing communities. Evidence in the US and abroad suggested it was far from an outlier. Catch shares let harvesters anywhere step out of rush hour to save precious fuel. Bering Sea mega trawlers managed to decimated their emissions ratio to 0.1 pound of carbon to one pound of wild pollock. That McDonald's Filet-O-Fish now boasts one of the lowest carbon footprints of any pound of protein, animal or vegetable, on earth: twenty times less carbon per pound of protein than tofu. In Alaska's fuel-intensive crab fishery, per Dr. Matthew N. Reimer, the process of rationalizing fleet size alone cut emissions by 70 percent. Skippers then began to: await smoother sailing in fairer weather; travel shorter distances between sets; idle their vessels; and make fewer diesel-powered lifts of their crab pots. As they did, net emissions per pound of crab further plunged. Across the US border in Mexico's Gulf of California, curvina fishermen who used to spend a gallon of diesel to catch four pounds of fish began to catch forty pounds with the same gallon, cutting their climate pollution by 90 percent. In none of these cases was emissions reduction the primary goal; rather, fishermen simply stepped up as catch shares let them reduce spending to fatten profits.

If reforms factored in a real or potential price on carbon, gains could be higher. In 2010 New England's historic groundfish fishery transitioned to catch shares. Once again, according to the research group CAPLOG, vessels of all classes burned 2.8 million fewer gallons than before, reducing carbon emissions by 27 percent while earning 18 percent more revenue per gallon. Despite a 50 percent lower catch limit, those fishermen absorbed a 9 percent reduction in income the first year after reform. If a carbon pricing scheme was in place, emissions markets compensated for climate-friendly fishing, harvesters could have recovered a third of their lost income.

If emissions rose as diesel fuelled overfishing, Buddy showed how to reverse these drivers. Scaled up, catch shares could spark innovation, build adaptation, and decarbonize what is already, pound for pound, a low-emissions protein source. Going further, some fishermen began to retrofit internal combustion engines with hybrid or even all-electric motors, with batteries recharged by hydropower or the sun. To supercharge fishing vessel emissions reductions, Buddy's revolution in the Gulf would have to accelerate nationwide and unite America's harvesters with their former adversaries.

Part IV

NATIONAL

Chapter Eleven
FEDERAL COHESION

Buddy's personal conversion, followed by his powers of persuasion, carried the promising story of catch shares from Wharf Road across Texas, Louisiana, Mississippi, Alabama, and Florida. But a regional, Gulf-wide alliance could only go so far. Red snapper, grouper and tilefish spend most of their lives in deeper waters under federal jurisdiction, so their fates would ultimately rest with Washington, DC. Those officials were strangers to Buddy, off his radar. He had no sense of their policy agenda for science, accountability, marine protection, public access, or the recreational angling sectors.

Yet if politics is the art of the possible, 2007 brought a convergence of possibilities.

First, starting in January, his snapper catch share engaged action across multiple states. Next, Congress reauthorized the 30-year-old Magnuson-Stevens Fishery Conservation and Management Act, with amendments that re-opened possibilities for more such programs. Then, as the presidential race heated up, the US suffered a massive financial collapse and slipped into what would be the worst recession in decades. Facing the prospects of massive unemployment, an incoming administration, whichever the party, would have to consider bailouts or stimulus packages to ensure the recovery of entire sectors. Yet despite the national downturn, Buddy's Gulf fishing industry was already recovering, fast, and on its own trajectory. As nature rebounded offshore, so did commercial life on shore. The federal government estimated that if America could rebuild all its depleted fish populations, the nation's waters could boost the economy by an additional $32 billion and create 500,000 new jobs up and down the coasts. The question was how to do so.

Authorities remained at odds over whether catch shares worked or were just an "ownership fetish." To resolve this debate, Christopher Costello and his UC Santa Barbara colleague marine ecologist Steven Gaines had led research that built on a global database of institutions and harvest statistics encompassing 11,135 fisheries from 1950 to 2003. The research team set out to "test whether catch-share fishery reforms achieve these hypothetical benefits." The data revealed that catch shares not only halted, but even pulled back the global trend of open access fisheries toward widespread collapse. The implications were staggering. Societies—consistent across geographies, laws, species and human cultures—who had undergone this institutional change had been able to slow, stop and even reverse overfishing. It was, said Costello, about the implications, like going from a monthly apartment rental to home ownership. Even, or especially, a leaky, run-down fixer-upper. "You take care of it—you protect your investment," he said. "When you allocate shares of the catch, then there is an incentive to protect the stock. We saw this across the globe. It's human nature."

It was a watershed moment. Catch shares had existed since 1968. Yet over the next four decades each unique program emerged only ad hoc in isolated pockets thanks to a smattering of public and private advocates. Now this broad and deep and irrefutable evidence could be translated into "effective and efficient institutions and governance structures" at the federal level. Supporters could help catch shares gain traction in the incoming administration and expand across US waters under "an integrated and comprehensive national ocean policy."

Born of tension, often as a last resort, catch shares initially seemed unlikely to broker peace. Controversies between America's traditional antagonists—fisherman vs. scientist; conservationist vs. preservationist; deckhand vs. monitor; harvester vs. angler—had long festered in a state of limbo. That stalemate was partly by design: the 1976 Magnuson-Stevens fisheries governance act balanced national principles against regional decision-making. In between, a confusing hodgepodge of 140 laws under a dozen different agencies and departments struggled to answer thorny questions. How should America reconcile the competing interests of oil and gas development, shipping, biodiversity preservation, or fisheries? What's the best way to hold US fishing vessels accountable? Where's the rationale for nationally unique places? Who can access the ocean's public resources, at what cost? Does optimal fishing mean several hundred commercial vessels harvest huge catches for public markets, or several million anglers land a few fish each for private consumption—or both?

Few could even agree if, how, or by whom these could be answered. Some sought the clarifying unity of one strong overriding policy. Others felt a remote authority could never appreciate or respect local nuances of coastal communities. It was the country's oldest philosophical and political fault line, one that has run throughout America's political history. Now it pitted federal supremacy against state's rights and set NOAA and the National Marine Fisheries Service against the eight Regional Fishery Management Councils over representation, rank, performance, and priorities.

The fissure, and resentment of federal intrusion, ran deepest in New England. The Atlantic coast, with a cape once teeming with its namesake cod, had in the twentieth century grown depleted, first by postwar foreign vessels, then (after MSA enactment in 1976) by too many domestic boats chasing too few fish. Under the broken open access system, cod and other groundfish were being drained from the sea. Struggling fishermen who couldn't make ends meet turned into easy prey for a few big players like New Bedford seafood magnate Carlos Rafael—who bought up permits to control 24 percent of the local fleet, then committed seafood fraud through excessive harvests, falsified quotas, and deliberate mislabeling. Though critics blamed catch shares for his rise and influence, it was improved scientific oversight, governance, limits and transparency under the new fishing system that ultimately helped authorities catch, prosecute and in 2017 convict the man known as "The Codfather." Indeed, similar cases of rampant illegality and delayed enforcement by regional managers finally compelled federal officials to draw the line.

In 2013, they cut the region's total allowable catch by 77 percent—the lowest level in American history. The toll on communities was immediate. Gloucester captain Dave Marciano prepared to sell his fishing boat, the *Angelic Joseph*. Plymouth captain Steve Welch predicted "the end of fishing as we know it." Sixty-five-year-old Russell Sherman, also of Gloucester, knew natural dangers came with the territory, and had survived twenty-foot seas in a storm that claimed the lives of two of his shipmates. Now he stared into an even worse fate, a federally imposed abyss. "Scared to death," he quietly confessed, "I'm scared to death." Once a symbol of inexhaustible plenty, cod had become an icon of depletion and collapse, fostering deep distrust by local communities of federal policies.

No fisherman alive could remember a darker age for the commercial seafood industry.

Yet going back, cod fishing prospects once looked far worse, and with far higher stakes. Its earlier collapse had spurred none other than Secretary of Treasury Alexander Hamilton and Secretary of State Thomas Jefferson into action. Hamilton, the gritty, scrappy, self-made New Yorker, sought an organized, efficient and muscular federal government to advance what he saw as the primacy of commerce and industry. The reflective and pastoral Jefferson wanted the opposite, trusting the agrarian ideal of his yeoman farmer to be the cornerstone of dispersed and democratic regional communities. As the brain trust of George Washington's first cabinet, and throughout their careers, the two men vied for supremacy and clashed over almost everything.

Yet despite their famously bitter rivalry these Founding Fathers did join forces in one consequential yet largely overlooked collaboration: an integrated federal policy to rebuild the nation's fisheries.

UNTIL 1776, NEW England's cod had anchored the aspiring nation's most indispensable industry. Harvesters produced enough dried cod for global commodity markets to make it the colonies' fourth largest export. Cod fishing's freedom and bounty caught the attention of Scottish economist Adam Smith, whose *Wealth of Nations* (published the same year) highlighted the fishery as "an exciting example of how an economy could flourish if individuals were given an unrestricted commercial environment."

Then, abruptly, war broke out. King George sought to punish, starve, impoverish and demoralize the "traitors." British forces targeted New England's cod fleet to break the backbone of the colonies' domestic prosperity. The cod trade was crushed, workers scattered, boats abandoned to dry rot. The industry was "annihilated...their vessels, utensils, and fishermen destroyed, their markets...lost."

Fast forward to 1789. Touring the New England coast, the newly inaugurated Washington saw hungry and idle men. He knew his legacy—the young country's food supply, the survival of this democratic experiment—would hinge on whether he could unite his cabinet and citizens to somehow rebuild, equip and staff America's founding fisheries. To marshal capital, train skilled labor and generate trust, the president turned to the catalyst of a federal fishing policy. That policy would have to be frugal; after years of deprivation, following a war against taxation without representation, American voters were in no mood to pay for a federal bailout of special commercial interests. As a general, Washington knew hunger nudged men to mutiny. As a plantation owner he knew how to grow hemp for rope, or cotton for sails. But he was out of his depth when it came to fishing. So, the President summoned Hamilton and Jefferson, his two most trusted advisors, to work out a plan—together.

Jefferson took the lead, hitting the books as soon as he returned from France. Hamilton worked behind the scenes, dispatching his right-hand man, political economist Tench Coxe, to support Jefferson's research. Together they began preparing for Congress the first *Report on the American Fisheries,* a detailed economic analysis of what had been a largely invisible trade. The report documented how—more essentially than tobacco or corn—wild cod (and to a lesser extent herring and shad) had sustained every facet of the colonies' pre-Revolutionary economy. Caught, salted, shipped and devoured by tens of thousands of families, fisheries galvanized crucial corners to the Atlantic triangular trade. With roughly 665 vessels crewed by four thousand men annually harvesting 28,000 tons, cod had fed soldiers, merchants and slaves alike. Indirectly it had comprised the single largest piece of America's gross national product.

War's legacy left nothing behind (save abundant fish, now scooped up only in foreign nets). Jefferson saw that a peacetime dividend—duties on restored harvests and exports—could lift the government back out of debt. But inventing the world's first fisheries policy had to resolve a fundamental question: whose cod was it? True to form, Jefferson envisioned easy access for small-scale, self-sufficient fishers who would bring home fish "to be salted by their wives and children." These local family businesses, in his vision, would require little capital investment and provide work even in winter as "household manufacture."

Hamilton derided that plan as picturesque but naive. Growing up in coastal seaports, with an early grasp of competitive economies of scale, Hamilton saw how a fishery could be a catalyst for real industry. Harvesting cod fueled onshore enterprises from timber to tar, iron smelters to salt extractors, coopers to cobblers, brothels to brokers, ship builders to waterfront developers, while also recruiting what John Adams called a "nursery of seamen and a source of naval power." He also knew all that would take serious money to stimulate a meaningful economy of large boats, gear, wharves, barrels, salt, processing, and trade. Hamilton and Jefferson agreed that excessive taxes would stifle any industry, large or small, before it had a chance to rebuild. Both opposed European-style subsidies. Instead, they converged on a policy that had dual objectives: "to give encouragement to our fishermen...to increase their numbers" and "to govern those fishermen by certain laws, by which they will be kept under due restraint."

On their advice, President Washington asked Congress to enact tax credits of up to $170 per ship for each year it went to sea. That payment (worth $4,500 in today's dollars) would help offset the tariffs that vessel owners paid to harvest cod, boosting their profitability and creating incentives for manufacturers to build more ships. However, legislators were soon warring, over whether those incentives would grow a robust fishing industry or prop up dying enterprises; go to waste on industries that would thrive anyway, unfairly favor certain entities over others, or encourage sloth among deckhands. And who would pocket the money—captain or mates; investors or wage earners; capital or labor? Jefferson's pragmatic answer, emerging organically out of America's seafaring legacy, would be based on customary fishing traditions, specifically an economic system self-organized by cod harvesters known as "sharesmen."

HAVING FLED EUROPE'S rigid class structures and penurious system of wages, colonial fishermen had been free to develop more egalitarian means for getting along and working cohesively packed in cramped vessels for weeks at sea. They'd settled on a system for sharing the fishing enterprise itself: divvy up the collective take on a merit-based system that reflected individual roles and responsibilities. The owner and each crew member, from cabin boy to captain, would hold rights to a portion of the fish brought to dock on a basis agreed to before the vessel set sail. The more fish landed, and the better its quality, the higher the value of each man's share.

Both deckhands and vessel owners favored this "cod sharing" over the old wage system. For fishermen it was fairer and fostered cooperation. For owners, it eliminated the risk of "loafers" counting on wages no matter the haul, dragging down a fishing expedition.

Of course, sharesmen did not materialize overnight. The sharing structure took a century to evolve. Nor did this system entirely escape the usual workplace grumbling and disputes over who deserved how much to do what kind of work: initial allocations, as always, were contentious. But while colonial sharing systems did not remain exclusive to the Atlantic Seaboard, New England's coastal ports—founded by seafaring families and fed by commercial cod fishermen—took the code of sharing beyond culture to be formally integrated as federal law.

Success wasn't just a hunch, or matter of ideology. The results of that governance system had been documented by Philadelphia's leading shipper and commercial trading house partner, Joseph Anthony. Over his career, Anthony had reviewed the records of hundreds of fishing vessels and found, as he wrote in a 1790 letter to Tench Coxe, that cod ships run by sharesmen performed much better than those without. "They [the crew] were generally found the most attentive, when their Dependence was on a Share of what they Caught" rather than fixed wages unlinked from the fishery's overall productivity.

Anthony's analysis (foreshadowing Costello and Gaines, 220 years later) elevated sharing systems from a local tradition to a tested basis for sound policy. Hamilton and Jefferson persuaded Congress to extend New England's sharesman system to the federal tax code itself. On February 16, 1792, Washington signed legislation that divided any tax credit payments proportionately among all those with a close stake in the fishery, distributing 3/8 to vessel owners and 5/8 to be shared by the entire crew. The law required owners of large cod vessels to document their sharing agreements before leaving port, signed by captains and all deckhands on board. The Founding Fathers thus expanded the concept of sharesmen: from a set of informal rights to fish caught by a single boat to a federal code guiding all fishing fleets.

Historian Joseph R. Blasi has argued that this first transformation of fisheries by Jefferson and Hamilton set an historic policy precedent for America's public and private institutions. The template of shared ownership grew into innovations such as profit sharing and employee stock options. "America's first political leaders recognized the rights to economic liberty of a broad group of citizens—the fishermen," Blasi wrote. By affirming how performance depended on shared incentives,

> "This case also shows the desire to encourage citizens to do the economic work of the country themselves rather than have the state do it for them. Congress did not take over the fishing industry…it did not control the prices…It did

not set up a state-owned company to rebuild the industry. Congress did not impose a tax to pay welfare to the suffering fishermen in order to redistribute wealth from the haves to the have-nots. The public did not organize a campaign of vilification simply to attack the owners and investors in ships. Many of those who [later] supported the profit-sharing idea wanted a fair rewards system consistent with the evidence of how well shared capitalism had worked in the [fishing] industry."

Within a few years, the unprecedented combination of incentives, transparency, and clearly defined rights of that initial federal fishing policy quickly achieved extraordinary gains. It revived coastal industries. It expanded the cod fishery well beyond its lucrative pre-war state of productivity and export value. It equitably created and distributed wealth and fed millions on shore. It pulled bitter rivals into harmonic cohesion.

And yet, offshore the "code of sharing" remained incomplete. It encouraged thrift and restraint only in the efficient harvest of cod. It did not rescue fish populations or habitats from the tragedy of the commons. Still, when America in 2009 tried to reverse a crippling recession and a collapsed cod fishing industry, its bipartisan leaders would again embrace a policy of shares.

THE COD FISHERY mayhem witnessed by incoming President Obama had very different origins.

No foreign cannons had smashed fishing vessels. The fishing industry was, if anything, *over*capitalized. Compared with harvest levels in the 1980s, New England fishermen in 2008 spent two thirds more time on the water, with deadlier gear, in bigger and faster boats, yet still routinely managed to catch a quarter less fish. By 2012 the accumulated threat from chronic overfishing, compounded by warmer waters, brought a 75 percent decline in cod populations in the Gulf of Maine over 1980. Ominously, New England appeared to be following Canada, which in 1992 eliminated twenty thousand fishing careers. Not because Canadians lacked skilled labor, capital, vessels or technology; they just had nothing left to catch. "Unlike other industries in which job loss is driven by economic decline or market contraction," explained Michael Conathan, director of oceans policy at the Center for American Progress, "in fisheries, productivity is limited by just one thing: fish. Not enough fish means not enough fishing. Yet here's the fundamental problem: There's not a single politician in the world—not a president or prime minister or poobah—who can regulate, dictate, or legislate more fish into existence."

The latter-day crisis of New England cod added new layers of complexity to the unfolding catch share story. No one blamed fishermen for doing their job too well. The region's Republican and Democratic mayors, congressmen, senators, and governors all campaigned to "rebuild the fishery." They got vague and uncertain about how to do so. Bailouts and buyouts, while popular, were expensive; lowering catch limits, while free, were politically painful. So, what did that leave as a pragmatic way to restore the wild through ethical resource stewardship? One American writer had devoted a lifetime to answering this question.

An ardent hunter, angler, and ecological scientist, Aldo Leopold had worked long enough as a public game warden to know the limitations of changing behavior through top-down enforcement. Durable conservation, he felt, must come from within the community that lived alongside and depended upon the wildlife. He believed that such ethical structures, or codes of conduct, evolved in three stages. In the first stage, individuals learn to coexist in harmony with one another, like men at sea on fishing boats. The second stage "integrates the individual to society" and "social organization to the individual," much as George Washington's fisheries policy had aligned competing interests of crew labor, ship owners, and taxpayers. The last, most difficult and most necessary, shapes "man's relation to the land [or sea] and to the animals and plants which grow upon it." A purely extractive ethic—seeing fish always to be worth more dead than alive—would erode nature's future integrity and thus human security. "The extension of ethics to this third element in the human environment is, if I read the evidence correctly," Leopold wrote, "an evolutionary possibility and an ecological necessity."

In 1792, when the fishing industry was flattened but cod remained abundant, harvest sharing systems helped achieve those first two stages: rebuilding trust both with neighbors and the larger society. By 2009, with groundfish almost gone, New England explored the third.

Cod fishermen weren't alone. By that point, modern sharesmenfrom Wisconsin, Alaska, and the Gulf of Mexico sought to ensure their new form of sharing—not just of landed fish but of the living marine ecosystem—could rise to become the solution across the US. Buddy saw that it was in his interest, and that of his fellow fishermen, to go to Washington and make it happen.

THE FIRST STEP was to pull together a notoriously fragmented industry. The each-against-all jealousies that had long dominated commercial fishing had weakened their ability to advocate for public policy or secure public resources. They lacked any unified voting bloc or political platform. They had no lobbyists to articulate the public benefits to be gained by their continued viability, unlike (to name a few) the US Association of Reptile Keepers, the National Association of Ordnance/Explosive Waste, The Balloon Council, the Cigar Rights of America or the American Dehydrated Onion and Garlic Association. The spread of catch shares began to change that.

Soon, Bering Sea crabbers shook hands with Alabama bandit gear fishermen. Florida spear fishermen traded notes with New England line fishermen. Oregon trawlers even spoke with their California brethren. Catch shares brought these scattered and seemingly disparate interests together under a national organization that would eventually evolve into the Seafood Harvesters of America. In 2009, commercial fishermen found a receptive audience in Obama's incoming Under-Secretary of Commerce for Oceans and Atmosphere, and Administrator of the National Oceanic and Atmospheric Administration, Jane Lubchenco.

Lubchenco was something of a rarity in Washington. Years of rigorous research in academic settings and leadership roles in academic organizations had earned her extraordinary scientific credibility. Yet she had enough contact with both fishermen and politicians to hold her own in negotiations. "My years spent diving with sharks prepared me for navigating the corridors of Congress," she deadpanned. "You need to be able to tell when they are hungry or just curious. You gotta read threat displays and know if there is something in the water that could trigger a frenzy."

The post-inaugural honeymoon period offered the best chance for action. On June 12, 2009, Lubchenco issued an ambitious White House memo setting out the terms and timetables for a task force that would, within 90 days, find ways to "protect and restore the health of ocean resources, improve coordination and collaboration among agencies, and prioritize objectives." Within 180 days it would propose a comprehensive, integrated, cost-effective approach "that addresses conservation, economic activity, user conflict, and sustainable use of ocean resources." Those memos set the framework for the first-ever National Ocean Policy, established July 19, 2010 under Executive Order 13547. The policy combined key ingredients for restoration, including "improved science that supports increased sustainable fishing opportunity," coordinated "coastal and marine spatial planning," and "clearly defined access rights that support sustainable, safe, secure, and productive access."

Finally, on November 4, 2010, Lubchenco threw the full weight of the administration behind rights-based systems. Crediting experience and lessons learned under the previous Bush Administration, she noted: "Catch share programs have proven to be powerful tools to transform fisheries, making them prosperous, stable and sustainable parts of our nation's strategy for healthy and resilient ocean ecosystems," she announced. "NOAA's policy encourages fishery management councils and stakeholders to explore the design possibilities of catch shares to tailor programs to best meet local needs."

The words made the administration's position crystal clear. They also galvanized immediate resistance across the political spectrum. Conservatives, including many philosophically predisposed to catch shares, grew instinctively hostile to any policy embraced by Obama; liberals objected on ideological grounds. Critics on both sides consistently raised suspicions about whether Lubchenco was swayed by her ties to EDF. As with George Washington in 1792, the next six years would be decisive in showing whether the new policy would get traction, forge lasting alliances among rivals, and earn bipartisan support. To an extent even he didn't anticipate, it would take Buddy's leadership and example to translate the debate in the nation's capital into an enduring new reality in America's waters.

Chapter Twelve
SCIENTIFIC CREDIBILITY

L ubchenco embedded federal ocean policy in a "comprehensive, ecosystem-based framework." Rather than focus on one species in isolation, managers now had to address the full spectrum of marine habitat interactions. They'd need to account for chemistry, temperature, shelter, currents and especially biology—the whole web of organisms eating and being eaten and otherwise shaping one another's world—and constantly adapt to feedback from the ocean system. Such an ambitious approach required far more intensive monitoring and research than any previous strategy. Yet even as she committed to it, Lubchenco saw that "we really don't have the fundamental science to underpin those decisions."

Under the best of circumstances, science is maddeningly difficult at sea. Start with the sheer complexity of gathering data from a vast and invisible world, with nearly endless variables in play. For natural or earth scientists, hypotheses rarely lend themselves to a replicable laboratory test. Protean and dynamic, the ocean resists control groups, confirming proofs, or close inspection by gill-free species like ours. In short, marine research isn't rocket science, brain surgery, or quantum physics. It's harder.

We know less about the ocean than we do about outer space. Yet "the social costs of miscalculations are enormous," as John McQuaid wrote in a Pulitzer-prize winning series for the New Orleans *Times-Picayune*. "Fishery scientists and managers operate on a razor's edge. They must allow as much fishing as possible without allowing the fish population to collapse and are under pressure to move in a more dangerous direction."

Those pressures fueled virulent disputes over the essential government sea census known as a "stock assessment."

Before officials could set a Total Allowable Catch to ensure long term sustainable yields, researchers had to first determine how much of what species was swimming around out there. That alone is difficult enough. As John Shepherd, a fisheries management specialist at England's University of Southampton, drolly explained: "Counting fish is just like counting trees. Except fish are invisible. And they move."

"And they eat each other," added Eric Schwaab, former administrator of the National Marine Fisheries Service.

If it was hard to count fish in the present, harder still was establishing a baseline against which to compare those current numbers. Working backwards through agent-based models and reproductive rate formulas, scientists tried to calculate "virgin biomass:" the inferred size of fish populations that would exist if there had been no harvesting, given current habitat conditions.

That could look like hocus-pocus to fishermen, who regard scientists with mutual mistrust. Buddy and his peers often felt they had the more accurate read on fish populations, since they're out on the water every day, with a built-in desire to count each snapper and grouper as they come off the hook. Some scientists, in turn, dismissed not only commercial but also local government and grant-dependent research as compromised due to "industry capture." They pointed to the work of researchers like Alabama Marine Resources Director Chris Blankenship, who regularly found that there was plenty of fish, at least for his state constituents. Each side accused the other of cherry picking data to promote their own agendas or distorting evidence based on their source of income.

At the mercy of all this contentious science were fishermen. Buddy allowed Gulf fishery researchers on his boats only when he felt he absolutely had to. He felt like they regarded his livelihood as, at best, a necessary evil, an encroachment on their otherwise pure or natural ocean ecosystem. "Just imagine doing your taxes," quipped one of his Wharf Road deckhands, "with an IRS agent looking over your shoulder and taking notes."

The parallel is apt. For the feds required basic information about activity. As was standard practice across US waters, Gulf fishery analysts gathered Buddy's catch data, log books, and even surgically removed from his catch some otoliths—fish ear bones that identify the age and ocean habitat conditions for harvested species. It galled Buddy that these researchers then turned around and used those logs to make the case that officials should reduce his catch. It wasn't just the Gulf. Nearly every US fisherman felt scientific evidence was used "against" him in some way. "The more data we provide them, the more it always seems to erode our opportunities to fish," said Puget Sound fisherman Ian Bryce. "You get gun-shy and cynical about that after a while."

The irony is that scientists and fishermen long shared a common approach to work. Both were toolmakers seeking to understand life: the most successful pioneers figured out how to use Petri dishes to probe microbes and cells, or to forge and refashion hooks or nets to extract protein from water. Both followed hunches (*what if we tried x?*), closely observed natural phenomena, and leveraged feedback loops (what credible professional peers are doing, writing, saying). "You rely on the color of the water, sea surface temperatures, and charts to make an educated guess," said Bryce, who compared fishing to playing 3-D chess in the dark. "You know the pieces by feel and the board layout, and while you can't see where they're going, you can rely on satellite downloads, surface/height anomalies, weather programs, being able to read your own electronics and interpret data points on a sounder for concentrations." Yet Buddy and his fellow fishermen struggled for scientific recognition. Even as they collaborated on research projects, deploying increasingly sophisticated equipment (radar, sonar, GPS, Fishfinder, Gulf Wild), they felt treated like second-class stakeholders, demoted in stature, discounted in weight. They resented this power imbalance and groused how, given years testing fishing hypotheses on the water, they might do science as well, or better. "Each time I set my gear," said Bryce, in a provocative mood, "I'm conducting an experiment."

There was some basis for this perspective. In his 1970s studies of desert Bushmen, anthropologist Louis Liebenberg found tracking animals required not only intellectual rigor but collective generation of hypotheses and informal peer review. "As perhaps the oldest science," he wrote of these hunter-gatherers, "the art of tracking may also be developed into a new science with many practical applications. One of these applications—at a time when wildlife management has become increasingly important—is nature conservation."

That insight into the value of traditional knowledge about wild animals in wild places, was slowly transforming ocean science. Academic researchers had begun tapping into what weathered hunter-gatherers of the sea can teach us about reefs, habitats, and fish species. Another early bridge builder was tropical marine ecologist Dr. Robert E. Johannes. In the mid-1970s Johannes traveled to Palau to understand and educate local people about the ways in which coral reefs were made vulnerable by overharvesting fish. Within a few months, Johannes realized that it was the Palauans who could educate him. These illiterate and innumerate fishermen displayed a far richer and more sophisticated knowledge of Pacific fisheries ecology than did any university-trained scientist, including himself. They routinely distinguished unique physical characteristics of hundreds of individual species. Most recognized behavioral linkages between (for instance) seasonal spawning aggregations, reproductive cycles and phases of the moon. Above all, the islanders integrated the human context. "I became aware of various political, cultural, and economic pressures impinging on fishing," he wrote in his landmark 1981 book, *Words of the Lagoon*, "in such a way as to make my purely biological explanation seem quite simplistic." Johannes sought to fuse Indigenous fishing intelligence with Western concepts of scientific management.

Commercial harvesters might welcome scientific insights as a boon, rather than a burden. In turn, researchers could gain credibility from incorporating fishermen knowledge in more robust outcomes. Without mutual respect, however, that goal remained elusive. "There's a lot more that commercial fishermen have to offer biologists and scientists about target and non-target species," said

Bryce. "But there's always been that great lingering distrust. How do you get past that? How do you get to the point where scientists' data won't be detrimental to the fishermen?"

BUDDY'S OWN THAW in his view of government research began in 2009, when a federal fisheries scientist hired him and his boat to conduct a longline survey off Galveston. It was hard to say no to extra income for fishing. The government would pay for his time, bait, ice, and fuel, and let him keep and sell his catch. The only drawback was that he'd have to fish it on federal terms and time-tables. He agreed, and not just for the money. As the most critical predator in America's ocean ecosystems, *Homo sapiens* might be hard to manage but was also irrepressibly curious. Now vested in the long-term outcome, Buddy was eager to discover what they might find.

That first willing scientific collaboration got off to a shaky start. The stock sampling was being run by the then-head of Gulf regional science. She rolled out a map for Buddy, highlighted all the randomly generated points on the chart, and gave Buddy clear directives. Please set your mile-long baited lines within half a mile of each point. Let them sit for an hour. Then pick them up, and we'll count what's on the line.

Looking at the chart, Buddy grew confused. With the entire Gulf to choose from, he wondered, why the hell would she want him to set lines in these particular spots, of all places? As he and every other grouper fisherman knew, *there's no fish there*. If he hauled in only a few tiny fish each time, the scientists could draw the wrong conclusion.

To offset that possibility, Buddy racked his memory for the sea-floor contours and tried carefully on each set to roll out the line in the direction that would land it over the best habitat below and thus maximize his catch.

The scientist watched, checked her bearings, and then politely asked him not to.

Buddy gave his rationale, based on his decades in this part of the Gulf.

She countered that the government has always set survey gear within a half mile of the dots without consideration of habitat or what fish may be swimming around it.

Buddy stared at this person, the best and brightest the scientific research establishment had to offer. Finally, he couldn't help himself.

Well, he said. That's just stupid.

To her credit, he recalled, she took time as the boat rocked out there on the water to explain how their work was all a test of repeatability. Scientists had to do the same thing over and over, following strict protocols, with all boats. Robust conclusions came from embracing randomness, not avoiding it. Year after year, they had to overcome fishermen's own powerful sampling and confirmation biases: First, by knowing and going where fish concentrate, a harvester may logically but wrongly conclude that a successful haul in one place, over one day, meant fish are abundant everywhere else, and always. Then, hoping for higher catch limits, he'd seek any signs that confirmed abundance, while ignoring or discounting any information to the contrary. That's why fisheries could often seem fine for decades, then "suddenly" collapse. Fishermen were indeed, as Bryce noted, experimenting and gathering vital information every time they set their nets, but they would never survive if they fished according to scientific protocols. "An experiment is controlled and replicated, and conducted in a random and unbiased way," remarked Jake Kritzer, a scientist chairing the science and statistics committee of the New England Fishery Management Council. "The fisherman who follows those principles will not be in business very long."

Eventually, Buddy came to understand and admire the scientist's approach, even as it ran diametrically against his own. "Only with these snapshots can they compare over time and see if fish populations are doing better, getting worse, or staying the same. I talked with her for a while, and we were determined to do this the right way, and get accurate results."

Both were surprised to find fish in places Buddy knew had once been barren. Paradoxically, this new growth now worried him. A decade earlier, Buddy might have cited that abundance to argue for a longer season and higher quota. Now, two years into catch shares, he wanted scientists to err on the side of *lower* counts. In any case, rather than just barely tolerating data collection he was now hungry for more and joined other Gulf reef fish shareholders in planning aggressive, collaborative, and exploratory research projects. One explored the ecological and economic costs of the lag between the time an animal hit their hook or net and the time they hauled it in.

AS A KID, Buddy felt it the instant a fish took his bait. Deep below, the animal's bite jolted up the line and triggered muscle contraction in Buddy's upper body. His rod jerked back. His pulse quickened in a primal adrenaline rush.

Commercial gear, however, often muffled that signal: fish action and human reaction could be far apart. Indeed, whether working with traps, purse seines, trawl nets or long-lines, few commercial fishermen could know the moment any one fish is captured, enmeshed, or hooked. Those seconds, minutes or (with nets or traps) hours of delay add up with each set, each trip, each vessel. If hauled in too late (or too soon), human and animal species suffered: exhausted, eaten or escaped fish reduced economic value; drowned bycatch left behind ecological wreckage. Distressed by ongoing, needlessly costly waste, Buddy and fellow Shareholders' Alliance leader Glen Brooks wanted to find out exactly how much was being sacrificed.

Brooks harvests grouper off Florida's Gulf Coast. As savvy and stocky as Buddy, if more soft-spoken, he's the kind of guy no one crosses. He's as comfortable chewing tobacco while talking to a congressman as he was negotiating deals with crews or fish buyers. While Buddy dominated the western Gulf, Brooks' skill at finding, catching and marketing grouper allowed him to amass the largest fleet of commercial vessels in the Eastern Gulf.

Brooks saw the multiple costs of his inability to know *when* grouper—or undesired fish, rare birds, turtles, or mammals—hit his thousands of hooks stretched out over several sets of longlines.

He couldn't know which target species of what size escaped or got munched by sharks (some of which themselves got hooked) while thrashing about on the line. Blind to what happened all along the strings he laid over the reefs, he wasn't fishing as clean or as profitably as he wanted to. His longlines might be *too* long. Or maybe too short. His hooks might be too many, or too few, or be spaced too close or too far apart, or be using the wrong bait. During race-to-fish days, "we might string out two sets of ten miles of line and leave it down there for five hours or more, waiting for it to fill up," said Brooks. "We knew we were catching fish, but we didn't really know *when*. It was just the way it had always been done."

For years, pushed to capture volume, the lack of temporal data hadn't mattered much. Now, with secure shares—as fishermen put more value on quality, accountability, and long-term health—it mattered immensely. So, in 2010 Brooks teamed up with two researchers at the federal fisheries science center labs in Pascagoula, Mississippi. Charlie Bergmann and Daniel Foster worried about rare species dying on so many longline hooks. They wanted to experiment with new electronic technologies. But they knew fishermen were likely to view them as antagonists, hiding behind the familiar hollow promise, "we're-from-the-government-and-here-to-help." They needed buy-in from a prominent fisherman—as a full partner, not just a borrowed vessel or catch data source. In Brooks, they found that newly motivated ally.

With a secure share, Brooks could now speak honestly. He could share what he caught and when, his experience of how gear, timing, season, sink rate, depth, methodology, sampling, and even bait affected his bycatch rate. With his knowledge and their methodology, Brooks, Bergmann and Foster co-developed an experiment— deploying a small, waterproof, electronic device known as a hook timer.

A hook timer, mounted between hook and line, recorded the moment a fish is caught. The force of the strike dislodged a tiny stopper, activating a digital clock that then ticked off elapsed minutes and seconds. The widget was too expensive for any one fisherman to afford. It also required rigorous protocols: randomized tests, controlled harvests, logging inputs, and linear regression models to interpret the data. But the fisherman-scientist team were able to analyze data sets as three vessels took ten trips, set 231 sets of lines, mounted with 155,521 hooks, using 30,416 timers. Accounting for such variables as depth, bottom temperature and barometric pressure, they tracked the mix (including size) of individual red grouper, red snapper, Atlantic sharpnose shark, Grey tilefish, Yellow-edge grouper, and Blacknose shark hooked on the lines. It was the first large-scale test in the wild answering a question weighing on conservationists' minds and fishermen's balance sheets: "How quickly do various animals bite on bottom longlines?"

The answer they arrived at had profound and far-reaching impacts. Half of one target species, Red grouper, were caught within the first thirteen minutes of the hook soaking in the sea; 90 percent were caught within forty-two minutes. Sharks were far slower to bite: 90 percent of them hit the hooks a full twenty-three minutes later than reef fish. A shorter soak time, then, would dramatically reduce bycatch death of sharks. It would also let fishermen free hooked turtles before they might drown. At the same time, it would boost profit margins. Shorter soak times meant Gulf fishermen could make more sets with fewer hooks and catch more target fish. By the time the results of this collaborative research were published in the journal, *Fisheries Research,* in 2017, Brooks and fellow Shareholders' Alliance members had already reformed their tactics, voluntarily: shortening soak time, reducing line length 70 percent, or setting them in the shape of circles or horseshoes. And since "the hook timers told us 45 minutes was more than enough," Brooks said, all sets brought back fresher meat.

Collaborative science can cut both ways. The data might just as easily have called for painful and expensive changes, the kind that in the past had led fishermen to avoid experimental research, or dispute results. Brooks knew those risks when he began. But with a longer view and more flexibility he was willing to share ownership of the problem, the opportunity, and the scientific approach. "Our motivations changed," he said. "Now we're concentrating more on quality than quantity. So, we can put the set down and pick it up quicker, and catch more fish in a ten-day trip than we used to in eighteen."

News of their experiments with Brooks spread faster and farther, Dan Foster reflected, than if his scientific team had done the work alone, for their own peer group. "The collaborative experiment has been a very positive and eye-opening thing," he said. "Even though fishermen are extremely knowledgeable, by teaming up with our scientific resources on things like hook timers, we can learn so much about their fishery that [even the] fishermen still don't understand...how to better target the things that are sustainable yet back off and have less impact on the others, while getting efficient for grouper and increasing their total catch per day."

THAT CATCH SHARES realignment of mutual interests, trust and respect had nationwide potential. Soon, Pacific coast fishermen felt equally inspired to collaborate on research experiments. One began in the shadow of Cannery Row, a once-booming part of Monterey memorialized by John Steinbeck, but which died after World War II with the collapse of the Pacific sardine fishery.

For three generations, the family of Giuseppe "Joe" Pennisi II had long been accustomed to fishing by feel and instinct alone. That was enough to get by. Yet every time Joe lowered his trawl net into the water, he was left to guess if and when it captured groundfish— or let them escape—right up until its contents were dumped on deck (with the exception, two decades earlier off Mission Point, when his father's boat was slowed, stopped, and then dragged backward, having snagged a US nuclear submarine going in another direction). He didn't know if his net billowed out at fathoms too high or too low, or if he was towing his gear at the right speeds. "It was always a mystery," he said. "Kind of like walking into a closet and picking out clothes to get dressed in total darkness. You don't know what you've got until you bring it into the light."

Like Brooks with his longlines, Pennisi knew that if he hauled in too fast or early, he'd miss the best catch. But if too slow or late, his target fish might escape, get picked off or, worst of all, his net might swallow rare species that would get him fined or locked down. To further complicate matters, scientists had set a Total Allowable Catch on dozens of groundfish species, each one unique. Some grew fast, matured young, and spawned early and often; others were late bloomers with weak libidos. But trawlers like Pennisi, unable to differentiate, caught all these fish, forcing them to discard millions of good (now mostly dead) fish at sea or pay heavy fines for "overages." That had left the fishery in shambles, plunging from 74,000 to 27,000 tons, losing $11 million a year, and eventually declared a federal disaster. The 2011 West Coast Groundfish Trawl catch share altered the equation, setting quotas for commercial fish. But it also tightly constrained Total Allowable Catches for more depleted species. Now, if a fisherman caught a rarer fish for which he lacked shares, he could lease those shares from a neighbor who'd been more successful at avoiding them. Precision, in other words, brought economic rewards.

So when two fisheries researchers, Huff McGonigal and former fisherman David Crabbe, approached Pennisi to test new experimental gear that might more precisely manage what his nets were killing, he was leery—fearing their findings might trigger new rules, more forms, heavier fines—but agreed.

The long-term experiment began by establishing a "before" dataset. First, McGonigal and Crabbe selected a specific area of the water and set of days, and documented Pennisi's current gear use in that time and place and what came up in his net. Next, they fitted GoPro underwater cameras and sensors to his trawl net—customized to catch the right species and release the wrong ones–then sent him out again into the same waters at the same times of year. They finally compared both those data sets against all the stuff scooped up by new, light-touch trawl gear that floated just off the seafloor, reducing drag, targeting the right species. "The idea is you reduce points of contact 90 percent, but still catch fish," said McGonigal.

After helping shape and execute the experiment, Pennisi said he felt "blown away" by the results. Even before converting gear, the scientific feedback from sensors and cameras unexpectedly transformed how he fished, allowing him to slow down and fish less. Those small adjustments in tempo led to big changes: reducing bycatch, increasing yield, and improving quality. "All these years I thought my gear was working well," he said. "But it turns out a few minor modifications can make a huge difference. I wound up trawling eight less hours each trip, at slower speeds. I'm dragging less and catching more."

The dramatic reduction in drag proved to be good for both the sea bottom and for his bottom line. By slashing several tons of dead weight, his engines required far less power, torque, and energy. "Here, look at my gas bills," he enthused. "I've kept the receipts, and in the last year I've saved $70,000 in fuel alone."

That initial experiment led Pennisi to seek out more research opportunities. Soon, other fishermen stepped up: volunteering their records, gear, crew time and fuel to the scientific process. The joint research outcomes altered the very understanding of peer review. Rather than die in a drawer or under the cloak of "proprietary advantage," this collaborative research was typically shared with the public, far and wide. "The point is to get the results spread up and down the coast as soon as possible," said Crabbe, "to engage more and more fishermen everywhere."

Pennisi hopes the new gear, with its documented ability to avoid bycatch, would allow America's fishermen into areas that have been off-limits to fishing. "We're going to only fish half as much, we'll catch all we need, and we'll barely be touching the bottom," he said. "I think we can triple productivity. What we're doing right now is the beginning of something huge."

Collaborative research on wild capture fishing soon emerged as a global trend, generating results that were both more credible and more broadly believed. A few hundred miles south of Pennisi, researchers at Moss Landing Marine Lab and Cal Poly-San Luis Obispo had tapped into fishermen's expertise to find clusters of fish to design a better sampling strategy. Elsewhere at that time, to reduce bycatch and expand fishing opportunities, The Nature Conservancy's researchers had begun working with fishermen to supplement camera data, submersible data, and trawl survey data with fisherman knowledge of "hot and cold spots" for depleted species. All these partnerships came together after Pacific groundfish graduated to catch shares. Why only then? The approach encouraged fishermen to collaborate, explained Canadian fisheries biologist Rick Stanley, to surrender their "independent cowboy" worldview. They set aside professional jealousies and help scientists design surveys, execution, analysis and documentation, right alongside researchers, "not acting as subordinates but as equal members."

The shift in this balance of power was profound. Before, observed Leiden University resource economist David Zetland, "fishermen had valid short-term reasons to oppose research (that threatened them), withhold data (keep prized spots secret from competitors), and challenge the veracity of scientists' conclusions (if they led to calls for reduced harvests)." Now, with a stake in future yields, harvesters themselves often become the most fervent advocates—and in some cases sponsors—of new data gathering and dissemination. "Instead of being supplicants to scientists," suggested Zetland, "catch share fishermen turn into their partners, or even bosses."

Chris Brown, president of Seafood Harvesters of America, went further. With thousands of individual vessels fishing US waters each day, he saw an opportunity to launch the largest scientific study on the planet. "Fisheries have gotten used to making decisions and policy based on very small amounts of data," Brown said. "Every boat is a chance to improve fishery science and to turn fishermen into partners in our effort to conserve fish stocks for future generations." To improve transparency and share information through trusted networks, he added, "we should harvest data at the same rate that we harvest fish."

Data-rich transparency was at the heart of America's central challenge of natural resource policy: how to hold private enterprises accountable for harvesting federal resources governed under the public trust.

Chapter Thirteen

SMART BOAT TRANSPARENCY

One spring day in 2005, while working in his cramped office above Katie's Seafood, Buddy was paid an unexpected visit by a fisheries law enforcement agent with a few questions to ask. Though a bit taken aback, Buddy wasn't worried. His files were in order, documenting his compliance with federal fishing laws and rules. He had his Gulf Reef Fish Permit. He'd kept continuous records of all notifications to NMFS each time his captains left Wharf Road, and again three-to-twelve hours before landing at Katie's with estimated haul. He'd completed all the exhaustive paperwork documenting the actual weight and sale price. So Buddy welcomed the enforcement agent upstairs and into the chair opposite his own.

This was two years before the introduction of catch shares, in the middle of a derby race. Which meant Buddy was not only irritated about the surprise visit but also eager to get back offshore. The official was in no such hurry. He sat quietly, looking around at the walls, keeping Buddy waiting—before finally coming to the purpose of his visit. The US government, it seemed, was prepared to make Buddy an offer he couldn't refuse.

"Look" Buddy recalled the agent telling him, "I hear you're a prominent, upstanding fisherman, and I know you don't ever do anything illegal offshore."

Buddy nodded and bit his tongue. He wondered who the hell the agent had been talking to. Years later he deadpanned a hushed confession: "I mean, just between the two of us, the truth is that I haven't always been as pure as the driven snow, exactly. Especially then. But hell, I wasn't about to admit this; I wanted him to keep thinking exactly what he was thinking about what a great guy I am. So I said, 'Yeah, sure officer, of course. What can I do for you?'"

"Well," the man explained, "there's this new pilot program, authorized by the Gulf Regional Council. A way to improve off-shore enforcement. So, would you mind if we installed a VMS on each of your fishing boats?"

It may be hard to recall but in 2005, not everyone could be reached, much less tracked, by their cell phone offshore. It was a different time. A Vessel Monitoring System would allow the government to electronically track Buddy's boats, constantly and always. Its on-board transceivers would send hourly time-stamped GPS reports identifying the vessels and their location to the computer screen of a technician in some distant federal office. The technology would enable fishery managers to monitor Buddy's movements, track violators harvesting at prohibited times or places, and record evidence should they need to prosecute lawbreakers. "You'd be setting a great example of accountability to the entire Gulf fishery," he added.

The precedent he'd be setting, Buddy thought, was letting Big Government watch everything he did offshore. He'd be giving up one of the things he loved best about fishing: being out of sight and out of reach at sea. Now he would surrender that anonymity to bureaucrats, and reveal his only competitive advantages to strangers. "Everybody would now know exactly where I was all the time."

Being watched on land was one thing. But damn, the ocean was different. If shore life got too crowded or wired, he could fire up diesel engines, roar out of cell phone range, and escape every noise but the hiss of wave on hull, motor vibration, grinding gear, crew voices and thumping fish. Heading out over the breakers blew open a pressure valve; it let him escape the nanny state. His radio could be turned off. But if he went along with the VMS system, this world would soon be tracked, involuntarily tethered to the intrusions and demands of strangers.

Once a VMS generated an unbroken record of where and when

he fished, what would happen to it? Despite strict confidentiality requirements, Buddy knew information, once gathered, had a way of getting out. "The guy assured me the records would be held tight and kept private," said Buddy. "I'm not a conspiracy theorist, and I'm sure people would do the best they could to make that happen. But I also know that data is shared with universities, and regional councils. Anytime someone's gathering information, there's a good chance it will get revealed. All my secret fishing places, all my activity. That's my life spread out right there, you know?"

Buddy didn't feel threatened by the law enforcement officer, but neither did he feel he could decline, exactly.

Like other commercial fishermen, he found himself caught between the competing demands for public accountability and private liberty. That was a tricky balance for officials, who had to ensure fishermen complied with the rules without micromanaging every haul of every boat. Buddy split the difference. He accepted installation of a VMS but quietly worked with other Gulf fishermen to sue the government to remove them.

OVER THE NEXT decade Buddy watched as VMS rules were clarified. America's system scaled up to cover four thousand fishing vessels, operating twenty-four-hours-a-day "with near-perfect accuracy," becoming over time the world's most electronically monitored fishing nation.

VMS-wired boats were only one layer of public demand for accountable fishermen. The halibut fishery explored the use of on-board cameras positioned to record everything pulled over the rail. The Nature Conservancy worked with federal fishery managers to provide West coast trawlers with iPads to record their harvest while still at sea, uploading data on each haul to a computerized mapping system shared by the fleet. Some fisheries experimented with aerial conservation drones to monitor nearshore seafood harvesting. To estimate their real time activity, Washington state co-developed the SmartPass system that combined shore-based cameras and artificial intelligence to automatically count and monitor recreational fishing vessels as they passed through key coastal bottle-necks like harbor entrances or river mouths. Through the scalable, cost-effective SmartPass, fishery managers could improve manage-ment decisions through more accurate and timely data on angler activity, which could then be cross-referenced with dockside inter-views to assess average catches per vessel.

In 2014, the satellite tracking system SkyTruth teamed up with marine advocacy organization Oceana and tech giant Google to establish Global Fishing Watch, an online platform aimed at promot-ing ocean transparency. It not only tracked large vessels equipped with Automatic Identification System (AIS) but also incorporated satellite radar to monitor dark fleets that operated without it. Global Fishing Watch provided free public access to near real-time maps and datasets, enabling users to identify the flag, direction, and activ-ity of individual vessels, thus enhancing efforts to combat illegal, unreported, and unregulated (IUU) fishing worldwide. Since incep-tion, Global Fishing Watch had monitored over sixty-five thousand vessels, mapping 300,000+ hours of fishing activity each day, and has helped reveal illegal fishing in protected marine areas. Mean-while Chile, Indonesia, and Peru integrated the platform into their national fisheries monitoring programs.

Pew Charitable Trusts teamed with a similar group based in Oxford, OceanMind, to use machine learning to sort and ana-lyze reams of big data from satellite observations, vessel tracking devices, and fishing licenses. With this array of information technol-ogy, a remote official could now observe not only where and when a given vessel was fishing, but also (in some cases) the quantity, spe-cies and size of its catch. For example, if they witnessed a fisherman working out of season, or poaching from within a protected reserve, they might dispatch law enforcement officers, impose fines, and/or confiscate the catch.

Big data technology can help weed out illegal vessels on the high seas. But as yet it couldn't shed light or reveal what happened aboard the vast bulk of fishing taking place legitimately, and legally. Higher levels of transparency required more intense surveillance, up close and personal. Each year the US had randomly deployed 891 on-board observers in 47 fisheries, who spent in aggregate 7483,000 days (about twenty thousand years) at sea. As catch shares elevated the obligation for accountability, it had meant the deployment of more observers offshore. For fishermen, the human pressure caused several pain points.

First, observers' salaries were typically paid by fees collected from the observed vessels. That meant fishermen had to swallow the fact that they were paying government agents to surveil and discipline their work. Observers also complicated life offshore. Deckhands sometimes welcomed human observers, if their presence nudged owners and captains to upgrade food, entertainment and sanitation (beyond a plastic bucket toilet doubling as a saltwater shower); or to tone down abusive words and harsh treatment of the crew. Still, the intrusion remained disruptive. Any extra body on a crowded vessel's working deck space (typically no bigger than a station wagon) could hamper productivity and generate friction, however skilled or sociable that body might be. In the stressful life at sea, crews had to obey the captain, but an observer answered only to the public.

Geoff Bettencourt, who once ran a compact fishing vessel out of Half Moon Bay, wound up sleeping on a foam mattress in his wheelhouse after surrendering his own bunk to observers. He used to have to shop and cook for them when they were on board; wait for them at dock if they were late; pay for their hotel if foul weather kept him in port. "All that," Geoff recalled, "I can bear. I may not like it, but I get it. But if the observer starts to leave equipment in passages, even after being asked twice not to, just as a way of showing me that he won't be bossed around? Well, that makes me snap."

Fishermen who complained used to find a reliably sympathetic ear among small-government conservatives like the late Alaska Congressman Don Young. Seafood harvesting is a 5.3 billion-pound, $1.7 billion chunk of Alaska's economy. But fish were also personal for Young, who in his youth worked as a commercial fisherman. The only licensed mariner in Congress, Young used to command attention by hammering down his gavel, an 18-inch walrus penis bone, or *oosik*. Serving on the House Natural Resources Committee, he exercised immense sway over federal forests, minerals and, above all, fish.

To rein in what he saw as an excessive federal appetite for spying on fishermen, Young organized hearings before the Subcommittee on Fisheries, Wildlife, Oceans and Insular Affairs. Young's own position had long been clear. "Observers are probably the worst thing that can happen," he had groused. "The observer is human. He can be corrupted. He can be put into the trawl net to solve some problems. He can be a drunk."

Young's joke landed badly with Liz Mitchell, head of the Association of Professional Observers and one of those called to testify. Young's "jesting in front of a bunch of fishermen that killing observers would solve the problem of having them on board is beyond contemptible given the reality of our already risky and vulnerable situation," she told the committee. Harassment, assault and interference were all regular and serious threats to observers' honorable service. "Transparency is the cornerstone of a democratic society and observer data has long been considered to be the cornerstone of fisheries management. Observers risk their lives to collect this data for the public good."

Transparency could take many forms, however. Young looked forward to more sympathetic testimony from the strong-willed and widely respected head of the Alaska Longline Fishermen's Association (ALFA). ALFA's members hauled in America's biggest fish. From as deep as 3,000 feet they might pull in sablefish, aka Black cod, which may live nine decades and grow as much as three feet or 55 pounds. Yet that was small fry compared to their other main target species, the Pacific halibut, which after six months as a floating larva spent the rest of its life lying flat on its side on the seafloor (its ventral side eye slowly migrating over the top of its head to join the other on the dorsal side), ambushing prey and growing as large as 10 feet and 700 pounds. There's little romance in such fishing: just weeks of punishing 18-hour workdays, in rough conditions, catching fish so monstrous they required a hydraulic winch and several men armed with gaffes to kill. It's no wonder long-liners had the reputation as the most hardcore of all fishermen, or that Young asked their hardcore leader to come tell Congress exactly what might emerge from this mandatory surveillance scheme. With approval from the family, including two young sons, ALFA leader Linda Behnken said she'd be honored to testify.

Behnken runs her small boat the *FV Woodstock* out of Sitka, a town of nine thousand that punches above its weight when it comes to fish. The town's Silver Harbor never freezes and offers deep-water access to the north Pacific. One in five Sitka adults earns a living from the sea, landing fish in the sixth largest US port by value of harvest. Though it still retains a few vestiges of its nineteenth century heyday, when its mix of languages and cultural life earned it the nickname the "Paris of the Pacific," Sitka is defined today by its remote isolation. Disconnected from highways, the town is reachable only by boat or plane, which is how three decades ago the young female Ivy League student arrived here for a summer fishing job and fell in love with the natural beauty and her fellow fishermen. "They're fiercely independent yet at the same time it's a really tight-knit community," said Behnken. "They may quibble on the dock, but if there's a big problem they're there ready to help you … [and are] incredibly resourceful and innovative." In turn, Alaska's longliners now counted on her ability to articulate their desire for regulatory relief. Going to Washington was a costly trip for a small organization with limited budget, but Behnken decided it was worth it to make their case for balancing the need for public accountability against the costs to small business. "This could be a good opportunity to deliver a powerful, hard-hitting message."

Behnken told the Congressional subcommittee members in no uncertain terms: Hurry up and install video surveillance systems. Now. "We can only ask—what can we do to make sure this proven technology is used in 2014. We are standing by to do whatever else is in our power to secure an electronic monitoring alternative for our fleet."

She urged the Members not to wait to sort out glitches. Compared with human observers, the perfect electronic system is the enemy of the good enough, she said. Mandate devices wherever appropriate. And yes, she added, since these electronic monitoring devices could save us money over the long haul, we are willing to help pay for installation, deployment, and operation.

One by one catch share fishermen decided to stop worrying and welcome higher accountability. They wanted to combine new incentives with richer information. Within months of Behnken's testimony, 150 fishermen around the country had stepped up to demand electronic reporting systems in their own fleets. Bob Dooley wanted them for the Bering Sea pollock. John Papallardo wanted them in New England for monkfish, haddock, dogfish, and scallops. Like reformed smokers, electronic monitoring's strongest evangelists were those who had initially been fiercely opposed, and nowhere had opposition been stronger than the Gulf. "We were the ones who sued the government over proposed vessel monitoring systems," said Glen Brooks. "But now, man, you couldn't pry them from our cold dead fingers."

To be sure, VMS was neither as intensive nor expensive as on-board cameras systems. Yet in both cases, catch shares triggered a change of heart, leading newly secure fishermen to demand richer data through more surveillance; in short: welcoming Big Brother aboard. Catch shares let fishermen coalesce around what would be known as "smart boat" technology. This combination of sensors, broadband communication and data analytics helped equip and surround fishing vessels of all sizes with digital tools and infrastructure that increased accountability through transparency. The system's adoption followed a remarkable template for resource governance that had been pioneered in Victoria, BC by Archipelago Marine Research Ltd.

FROM AN UNDERSTATED two-story office, Archipelago has defined an entire industry unto itself. Starting in 1978, in response to Canada's own need to carry out new fishing laws, the company pioneered the placing of human observers on a random sample of fishing boats. Over time, as catch shares in a dozen nations created demand, it had trained thousands of observers, and equipped fishermen with tools and techniques to monitor themselves. The company had crunched reams of data to help managers set future catch limits, and over four decades grew into the undisputed leader in electronic monitoring for fisheries worldwide.

That said, you'd never mistake its executive team for titans of capitalism. On a drizzly morning in autumn 2013, co-founder Howard McElderry shared his warm home-baked chocolate chip cookies. CEO Shawn Stebbins later offered chinook salmon he had caught and smoked just a few hours earlier. Sure, they could lobby governments more aggressively, relocate to Toronto, New York or London, or strive to dominate global market share. But they don't. "We like it here," Stebbins explained with a gentle smile, "and maybe we're just, well, too Canadian."

Archipelago occupied a position halfway between the fishing industry and government regulatory agencies; it bound both parties yet held each at arm's length. As Canada's leading service provider of at-sea and dockside surveillance, the firm's reputation for trust rested on the quality of data it simultaneously provided both private and public interests. Archipelago worked within rules defined by the entire stakeholder community.

Archipelago maintained the anonymity of proprietary catch data from individual vessels but kept no secrets of its own. Their operations were an open book, where on a random July day a visitor could wander freely, pausing by Roth Wehrell's cubicle to watch while, with a few clicks on his keyboard, he transports them both to sea. Through a camera lens mounted off the stern of a longline vessel, they watched in real time as two men hauled in hooks loaded with groundfish of various sizes and species, pinpointing exactly where in the Pacific they are. This was what Buddy, Behnken, Brooks and Bettencourt all wanted for America's future. If they could sort out questions of who paid what costs, many see this smart boat capacity for government scrutiny as strangely liberating, having lifted the physical weight of an expensive, hungry and sleepy judge hovering on deck, peering over their shoulder.

Those fishermen on camera didn't smile, wave, or offer a middle finger. They simply fished, with no wasted motion: haul in, hold each fish against a painted measuring board, keep it if it's big enough, gently release it back to the water to grow bigger if not. The camera had become for them an extension of the boat. The fisheye lens switched on only when the net or hook-and-line gear triggered it upon motor release into the water; so, it captured no images of any activity except fishing. "Initially some fishermen were worried that we'd be here perving out, tuning in to watch them doing stuff with their wives or girlfriends on board," said Wehrell. "But with this integrated system we were able to put those concerns to rest."

The camera allowed an observer a second take or set of eyes, so that, as in televised football, fishing referees could say, "The player is questioning the call. So…let's go to the videotape!" Wehrell could slow down the camera speed in heavy seas, sleet or the dark of night. He could stop, rewind, and replay scenes when something odd caught his eye, zooming in on a discard or a keeper or a species that doesn't look right. He could watch for unusual crew behavior, high grading (tossing back legal but small fish to maximize value of the quota share), accidental harvest of rare species like Yelloweye rockfish, interactions with mammals, or a weak moment on an off day. If the recording didn't match up with the report filed dockside upon landing, a red flag went off. To ensure fishermen didn't cram in a bunch of noncompliant fishing before the observers caught up with them, the data from their first trip must be processed before they can take their next. "Archipelago understands the fishing industry," said Behnken in a strong endorsement, "they respect fishermen and know how to plan, implement, and integrate at-sea monitoring programs." Crews knew exactly where the camera was installed, and what it's for. But they don't know when, or even if, they're being watched. Any video can be reviewed, only a small percentage is. This uncertainty, Stebbins and McElderry explain, underscores a crucial advantage of fixed electronic monitoring over an on-board human observer.

Beyond being fallible and expensive, humans could by their presence breed evasion. Before catch shares, some regulatory agencies required randomized human observer coverage of fleets. But that just meant that any boats not assigned someone—or any hours when an observer had to sleep, eat, puke or take a leak—were essentially unaccountable. Even the extreme practice of sending an observer out on every boat still yielded mixed results, compared with the behavior change on smart boats. When they knew their activity was being recorded and might be checked, fishermen also know they couldn't avoid, influence, or deny the evidence of their actions. Much as drivers behave better under inactive intersection cameras than a motorcycle cop, that uncertainty nudged the better angels of human nature to fish honestly. And a virtuous circle kicked in. The more a fishing boat could prove cleaner fishing, the less their surveillance videos got reviewed. Fishermen could potentially save time and decrease compliance costs, while stock assessments could be more responsive in the face of a fast-changing climate.

Not surprisingly, Liz Mitchell, head of Professional Observers, took a dissenting view. If "humans sometimes come with negative variables," she said, "so do cameras, with much more ease and likely with less consequence, not to mention less oversight." Mitchell saw electronic monitoring as yet another job-replacing technology with "risk of lowering standards of data collection and oversight." Before you can build trust, she argued, you need face-to-face accountability. The presence of solid, scientifically trained observers, "in the belly of the beast," offered immediate checks on bad behavior. People could sniff out the grey areas of wrongdoing, detect the quiet killing of an albatross, turtle or monk seal that cameras might miss. "Electronic monitoring systems can't do what we human observers have been trained to do."

Interestingly, Behnken and Archipelago shared these sentiments. A consensus has emerged about what tasks smart boats can't perform; machines can't replace some human skills. Rather than call for "either-or" oversight, some fishermen support a "both-and" system where federally trained fisheries managers reviewed a larger sample of richer data, drawn from human *and* machine sources.

For his part, Buddy considered surveillance technology to be a means to an end: as a shareholder, "you now have a vested interest in doing the right thing, and financial reward if everyone does the same. The best way to do that is to monitor what you all do. Hell, nobody wants a camera on their boat, *unless* they start to see it as a valuable piece of equipment to help them." That help came in the form of three critical levels of trust.

The first was political. A system with even the best-trained on-board human observers may still be inefficient, slow, and flawed. Smart boat technologies and networks equipped both fishermen and enforcement agencies with an opportunity to capture activity through an impartial lens. This documentation let private companies prove, and *improve*, compliance, thus (ironically) shrinking the size of government. As Gulf Shareholders' Alliance vice president and Florida grouper fisherman Jason DeLaCruz says, "video cameras don't sleep. They don't eat. They never slow down the process."

The second level of trust was economic. At Archipelago, Roth's ability to fast-forward means he could oversee two weeks of fishing on two dozen vessels in the space of a few hours. The same level of observer work, if carried out by twelve human observers on board, would have cost both taxpayers and industry tens of thousands of dollars more. Those savings could finance more and better-trained reviewers, which could in turn translate into more profits for industry. As Gulf Wild demonstrated, profits rose when fishermen could verify who caught which fish, how and when and where.

A third level of trust was ethical. Catch shares worked best if every stakeholder knew they'll be held to the same level of accountability as every other vessel out there: that all parties operate at the same sea level. Fishermen could work two states or two hundred miles apart yet through surveillance feel like they are fishing within sight of one another. Transparency shrank social distances, reduced suspicion, and fostered integrity. "I know that if I can break the rules and get away with it, then any other fishermen out there can too," said Florida grouper harvester John W. Schmidt. "But now it's pretty neat to know that your neighbor's not cheating. That you all now have to—and so will—follow the same policies under the same system as everyone else."

Back in 2005, Buddy had caved under pressure and accepted the VMS. For two years he fished with misgivings about that choice, but looking back two decades later, he's glad he did. His early fears of intrusive, Big Government surveillance melted away. "I had traveled all over the Gulf and had my own readings from my historical fish catches," he said. "Every fisherman did. But after catch shares there was no need to hide my honey spots from competitors." This new support for surveillance improved compliance, which sped recovery, which in turn boosted catch limits, income, and prosperity. "No one today is as secretive as they used to be."

America's fishermen now shared precious information with former rivals. That astonishing new development would also alter America's approach to preserving the most extraordinary and valuable "wildernesses" of the sea, supplanting the traditional top-down fortress approach with a bottom-up effort by fishermen to protect vital, teeming, ocean conservancies.

Chapter Fourteen
BOTTOM-UP CONSERVANCIES

Fans said it was inevitable, given his Hawaiian bodysurfing childhood. Critics fumed at his reckless executive overreach. Both were caught off guard at the massive scale of his efforts when, between his inauguration and leaving the Oval Office, Barack Obama achieved a legacy by locking up more ocean than any predecessor, creating new marine sanctuaries, marine monuments and quadrupling US waters under federal protection.

Protection, of course, is in the eye of the beholder. Both Democrats and Republicans had used the Antiquities Act to ward off perceived threats to natural landscapes and seascapes. Yet each top-down decision stoked debate about who benefits and who bears the burden from putting places off-limits. Even after extensive consultation, America's fishermen and resource producers chafed at being nudged out of the resources they depended on. They pushed Congress, courts, and federal agencies for relief. The question was whether catch shares could defuse entrenched "us-versus-them" polarization and unite harvesters and environmentalists under a shared approach to protection—from below.

Offshore friction had origins on land. For more than a century, debates over how best to protect America's millions of square miles of public lands had often turned people who care about nature against one another. Beginning with the first Chief of the US Forest Service, Gifford Pinchot, "conservationists" viewed federal lands as resources—to be used by loggers, hunters and ranchers but with care and economy to keep the whole undiminished for future generations. In contrast, "preservationists," embodied by John Muir, sought to cordon off sacred places, wilderness and reserves, which prohibit commercial extraction and allow humans only as temporary visitors. So, from dams in National Parks to logging in National Forests, users had for a century clashed with savers. A parallel debate now roiled America's largest public space: the sea.

It began harmlessly enough. On March 14, 1903, President Teddy Roosevelt established at Pelican Island, Florida, not only the first National Wildlife Refuge but also, simultaneously, America's original marine protected area, or MPA. That first MPA set out to protect birds; it made no mention of the 200 fish species swimming below. But in the decades that followed, America would ban catching fish in favor of protecting them—like at Hanauma Bay MPA, Hawaii; create the first National Marine Sanctuary; and integrate in the world's first legally-defined MPA System. The economics of doing so were often irrefutable. While local Hanauma Bay fishers once hooked $2,500 worth of seafood a year, visitors with masks and snorkels soon annually forked over $35 million to see live fish on that same reef—a 14,000-fold increase.

Unfortunately, those lucrative gains from ecotourism seldom reached displaced fishermen. And by 2008, when Lubchenco joined Obama's team, some 1,700 MPAs had been designated up and down America's coasts. With confusion growing over which places to secure for which interests, the US Ocean Policy, combined with a catch share policy, sought to enable more deliberate sustainable use and development.

PUBLIC TENSION CAME later to seascapes than to landscapes. For starters, until the 1980s the ocean's federal resources weren't technically even America's to squabble over, let alone protect. Also, potential MPAs were often out of sight, out of mind: unlike a Yellowstone or Gettysburg, their hidden value wasn't immediately obvious. Yet Lubchenco, a scientist, knew that the seemingly undifferentiated ocean was in fact more varied in topography and complex in natural history than the terrestrial world. Those pockets of exceptional biodiversity deserved "a framework for effective coastal and marine spatial planning."

Like Teddy Roosevelt a century earlier, Lubchenco soon found herself whipsawed between powerful conservation and preservation camps. Yet, also like Teddy Roosevelt, she believed it possible to "conserve natural heritage values such as biodiversity, ecosystems, and protected species" shielding them from excessive "commercial pressure." She had long championed setting aside "areas of the ocean completely protected from all extractive and destructive activities," with "explicit prohibitions against fishing and the removal or disturbance of any living or nonliving marine resource." The goal at that time, to set aside 20 percent of the world's ocean by 2020, would increase by half to "30 by 2030." Yet this time no-fishing MPAs had potential, in the government's view, to do more than merely preserve life for its own sake. As fish banks or ocean insurance policies, they would accumulate interest to the benefit of seafood harvesters by spawning, growing big, and swimming out into fishable waters.

It made perfect sense on paper. But this "spillover effect" rarely worked fast enough to help those fishermen competing in open access derbies. Harvesters understood how protected nurseries could rebuild stocks over time, but felt preservationists ignored the question of where those displaced by an MPA were supposed to earn a living, in the meantime. By the time MPAs rebuilt fishery health, the fishermen might have gone belly up. Critics opposed what they considered a blunt, slow tool. "Is it better to lock up small areas that are completely protected (to the extent that any area can be completely protected)," asked one. "Or to manage all areas as well as we know how?"

The overwhelming answer from the public was the former. Under "fortress" protection, officials walled off swaths of biodiversity to be preserved in a relatively pristine state. Ideally, these could generate more sustainable local revenue streams from recreation than extractive activities could have earned. While popular, that approach risked displacing communities that depended on the resource. More than 285,000 protected areas now blanket 16 percent of the planet's surface. Of that total, roughly 18,000 MPAs cover

6 percent of the global ocean, some with no-take zones that prohibit extractive activities such as fishing and mining. Yet there was a
tradeoff. That worthy achievement on land and at sea meant evicting
five to fourteen million people, a vulnerable caste of humanity Mark
Dowie has dubbed "conservation refugees." Many resisted in vain.

FOR BUDDY, MPAS posed less of an economic constraint than an
emotional, or maybe spiritual one. He had always cherished his liberty to fish anywhere. While traffic signs made him Stop, Yield or
Do Not Enter, those markers vanished in the Gulf. Over time, he'd
learned to live with the 40 percent of the Gulf under some form
of MPAs. Most were multiple use, while only thirty-five, covering
just half a percent of the Gulf, were strict no-take zones, centered
on spawning aggregation sites. Still, it frosted Buddy that, no decision-makers drawing lines in those waters "had felt a need to ask
my opinion."

It riled him even more when in 2010 the National Ocean Service and the National Marine Sanctuary Program drafted a concept
paper urging President Obama to designate a vast "Islands in the
Stream" MPA network covering nine priority areas—hard-bottom,
soft-coral habitat for ninety fish species, all linked by the Gulf Loop
current—across Buddy's prime fishing grounds.

He figured, *this is how it begins*. Not only was Lubchenco arguing from her perch in DC for protecting more areas, Buddy's ally,
EDF's Pam Baker, was urging "that well-designed Gulf closed areas
be created to address fishing gear impacts on habitat, provide an
area free of fishing to allow scientists to obtain accurate estimates of
natural or fishing mortality critical to fishery stock assessments, and
protect source populations." Famed oceanographer Dr. Sylvia Earle
and her influential alliance, "Mission Blue," soon upped the ante:
recommending preservation of 200 Continental Shelf-edge reefs
and banks in the northwestern Gulf, which she called biodiversi-
ty-rich "Hope Spots."

One of those spots—the Flower Garden Banks National Marine
Sanctuary (FGBNMS), designated in 1992 a hundred miles off Gal-

veston—was particularly galling to Buddy. He'd heard its Superintendent G.P. Schmahl wax poetic about how the sanctuary "provides critical habitat for a variety of biological communities and fish species" including whales, rays, sharks, sea turtles and an extraordinary diversity of sponges, soft corals, white curly whip corals, orange deep corals and large black corals. Biodiversity is great, he growled, but its protection always falls heaviest on guys like him. Fishermen who decades ago had discovered Flower Garden now wished they'd kept quiet. The restrictions weren't terribly onerous: he had to hook to moorings rather than anchor; and use bandit gear instead of longlines. But Schmahl had announced plans to expand Flower Garden eightfold to 383 square miles, adding and linking 15 prime snapper and grouper reefs, which would restrict his fishing freedom.

Stepping in, Buddy got himself appointed to the Sanctuary's Advisory Council. But there were fifteen other members, from universities, research institutes, conservation groups, and diving and recreational fishing interests. Most pushed the preservationist agenda. When they chose the biggest expansion as their "preferred alternative," Buddy felt outnumbered and besieged.

Buddy had lost the catch shares vote—to other fishermen. This felt different: serving on behalf of fishermen, he'd lost to strangers, outsiders whose focus transcended his region. He admired the goals of conservation groups "to protect all corals everywhere is a worthy ambition, if that's what you want to do with your life." But he wished they had "empathy toward those of us who make our living from the sea."

Flower Garden suggested how the backlash to the race to fish often gave rise to the race to fence. Over 30 years bipartisan governments had walled off 3 percent of the sea and set sights on more expansive protections, especially MPA networks linked by fish migration corridors. A nearly California-size chunk of the Pacific Ocean had gained the highest level of protection through presidential creation (under George W. Bush) and then expansion (under Obama) through two of the then-largest marine reserves on earth. The 490,000- square- mile Pacific Remote Islands Marine

National Monument–larger than all land-based parks and closed off to drilling, mining, and commercial (but not recreational) fishing– was surpassed only by the Alaska-sized 583,000-square-mile Papahānaumokuākea National Monument in the Northwest Hawaiian Islands, holding seven thousand (including some endemic) marine bird, mammal, reptile, and fish species.

Other nations rose to the rivalry. Australia's new Coral Sea MPA covered 382,178 square miles, while the UK set aside 413,129 square miles east of the Falklands and another 322,138 around Pitcairn Island. New Zealand blocked out 598,458 square miles in the Ross Sea—the size of two Texases. Less developed countries joined the competition. Kiribati set aside 157,626 square miles of ocean around the Phoenix Islands. Most restrictive is Palau, which banned all commercial fishing across 230,000 square miles, a no-take reserve the size of France.

The vast expanse and rapid deployment of "sea fences" made Buddy nervous enough. More worrying was how global targets kept rising. Initially preservationists wanted MPAs for just 10 percent of the ocean. Very quickly influential environmentalists at the World Parks Congress and 2016 World Conservation Congress were demanding "highly protected MPAs and other effective area-based conservation measures," with the aim being "a fully sustainable ocean, at least 30 percent of which has no extractive activities." In his book *Half Earth*, famed Harvard biologist E. O. Wilson pushed for far more. "We need to stop fishing in the open sea and let life there recover," he argued, calling for a "Grand Retreat" from 50 percent of oceans letting those waters revert to wilderness. "If we halted those fisheries, marine life would increase rapidly."

Halt fisheries. Stop harvesting. No take zones covering at least 30 percent of the ocean—within the next five years. To a fisherman, those words triggered fight or flight instincts. Feeling overwhelmed, Buddy fought MPAs as hard as he'd fought catch shares. But once catch shares were in place, he began to reconsider. With a secure stake in future harvests, fishermen could (unlike in a derby) afford to be patient; reef fishermen found that in two to six years they could indeed collect interest from no-fishing areas. Seafood harvesters even began the unthinkable: voluntarily fencing themselves out of sensitive habitats, creating new *de facto* MPAs. This turn-around was especially pronounced among Pacific coast trawlers.

SITTING IN HER Fort Bragg office, on California's northern Pacific Coast, Michelle Tarantino Norvell opened her laptop and pulled up an image of the sea. The picture wasn't of swirling currents or nutrient-rich upwelling through rocky shoals and kelp forests. Instead, across an intricate grid of state and federal waters, a splatter of green, orange, blue, red, yellow, grey and black blobs blotted out all the places where her family is forbidden to fish. Among the largest of those closed-off zones were thousands of square miles in the Rockfish Conservation Area (RCA), a coastwide ribbon of ocean between 100 and 150 fathoms (600 to 900 feet deep), that federal officials established in 2002 to minimize catch of depleted species such as darkblotched and canary rockfish.

Norvell grew up here when the sea was wild, open and free. Like Buddy, she chafed against recently imposed limits that eroded her bottom line. She oversaw one of the region's few remaining trawl operations, after bankruptcies and buy-outs shrank the harbor's trawl fleet and worried she too could be the next pushed into permanent dry dock. Trawling critics might cheer if her fleet management and operations shut down, but Norvell had refused to be marginalized. Now, citing critical habitat of rare and overfished species and the need to protect deep sea corals and sponges, their no-take zones might simply box her in.

A third generation Californian with fishing roots extending back to Sicily, Norvell was the first female to carry the torch of her family legacy and wasn't about to let the flame go out. Surrounding her desk were old black-and-white portraits of pioneering Tarantino ancestors, part of Steinbeck's rugged Westering breed who pushed back the American frontier here, and carved out a fishing life on, and beyond the continent's edge.

Fort Bragg sits on a high bluff overlooking a rocky coast. Today its scenic value had grown more valuable than its timber, minerals, grass, croplands or fish. The main drag was lined with coffeehouses and boutiques, motels and mini golf, attracting urban weekenders, hikers, foodies, surfers and retirees who prize the picturesque. Groundfish—the sole, flounder, halibut, rockfish and whiting that live on or near the seafloor—formed the cornerstone of Norvell's business. Her family's *Donna J* is one of the last four trawlers on the Fort Bragg waterfront. For roughly 100 days of the year her skipper, Charlie Price, would guide the *Donna J* out of the town's gorgeous natural harbor, through marker buoys and open throttle out to sea.

To stay afloat, *Donna J* and other trawlers had overcome massive swells, gale-force winds, riptides, submerged rocks and market gyrations. What may sink us, Norvell feared, were decision-makers from Washington, DC, who drew trapezoids on waters they'd never seen—Point Arena, Saunders Reef, Stewarts Point, Bodega Head. All seemed bent on one outcome. "There was talk in some circles," said Norvell, "that the state, or the feds, or some environmental groups out there were trying to do away with trawl fishing altogether." During interviews, otherwise neutral journalists trashed her proud family heritage as a "horrible," "marine life altering," "destructive force" that needed to be drastically reined in or phased out. She worried for her family but also her crew. "Fishing is all I know," said Charlie, who had spent four decades as a commercial harvester. "If I could do something else, I would. But I can't."

California and Washington had already completely banned bottom trawling in state waters; Oregon remained open and largely unprotected save a few fragments; but fishermen up and down the West coast grew increasingly wary of what they saw as arbitrary protections and de facto regulations. "They said they'd allow boats to come in, but you can't fish," said one exasperated fisherman, Bernie Bjork. "Then they said the crabbers could come in, but not the trawlers. They can change the rules at any time. It really got confusing." Even advocates recognized the shortcomings that could arise from a top-down fortress approach to MPAs, like the vast ribbon for rockfish. "Although appropriate for its time, the RCA was a blunt regulatory instrument," said Shems Jud, of EDF. "While it closed some areas of sensitive, high value habitat like underwater cliffs, rock piles and pinnacles where several species that were considered overfished congregate and reproduce, it also prevented access to vast areas of sandy, soft-bottom seafloor where more plentiful target species like Dover sole and sablefish are found."

MPAs often proved easier to proclaim than maintain. Over time, monitoring and enforcement grew increasingly expensive. Even affluent nations like America struggled to afford the science needed to design, guide, adjust and patrol boundaries in the right place at the right time to keep up with evolving habitats, threats and conditions. Economies of scale meant that net gains from tourists or harvests only paid for no-take zones after a country fenced off more than 8.5 percent of its waters. If excluded from the initial creation of a reserve, alienated fishermen like Bjork or Buddy may simply intensify efforts to hammer fish all along its perimeter, reducing the spatial and temporal benefits of any spillover.

In short, MPAs never existed in a vacuum. Even in the US, many have fallen short of their goals. A review of sixteen Gulf of Mexico MPAs (which restricted harvest of various species) found that "most have not provided anticipated protection for exploited species." A global study of eighty-seven reserves in forty countries found biodiversity and fish populations at fifty-two of them were in as poor shape inside as outside, that size alone matters little. Finally, there was a problem of "leakage." Banning fishing inside a Gulf reserve or restricting trawlers along the Pacific may simply shift harvest pressure somewhere less visible or regulated, resulting in a net negative impact on the sea. "It's not that we should necessarily forgo large MPAs," concluded University of Washington fisheries professor Ray Hilborn, "but rather that we need to broaden the conversation and analysis to understand the global environmental consequences of such actions. The world is irrevocably connected, and nowhere more so than in food and especially fish."

Thankfully ocean protection need not be a zero-sum game. Wherever there's a catch shares fisherman, there's hope. Fort Bragg demonstrated this potential as well as any corner of the ocean.

When she first heard about catch shares, Norvell's reaction was like Buddy's: *fear*. Hers would be one of more than a hundred vessels divvying up shares for 90 or so distinct groundfish species strung along the Pacific from the Mexican to Canadian border. A secure amount would allow flexibility to plan her season, but to reduce harm to the fishery, it also meant she and other trawlers were now totally accountable for dealing with everything that showed up in her nets. Any well-intentioned trawler might still scoop up rare, undesired and overfished species like Yellow-eye rockfish, Boccacio, or Cowcod. Such a "disaster tow" was akin to a hunter of Canada geese mortally wounding an endangered whooping crane. Norvell's boat would be fined or shut down, unless she could buy an offsetting share—assuming she could find it. "There were a lot of uncertainties going into the first year of the catch share," she said. "Above all, we were concerned about the potential for accidentally catching something which could torpedo the entire fishery."

To avoid that terrifying prospect, in June 2011 Norvell worked with The Nature Conservancy, EDF and various ports to form the Fort Bragg Groundfish Association. The idea was to increase awareness of who was catching what on the water, and make sure the cohesive group had enough quota to absorb any individual's potential "disaster tow." It worked like an insurance policy, within the trawl fishing community. Our goal, she said, was to not only "pool our risks, but to document where those risks were, so that we could avoid going there in the first place." Their first step was to deploy eCatch, a Nature Conservancy app that enabled trawlers to upload real-time data on the species, time and location of their catch: that electronic record of all fishing activity could be accessed and shared, aggregated and anonymized. "By serving as a shared database," said Norvell. "It's better than the state's paper logbook because it has capabilities for spatial mapping."

The resulting display was a living dynamic map, one that showed fishermen where *not* to go and what depths to *avoid*. The voluntary choice to stay out of those places reduced both individual and collective risks. It was in harvesters' self-interest to adjust the boundaries each day with ever-richer data. So unlike the static no-go blocs locked in by regulators, the grid on Norvell's computer functioned like a living, breathing, climate-adapting MPA—designed, owned, refined, updated and championed by, of all people, trawl fishermen. It took cooperation and sacrifice, but since the advent of catch shares in 2011, discarding had dropped 80 percent, and species like Boccaccio, Darkblotched, and Canary rockfish, along with several other once-depleted species, had been declared rebuilt. As Shems Jud explained, "the policing effects of the Rockfish Conservation Area were effectively rendered obsolete, because the new system strongly incentivized fishermen to avoid overfished species of their own volition."

What's more, the recent years of new, rich data about the seafloor helped stakeholders pinpoint the most sensitive essential fish habitats that deserved to be protected and which soft sediment muddy areas could be opened as safe for fishing. When the Pacific Fisheries Management Council next addressed fish habitat as a result of a Magnuson-Stevens Act habitat review requirement, instead of a zero-sum fight, the result reopened 2,739 square miles of prime fishing grounds in the formerly closed RCAs, 95 percent of which is soft sediment. While permanently protecting more than 12,240 square miles of sensitive, priority habitat such as reefs, pinnacles and coral and sponge aggregations, plus establishing an un-fished, deep-water area the size of Norway. Fishermen and environmentalists agreed on just over 135,000 square miles of new protection, and just under 3,000 square miles of re-opened access. Both sides walked away thrilled at the outcome.

As catch shares helped bridge the preservationist/conservationist divide, harvesters elsewhere similarly stepped up to work together on closing areas to protect fragile or important habitat and biodiversity. Pollock fishermen went beyond imposed Bering Sea MPAs to create and self-enforce no-take zones designed to avoid bycatch of Pacific salmon. Any pollock vessels who pulled up undesired salmon let others in the industry know. "When alerted by radio of a potential risk, the entire fleet can stop fishing within minutes," said Bob Dooley, "and avoid an entire area in ways that would have taken months to zone."

Beyond the US, some nearshore, small-scale fishing communities in the Caribbean, Asia Pacific and Atlantic coasts were fusing preservation and conservation through a type of catch share known as a territorial use right for fishing, or TURF. Rather than divvying up pounds of catchable fish, TURFs allocated to communities, groups or individuals the secure, exclusive privilege to harvest from particular stretches of water. Holding their own fishing grounds gave these often impoverished, food-insecure communities strong incentives to put the richest nursery waters off-limits, since fishermen can then be sure of reaping the future harvest. In ten countries, the establishment of TURFs turned opponents of no-take zones—including poachers—into effective sponsors for the creation of small-scale MPAs of their own design: a combination known as a TURF-reserve. Having demonstrated their capacity to create, monitor and enforce those reserves, they began expanding and integrating them into national networks with the support of conservation groups like Rare.

Some TURFs have formalized into law what had been customary, Indigenous, unwritten codes of protection. In Samoa, for example, coastal districts instituted village-level reserves within TURFs based on traditional closures known as "*sa*," a word for what has been culturally regarded as sacred. To allow oversight, these sacred, off-limits reserves tended to be kept close to shore and are demarcated by buoys, covering on average 4 percent of the TURF's area – a highly replicable and scalable approach.

Whether in the US or developing world, the surest way to win support for no-take reserves among even the most resistant fishermen was to grant them secure, exclusive harvest privileges or rights. Galveston fishermen, formerly lukewarm about protected areas, described their change of heart after catch shares. An MPA is "like having money in the bank," said one. "You've always got those fish protected, and they're going to be there producing new fish."

There are other reasons to protect underwater habitats: for their rarity, beauty, and vital role in the planet's survival. Shared, long-term incentives could convert twentieth century adversaries—Muir's descendants v. Gifford Pinchot's—to become twenty-first century partners in ocean protection. Sportsmen on land have came to support Yellowstone, where hunting is banned, because they valued the trophy elk who wander out of the park into surrounding national forests. Similarly, when the Trump administration made clear its hostility to new and existing MPAs—revoking his predecessor's 2010 Oceans Policy executive order and replacing it with an emphasis on use and energy extraction over conservation—Buddy stood with their defenders. Michelle Norvell best described this integrated effort by conservationists and preservationists to create more, bigger, and integrated habitats for wild food and biodiversity to flourish offshore. "The days of the individual fisherman are nearing an end," she said. "This collective approach is really the future, and we want to share this concept and model with other port communities to ensure their success."

Chapter Fifteen
A SHARED DOMINION

A mile and a half separates Wharf Road from the Galveston Yacht Basin. It's a half-hour walk up Harborside Drive, or six minutes by car. But between them, the political distance yawns wide.

Where Wharf Road serves bloodstained harvesters like Buddy who talk price per pound, the Yacht Basin caters to saltwater recreational anglers: men and women who cast from small pleasure boats seeking gamefish for sport. Both sides saw themselves as conservationists to the marrow. Yet while their fishing economies may appear different on the surface, both had since World War II competed for the same species below: red snapper. Each year, ever-growing numbers of sportsmen descended on the Gulf coast to haul in roughly seven million pounds of the legendary fish. As a result, tension escalated on and off the water over who can catch how much seafood. The rivalry opened deep and emotional wounds between America's offshore stakeholders who could, if ever reconciled into an alliance, become the ocean's strongest defender.

Caught in the no-man's-land between commercial harvesters and recreational anglers were millions of Americans like Bryant Thomson. Bryant was an amiable, heavy-set guy who for the last two decades has managed the facilities and coordinated missions for a large Baptist Church on the eastern shore of Mobile Bay, Alabama. Bryant drew inspiration from the Bible, his "doorway to salvation." He felt much the same when it came to fishing. "I've fished my whole life all over the place: inshore, offshore, bays and estuaries, from Maine to South America and much of Arkansas in between," he explained, "but where I truly love to fish is heading right out in the Gulf."

The wide-open waters recharged his spirit. The vastness of God's Creation humbled him. Bryant found deep parallels with the fishermen in the Scriptures, even if he found no chapter or verse describing fish brought to the point of depletion like several species in the Gulf. "I look at the world from a biblical perspective," Bryant explained, "that we were put here on earth to have dominion over these fish in the sea." Dominion is an old and often misinterpreted word, he adds: it does not mean we can destroy species and take advantage as much as we want. "What God's dominion means is you've been given responsibility to take care of it, which is something that for decades we failed to do."

As a boy fishing off docks with his father, Bryant figured snapper were ghosts. He saw pictures and heard stories of big ones—but never caught any. "When I asked my dad what he'd pay to have a red snapper come back and grow big, he said 'I'd give $5,000 to make that happen. But you won't be able to do it, son.' We thought the red snapper was gone for good."

Ten years after catch shares, Bryant and his father couldn't *avoid* reeling in red snapper. "I love to look at them, study them, think about what makes their world tick," he said. "Catching one's always a source of pride."

Pride was contagious. Today there are far more fish offshore, chased by far more recreationists like Bryant who seek from red snapper a personal, or spiritual, link to the wild. He was far from alone in that. "Fishing is about spending quality time with family and friends," NOAA Administrator Lubchenco proclaimed in the fall of 2009, "helping people connect with each other, with the natural world." Beneath the scientist and federal official, Dr. Lubchenco was, at root, an angler herself. She had caught salmon off Oregon, bonefish off Cuba, striped bass off Maine and shaped the national fishing policy to "ensure one of America's most treasured pastimes endures for future generations."

That gentle individual pull to cast a line can, when scaled in aggregate, turn into a more aggressive political push. In a few short decades America's fifteen million saltwater anglers rocketed into a force to be reckoned with, contributing $100 billion to the US economy, and spurring more than a dozen powerful membership groups to exert influence on their behalf. The rapid rise of these competing interests increasingly could set anglers and harvesters at odds with each other. Under the Magnuson Stevens Act's rules to end overfishing, coupled with catch share incentives, fisheries were rebuilding along America's shores, rapidly increasing abundance that filled all boats, commercial and recreational. For the latter, though, it wasn't fast enough. Rather than rejoice at the growing pie, some wanted an ever-bigger slice of it. The surging political clout of recreational boat and equipment manufacturers, combined with large angling organizations, have pushed to correct what they perceive as laws that inhibit their constituents' freedom to catch fish across America's sea. "Fights over allocation of the total allowable catch of species like red snapper in the Gulf of Mexico and summer flounder in the mid-Atlantic," wrote a recent think tank report, "have pitted anglers, charter boat captains, and some recreational gear and boat manufacturers against their commercial counterparts."

A showdown was a long time coming and the rivalry had only intensified. As ever more saltwater anglers like Bryant crowded into the prime fishing days and spots in the Gulf, commercial guys like Buddy felt outnumbered and scorned for "making money off of a public resource." The animosity ran both ways, hardening into place after 1990 when—based on historical landings—federal officials split the bounty (almost) down the middle: allocating 51 percent of the Gulf snapper catch to commercial fishermen and 49 percent to recreational interests. Naturally, each side felt they should have gotten a bit more of what went to the other.

It got worse. Regulators had put in place three distinct sets of rules and fees: one for commercial harvesters, a second for the for-hire charter vessels and head-boats that guide people to fish, and a third for private anglers with their own craft. Partition brought perverse incentives to each group. For example, individuals like Bryant had bag limits on how many fish they could take home. Fair enough. Only his group's overall catch limit was set in pounds. That meant as the average size and weight of recovering red snapper population rose, the whole recreational sector could exceed its limit even as anglers bagged fewer fish.

Initially each side kept to itself, to live and (sort of) let live. But as demand for fish kept outstripping the live supply—leaving commercial holds half-filled and anglers empty-handed—the simmering us-versus-them rivalry began to boil over. By 2009, as Lubchenco's policy took shape, Wharf Road and the Yacht Basin had come to see each other less as local adversaries than as existential threats in a national struggle for survival.

WHEN BUDDY SHARED his suspicion that recreational interests "are coming after us" and "want to end all commercial fishing of red snapper," he wasn't being paranoid. The angler lobby openly acknowledged that agenda. The American Sportfishing Association (ASA) had suggested federal fisheries should reallocate Pacific halibut, Gulf red snapper, and yellowtail flounder in New England from seafood harvesters like Buddy, and gift them to anglers instead. In some political circles, calling for "local management" rather than "federal regulations," had proven a winning strategy to accomplish that goal. Already, several coveted species—including striped bass, speckled trout, and redfish—had disappeared from supermarkets and menus. Why? Because advocates succeeded in reserving them for guys like Bryant. Growing fast, increasingly well-financed, and generating $68 billion in sales and 472,000 jobs, the saltwater recreational fishing lobby was in no mood to compromise. "We are not a conservation group," the ASA's Mike Nussman told a *Managing our Nation's Fisheries* conference in Washington, DC. "We're an industry, second only to running and jogging. We need a recreation policy" that supported that industry.

Buddy was all in for any fishing policy that created jobs—if they didn't eliminate his own. What galled him was the recreation lobby's reflexive habit of blaming harvesters for fishery declines while refusing to look in the mirror, acknowledge angler impacts, and accept or put in place effective monitoring measures that would hold Yacht Basin clients as accountable as Buddy now was. He set out to fight what he saw as a metastasizing political juggernaut that had become—more than the scientists, officials, preservationists, or social critics he'd made peace with—America's most formidable force at sea.

BUDDY KNEW, OR at least hoped, that no one ever just woke up and sets out deliberately to overfish—to fill their cooler boxes one way or another. He felt a kinship with the average angler, like Bryant, swapping fish stories when he met them on the docks or in the bar. He never forgot the hours he'd spent begging his own father to bring him along fishing (now those roles had reversed), his early years sharing fish he caught for fun. But Buddy and Bryant both know how a broken system, with the best of intentions, could wreak havoc.

In other parts of the US, anglers had also swelled in number. His native Great Lakes states registered 2.2 million private motorized fishing boats, versus a few hundred commercial rigs. New York City had seen a similar triumph of the amateurs. For 183 years, its Fulton Fish Market supported hundreds of vessels unloading their catch on docks below the Brooklyn Bridge, much of it for local consumption. By the 1960s most New Yorkers were eating fish trucked in from elsewhere, and by 2005, the wholesale docks had shut down, gone online, or moved indoors in the Bronx. New York City's waters were surrounding mostly crisscrossed by fishing vessels that charged $900-$2,200 per person to take Manhattanites and tourists out in pursuit of striped bass or tuna. In the Gulf States, where Bryant fishes, the recreational angling economy was more significant still: 3.2 million private anglers made 24 million fishing trips, launched from thousands of public and private docks. They invested billions into local purveyors of boats, marinas, gear, food, and lodging. They bought fishing licenses for thirty-five dollars (resident) or sixty-eight dollars (out of state), filling cash-strapped state coffers. At the ballot, their votes added up to a potent constituency; at sea, their rods add up to an unprecedented threat.

That threat may be hard to fathom for someone out in a small motorboat with his kid. While waiting for a bite, it was unimaginable that he could diminish the surrounding sea. Comparing even a good day's paltry catch—a couple of groupers bagged for dinner, the rest released—to Buddy's massive hauls, any oversight might feel like overreach. "Recreational anglers like to be left alone on the water free from rules," as one angler put it. "That's the whole point of it."

Yet as Bryant came to realize, the impacts of hobbyists like himself at sea were real and, in some regions and species, potentially devastating. As Americans kept migrating toward the coasts and Sun Belt, angler pressure on those species was projected to double. Federal fishery managers estimated those 15 million saltwater anglers took seventy-five to one hundred million trips and remove 100 to 150,000 tons of fish from the water. No one knew for certain which end of the range was closer, but fifty million tons offers an awful lot of wiggle room. That's why fisheries managers kept trying to augment flawed dock surveys with more accurate, credible and timely data. Even low-end estimates threatened the survival of the most desired fish species. Sport fishermen might land just 10 percent of all seafood harvested in US waters. But when it comes to popular stripers, bluefish, tautog, black rockfish or prized red snapper, the recreational take was by far the largest proportion removed from the sea..

Since recreation was driven by competitive evolutionary forces, size clearly mattered. Anglers tested their prowess by going after gnarly old trophies that conveyed bragging rights. By high-grading—keeping only the biggest and throwing back the rest—anglers collectively killed 20 to 65 percent of the most fertile adults. Those several million anglers who roared out on the Gulf the moment the recreational red snapper season opened could churn through their collective three to four million pound limit in a matter of months, weeks or, it turned out, days. Someone on a boat with a rod and reel could now catch his two allotted snapper in the first half hour—a thrilling but addictive new wrinkle complicating how anglers spent the rest of their day on the water. Add that up over a season and "you put a real dent in the population," said Bryant. The question he asked of himself and others, was how conservation-minded anglers could reform a broken system to exercise dominion.

There was no quick fix. Most anglers adhere strictly to legal limits on what they could put on ice, "catching and releasing" the rest. Yet even they may still unwittingly rack up a death toll all day long. Released fish stressed by severe hooking, overexertion, rapid thermal change or exposure often don't make it, leading to huge losses through dead discards. A deep-water fish like a big old fat fertile female sow snapper could experience "barotrauma": the stunning shock when—yanked from dark cold pressure of the depths into the bright hot sea level air—her internal swim bladder exploded out her mouth. For such instances, Bryant kept a hypodermic needle handy, and trained others how to puncture the bubble prior to release. "Otherwise, it all happens so fast they lose the ability to go back down, and just float there, easy targets for porpoises and sharks and large mackerel: boom." On board the *Falcon* all snapper counted toward Buddy's quota. But however a catch-and-release angler handled that same fish—wet hands, pose for photograph, release the air, and gently lower her back into the Gulf—there was still a fair chance she died an unrecorded death. Far from exaggerating "the one that got away," a 22-year study found US anglers routinely lowballed the number of fish they threw back and what happened to them. Anglers not only collectively exceeded their quota (in some years landing twice the amount commercial guys harvested), but on top of "overages," lethal discards often went uncounted, thus underestimating fatalities.

Anglers' diffuse activity posed its own problem. Even with Vessel Monitoring Systems, it was hard enough to monitor those few hundred commercial vessels in a dozen Gulf ports. Now imagine trying to inspect the contents of every icebox aboard smaller vessels launched from countless private slips and town docks. Federal authorities fell back on the default option: shrinking and then shrinking again the recreational red snapper season. Under President

Clinton, the Gulf Council reduced anglers' days to catch snapper from 365 to 200; under Bush, it cut the season to 60 days; by the end of Obama's term, officials pared it to just seventy-two hours. They also reduced anglers bag limit—the number of fish they could keep each of those days—from seven red snappers to two and increased the minimum size from 13 to 16 inches (generating even more dead discards). None of those measures curbed anglers' growing numbers, appetites or impacts. In the two-month recreational derby in 2011 anglers landed 4.6 million pounds, or 25 percent more than their limit; two years later, in a 28-day derby they landed 8.8 million pounds, 67 percent over limit. From 2007 to 2013, as new management for commercial fisheries rebuilt red snapper, anglers kept overshooting the mark, with overages severe enough to undercut the gains achieved by commercial sector reforms.

Escalating risks. Racing. Dysfunction. Discards. Opacity. Overfishing. Buddy knew the symptoms of competitive derby madness all too well. And though he'd started his fishing life as an angler, he now felt constricted by the recreational fishing industry's unchecked hunger. So, as always, Buddy fought back. He called in support from the Seafood Harvesters of America group he'd helped form, and gathered a new coalition of fish shops, chefs and seafood wholesalers in a "Share the Gulf" campaign to keep fresh, local seafood on the menu. He brought fishermen to Capitol Hill to sit down with their own representatives as well as with Congressmen from inland states whose constituents wanted continued access to Gulf seafood. Instead of his fists, Buddy fought through his attorney, becoming in 2013 the lead plaintiff in a lawsuit against the federal government for failing to rein in "chronic overharvesting" by recreational anglers. That one, he won: After an eighty-minute hearing, US District Court Judge Barbara Jacobs Rothstein sided with the plaintiffs and ordered NOAA to develop a better plan. He also helped win multiple electoral upsets, ousting some of the angler lobby's biggest champions, including Florida Congressman Steve Southerland.

Buddy wasn't alone in this fight. For commercial fishermen all over America, red snapper became an icon of danger, a rallying point: if the recreational sector could take over a species so highly valued by consumers, they reasoned, no commercial species would be secure. Buddy also enlisted his sons, believing the battle would outlive him. "Until recently I didn't really even want my boys to get into fishing," Buddy said, "to go out there and risk their life, and for a pittance. But now it's no longer a risk, and not a pittance. The future's at stake. No one ever wanted to do what we did, back when it was hard work, and we were all going under. But now that we're taking care of the fishery, and it's thriving, it seems everyone wants a piece of what we've rebuilt, even if taking it might bring the whole thing down again. And there's no fucking way we can let that happen."

As it turned out, in this long battle between Yacht Basin and Wharf Road, Buddy would find one of his strongest allies across enemy lines, together helping generate a new outcome that allowed Bryant and other recreational anglers to go fishing for red snapper in a state of dominion.

FOR TWENTY-NINE YEARS, Scott Hickman was part of the Gulf's recreational sector: one of hundreds of captains running "for-hire" charter vessels (with five to six paying guests aboard) or larger group "party" or "head" boats (carrying twenty to one hundred). For decades he'd never met Buddy. But he'd heard of him, and not much of it was good. "Everybody thought those guys were criminals, fish thieves who broke every rule they could," he recalls. He knew derbies pushed commercial harvesters to cheat: sneak out early, surpass limits, hide excess. "We saw how they were absolutely poaching and abusing and depleting our shared fishery, taking from us, from our future." He paused. "I saw they were pirates, and I knew who caught the most. I'd heard that Buddy was a bad guy, someone to avoid."

A former Marine who still sported the buzz-cut, Hickman met you with a firm handshake and hard-ass manner. But he quickly softened into a self-effacing chatterbox, prone to share the latest awful joke; then became dead serious as the conversation turns toward natural resources, personal ethics, family values, and civic life—which for him all amount to the same thing. He grew up hunting and fishing and in college studied two seemingly unrelated subjects: wildlife management and criminal justice. He'd considered a life in law enforcement, but then learned of a game warden's paltry salary, so decided he could earn more and laugh more by bringing anglers out to sea. "I recently had an African-American kid come on board," he recalled. "He'd never been on the ocean before. And I watched as he put the whole thing together, reeling in his first big fish, grasping the enormity of what the environment is, the planet we live on. Seeing how children react to the experience like that, well, it's something I cherish. It's why I do what I do."

As an outfitter on both fresh and saltwater, Hickman noticed something curious among his clients. When casting lines into creeks or tracking birds through forests and meadows, he saw hook and bullet groups and state game wardens agree on codes of conduct designed to constrain human impacts on finite populations of game. Self-organized into groups like Ducks Unlimited, Trout Unlimited, Boone & Crockett, and BASS anglers—these sportsmen self-imposed norms of fair chase and limited take. But that landlocked conservation ethic was missing at sea. "The same sportsman who will clip barbs from hooks on a trout stream or spend ninety minutes trying to find a downed mallard," observed Jack Sterne, a national conservation consultant with Rising Tide Strategies, "will out in saltwater toss fish after fish overboard until he gets one he likes and can brag about."

Hickman saw this play out many times. One winter, his hunting buddy Tom shot a Northern shoveler duck out of the sky but despite searching could never find it, which gnawed at him. Yet the very next summer, out on the Gulf in Hickman's boat, Tom hooked a big snapper. He'd exceeded his limit for the day, but instead of handing the rod to a colleague who hadn't he just tossed out a smaller one from the ice chest to make room for his own bigger trophy. Hickman recalled glancing over in time to see the dead fish float by. "I got mad at him, but he just smiled at me and said he wasn't doing anything illegal. I told him, 'Sure, but it's also not right. A dead fish is dead. And now neither of the ones you killed can spawn. You should know that, after how hard you work on land to conserve fish and game'." Tom still shrugged that 'it's different out here,' sweeping his arm in a circle. 'I mean, look at all this!'

"And *that's* the huge disconnect when these guys go offshore," concluded Hickman. "Because of the size of the sea, the perception is that the fishery resource is *not* finite. People can't *see* it. They see ducks in a marsh; they see deer against trees. So, they get it how on land there's not an endless supply. But then they look at the ocean, at all that water, and get a feeling of saltwater fish being inexhaustible—something they can't overfish with just a single rod and reel."

Hickman's anecdotes about perception versus reality were supported by research across the US and Europe. In 2004 Duke University's Larry Crowder made a comprehensive assessment that included red snapper. "The large impacts of recreational fisheries surprised us, and they may startle many people, including fishermen, concerned about the health of our oceans," he noted. "But if anything, our results likely underestimate the true impact of recreational fishing because we did not include fish that are discarded at sea or die from the effects of catch-and-release fishing."

For the decades Wharf Road and the Yacht Basin were equally guilty of overfishing, Hickman's tribe could blame snapper decline on Buddy's. Then catch shares happened, making it far harder to point fingers. Now everyone could see that the commercial guys were taking exactly as many fish as they were allocated, while the rec guys were taking many more—depleting the spillover effects. "Once we had 100 percent accountability," said John W. Schmidt, a commercial skipper who harvested grouper and snapper off Florida's Gulf coastline, "we were able to take all the records and data of what we were doing, and show exactly how much we caught and killed, and how we reduced discards. And we could take all that to the recreational guys who were complaining about our impacts and put it on the table, and say, 'here's what we've done. What've *you* got?' And they had nothing to show. No records. No data. Nothing."

Hickman had once looked to recreational fishing lobby groups like the Coastal Conservation Association, where he'd been a long-time member, to fill the gap, but in recent years he'd begun to sour. Rather than seek long-term solutions that would keep growing the pie, they seemed to be fighting to just grab more of it: petitioning the Gulf Council to take fish from the commercial sector and give it to themselves instead. To Hickman, that zero-sum approach defied logic and long-term self-interest. "To be responsible you need first to acknowledge that there's only so many deer we can shoot, only so many ducks or fish we can harvest," he said. "You need to make hard choices and accept the consequences that you're not going to please everybody." It was easy to keep blaming commercial fishermen, but after catch shares, "our relationship had flipped. Now we're the bad guys, making the resource worse off, while they're in compliance, doing it right."

For Hickman, a tipping point came from his seventy-five-year-old mom. Bonnie Conrad's overflowing patriotism led her to clean soldiers' tombstones on national holidays. Prone to seasickness, she wanted no part of fishing with her son. But she loved fresh seafood, and every Sunday after church treated herself to fresh-caught wild snapper. If seafood harvesters like Buddy could provide landlubbers like Bonnie every Sunday's fish, Hickman wanted to ensure that he and his peers could also offer Americans like Bryant the year-round fishing experience. Around 2008 Hickman finally reached out to Buddy—and the former rivals shook hands. "I mean, Scott never shuts up and he's a real pain in the ass," said Buddy, smiling broadly. "But I came to realize he was pretty damn intelligent, motivated and hard-working. And a prior service marine like myself, which gave us camaraderie. He's not afraid to say what he feels about people, including legislators, who need to hear it when you think what they're doing is stupid."

By 2009, Hickman started to talk with other for-hire captains across the Gulf, all equally concerned about their future. He found allies in Gary Jarvis of Destin, Florida; Michael Jennings of Free-port, Texas; and Steve Tomeny of Golden Meadow, Louisiana. They were soon joined by Randy and Susan Boggs of Orange Beach, Alabama, whose two big head-boats took customers on day trips to chase vermilion snapper, lane snapper, white grunt, and trigger-fish—and who had found a recurring client (and occasional volunteer deckhand) in Bryant Thompson. Bryant used to fish out of his small private vessel, but after a while that no longer penciled out. "It just doesn't make a lot of sense to me," he said. "You get fired up and something goes wrong with the motor; there's always an expense. The two happiest moments for a boat owner are the day you buy it and the day you sell it. Instead, for eighty dollars a trip, a head-boat like Randy's provides it all."

For years, those for-hire captains felt trapped. Outside the increasingly brief season, they had to make their customers release any big red snapper, which they knew usually wound up dead, a sickening waste. They also resented the ever-tighter punishing restrictions imposed on their businesses as unfair, keeping paying customers off the water while unregulated private anglers kept going over the sector's quota. Rather than try to impose change on millions of amateurs, this small renegade band of professionals explored the possibility of breaking away, into a third sector all their own. As Captains like Randy Boggs envisioned it, a portion of the recreational total allowable catch could be carved out just for for-hire vessels. His clients, like Bryant, quickly warmed to the idea. "There needs to be a sector separation," he said of anglers, for-hire charters, and commercial vessels, "let each be managed in a way that is productive for them."

Still, early on even the idea of "sector separation" carried risks of ostracization or worse. Industry groups had muscle, and numbers, and wanted to stay united to persuade members of Congress to give more commercial share to the recreational derby. If that happened, the for-hire group knew, they might enjoy a brief boost, like a sugar high. But then what? The precedent forced a hard decision: stand with the few hundred harvesters rebuilding snapper with catch shares, or the few million anglers under management that was eroding it.

Despite federal treatment as a single legal entity, charters and private anglers rarely overlapped. For-hire captains sought income and business certainty; private anglers sought fun, trophies and tonight's meal. Federal permits capped the number of for-hire vessels; private angler licenses were unlimited. For-hire captains were carefully watched in federal waters and had to file paperwork tallying what they landed; private anglers faced no such oversight. "It makes good sense that the different fishing groups would be managed separately," said Jarvis, "because they each operate very differently. Commercial fishermen provide food to Americans. Charter fishermen run tourism-driven businesses. And private boat recreational anglers fish on their own for fun."

In 2010 these for-hire captains formed an official entity, the Charter Fisherman's Association. Committing to explore ways to "increase fishing time, improve businesses, and ensure a sustainable fishery," the Association contrasted its goals against angler lobbyists who "advocate doing nothing, or worse: 'Quick-fixes' that lack any conservation considerations in order to avoid responsibility." Charter Fisherman's Association grew fast, attracting 600 members out of 971 total charter vessels in the Gulf. Backed by such numbers, they petitioned the Gulf Council to grant them freedom under "Amendment 40: Partitioning the Recreational Sector."

The lead up to the vote set off an ugly, drawn-out fight. Angry anglers "blacklisted our businesses," Hickman recalled. "They made threats, vandalized boats with claw hammers, pushed boats out of the marina, and put water in fuel tanks to ruin our motors. We paid an enormous financial price, and suffered personal attacks." Still, Charter Fisherman's Association refused to retreat, and after four tough years, on April 13, 2015, won a 10-7 victory. Now separate from the rest of the sector, for-hire vessels were granted 42.3 percent of the recreational red snapper quota, leaving private anglers the remaining 57.7 percent.

The CFA didn't break off just to continue business as usual. For-hire captains had been learning lessons from Buddy's commercial sector. Soon, a vanguard set out to design and demonstrate their own recreational catch share, the first of its kind. Seventeen captains signed on to the (take a breath) two-year Gulf Headboat Collaborative Exempted Fishing Permit Pilot Program. Beginning on New Year's Day 2014, the Gulf Council allocated those captains their own quota of snapper and grouper—5.5 percent of the recreational sector's portion, or 286,457 pounds—apportioned among the individuals based on their 2011 harvest records. In exchange for electronic monitoring and other new accountability measures, those pilot participants would be allowed to take out clients all year round, until each reached his quota. That flexibility let them focus on peak weekends, tourist seasons, and optimal weather conditions. "Our program goal is that once we prove this fishery management model to be successful," said Boggs, "that the powers-that-be will expand it to all recreational fishing charters."

The pilot performed better than expected. As headboat captains could spread red snapper fishing across the year, they achieved the often elusive triple-bottom line. More people had more time to fish a healthier sea, generating more profits for the recreational fishing sector.

The Gulf pilot's lessons had bigger implications. Against shrinking or closed seasons and forced constraints, the pilot catch share raises questions about the value of freedom. Namely: What is it worth to anglers to have the choice of when to go fishing for species they want, when they want? The answer is that allowing guys like Bryant year-round trips to catch and keep the fish he prizes most could add "a minimum of $139 per year of benefits per angler." In the Gulf of Mexico headboat red snapper fishery alone, that added up to $12 million per year. Replicating and scaling such a system could generate an additional $1.2 billion per year for US saltwater anglers, and $30 billion per year worldwide. Those numbers may be conservative; they don't include the usual industry multipliers related to tourism, equipment, bait, boat, gas, food, lodging. It's also limited to the status quo of today's existing baselines. If a depleted recreational fishery recovered as red snapper has—so that more people can fish more often over more days—the long-term economic benefits would be substantially higher.

The promise of catch shares had now proven itself in two of the three fishing sectors. Following Buddy's example, for-hire captains like Hickman or Boggs could readily absorb the cost and time required to practice dominion. To expand opportunities for paying clients, they could invest $2,000 in a VMS to demonstrate accountability, or spend hours filling out forms, checking tags and listing all the fish caught on board by date, vessel, and angler's name. But for amateurs whose income didn't depend on catching fish, such measures might feel too burdensome. Private anglers would need to track fish in a quick, cost-free way, like fitness buffs track steps or calories.

BRETT FITZGERALD RAN the Snook and Gamefish Foundation. His West Palm Beach, Florida non-profit works to protect saltwater fish by coordinating anglers, researchers, and policy makers. Snook is a tropical fish that ranks alongside permit fish and bonefish as a coveted catch-and-release trophy. It first introduced him to the deep rewards of sport-fishing. A Special Forces veteran of overseas wars, Fitzgerald found the solitary quest for these elusive fish eased his mind—if he was left alone with that experience. He was exactly the kind of angler who chafes at regulators' intrusions. "Most of us everyday anglers enjoy fishing for more intimate reasons than we generally admit," he explained. "I'd also say that most of us would rather just go about our business, and don't feel the need to share the day's experience with more than maybe a close friend or two—usually someone who we know 'gets it' the same way we do, whatever that might be."

Fitzgerald acknowledged that private anglers could damage the resource. But he resented their portrayal as free riders, enjoying the fruits of red snapper recovery work done by commercial fishermen, with no contribution of their own. While a few rogue vessels might stash extra meat in their coolers, he knew the overwhelming majority of anglers bought permits, obeyed rules, and invested in the fishery every time they shelled out cash from their pockets for bait, tackle, ice, or permits. And in recent years, he noticed, those pockets held something even more valuable than money: smartphones. That gave Fitzgerald an idea. Private anglers may not want distant officials to track or restrict their efforts but one thing they *did* want was bragging rights. Smartphones let them swagger while still at sea. They could snap a selfie holding their vanquished quarry, add text about how big it was and how they caught it, then share the triumph via email, Twitter, Facebook, Instagram, Snapchat or Pinterest. It might take thirty seconds, before releasing the live fish back into the wild.

What if all that data, wondered Fitzgerald—enriched with a few more details like the vessel's GPS coordinates—could serve both private ego and public good? Fisheries scientists hound state and federal agencies constantly for better data on anglers' "catch per unit effort," meaning how many each land, in this or that location, in an hour's fishing. Gathering together all those fishermen selfies could provide exactly that data with unprecedented granularity, enabling richer insight into the relative abundance and size distribution of target species over time. Fitzgerald envisioned a web and mobile app that would capture the anonymous experiences of these "citizen scientists" on a standardized platform to ensure reliable and comparable inputs. Aggregating the data would smooth out outliers. An opaque world rife with suspicion would give way to an age of offshore enlightenment.

Thus was born iAngler, the cornerstone portal of a nationwide Angler Action Program—an effort that would soon number ten thousand participants logging 100,000 catches across 150 target and non-target species, some via species-specific apps, including iSnapper.

Early on, iAngler participants represented a microcosm of private anglers. Yet feedback loops from those early adopters help make tools user-friendly. They also grew the numbers through network effects. It now takes an angler just two minutes to log information about her trip: where she went, for how long, how deep she fished and in what kind of weather; and about herself: her age, income, hometown, distance traveled and dollars spent on the fishing trip. Why bother? Self-interest is a powerful force. First, her fish stories gain broad and deep credibility through a third-party platform. Second, her accurate and near-real-time data enriches information fishery managers collect elsewhere—via marina surveys, boat ramp interviews, and random checks of what's in the creel—to reduce or eliminate built-in assumptions against overfishing. Third, she could access the rich anonymized data to see where others were scoring bites, improve her own experience, and even spark innovations in angler self-management.

Since 2015, for instance, thousands of anglers on both Florida coasts had been using iAngler to document their catch of the popular and delicious speckled sea trout. Florida rules allowed licensed anglers to keep up to six trout each day, measuring 15 to 20 inches: a range called "slot-size." Under those rules, hundreds of iAngler users tallied a statewide daily haul of 2,700 seatrout, over trips on average three hours long, for a catch rate of 1.75 per hour. That was new, rich, useful data. It also revealed an important wrinkle. On the Atlantic coast, ninety-two percent of private anglers released their "slot-sized" keepers; on the Gulf coast, half shoved them into coolers to throw on the grill. Then the iAngler platform also documented something else: the Atlantic coast supported far more gator sized speckled trout, while only smaller members of the species still swam on the Gulf coast. Did angler restraint result in the larger size—or was it a function of genetics, habitat, or prey base? The beauty of it was that iAngler didn't pass judgment. It let users draw their own conclusions, harnessing shared knowledge and peer pressure to shift collective behavior. Anglers might vote with their feet to enjoy the Atlantic shore's big catch-and-release action; others might change their consumptive habits on the Gulf shore.

Rather than just belly-ache about catch or short seasons, iAngler users could voluntarily contribute to enhancing them both. "Never before has there been a greater need for us to prove our value, demonstrate our release ethics, and help managers obtain a 'census' of the fish we target and catch," wrote Fitzgerald. "If we want to ensure those idyllic episodes don't get flushed away by the different forces that press against recreational fishing—sloppy land development, degrading water quality, industrial fishing—the days of locking your fishing memories in your private vault need to be over."

Scaling remained a challenge. When it pioneered in 2015, anglers on iSnapper logged just 163 trips and a seasonal catch of 1,519 fish. But technology wove a remarkable net—and network effect. "Programs such as iSnapper, iAngler and Tails n' Scales have been used by state governments to capture recreational data for fisheries management," explained Michael Christopher, managing director of Elemental Methods, a consultancy. "As the prevalence of these technologies grows, the amount of catch data captured by such self-reporting programs has the potential to surpass the volume of data from traditional federal and state programs."

And these apps proliferate. Fisheries managers acknowledged they can't keep track of how many have appeared in recent years, each covering a given location, species, or type of angling. Other studies reinforced qualified support for smartphone apps as a feedback tool; correcting for early biases, these may "improve data information quality and provide valuable catch-rate data to fisheries managers." Meanwhile, anglers kept building a code of ethics with each new cast.

BRYANT FELT HOPEFUL that these tools and advocates of dominion would prevail. "In commercial and for-hire sectors, the collaborative pilots have proved without a doubt that a catch shares approach to fishing works," he said. "The recreational guys should follow that course. But it seems like they've got the envy thing going; they just want to complain about it and see what they can get."

Indeed, rather than support or expand the proven pilots, recreational fishing groups instead pushed the executive branch for more of the same failed, short-term fixes: reallocation, longer seasons, or the hand-off of management authority to the states. The angler lobby found a new window of opportunity with Donald Trump's first inauguration. On June 19, 2017, the White House announced that it would unilaterally extend the federal recreational red snapper fishing season for private anglers in the Gulf of Mexico from three to 42 days—ignoring the Gulf Council, evading any public consultation, and dismissing the need for scientific justification. Scientists projected that this season extension would lead private anglers to exceed their annual catch limit by 197 percent, jeopardizing the entire fishery. The Commerce Department's own director of Policy and Strategic Planning concurred in principle: a June 1 memo warned Secretary Wilbur Ross that this "would result in overfishing of the stock by six million pounds (40 percent)." The Secretary shrugged, forging ahead even while conceding the longer season would delay rebuilding of red snapper stocks by six years, a clear violation of the federal law. Buddy contemplated heading back to court. "We had standing and could have sued and stopped the longer rec season in its tracks," he said. Instead, he deferred to his Shareholder Alliance colleagues in Florida, who opted to play the long game, head down, keeping recovery on track.

All the while, Buddy and his former rival Scott Hickman continued to mount a united front in Austin, Texas and Washington, DC, sauntering through the Statehouse and Cannon House Office Building shoulder to shoulder, working their governor and key congressmen to advance the for-hire catch share. Buddy would start drawling about how he'd grown up sport-fishing on the Great Lakes, and then always loved taking his family out on the Gulf, fishing for fun. "Everyone should have that opportunity," he said, "not just guys like me with a boat. That's why for-hire captains need more freedom for their clients, along with sticking to limits." Right about then Hickman would lean in with a plug for his commercial ally, talking about how his mamma loved to "order snapper off the menu, even if—unlike guys with their own boat and dock—she can't catch it herself." Pretty soon the Congressmen would be laughing, sharing fish stories of their own, pointing to a stuffed snapper trophy on the wall, and asking: What the hell's all this fuss we're hearing from some recreational guys?

Despite their efforts, the national policy fuss grew more vitriolic. Recreational fishing lobbyists urged Congress to shelter anglers from federal catch limits and controls, arguing that "recreational fishing and commercial fishing are fundamentally different activities, therefore requiring management approaches adapted to the characteristics of each sector." For anglers, that "modernizing" approach meant exemptions to give snapper management to angler-friendly state officials who don't even have jurisdiction over the deep federal waters where snapper swim. Complicating this rivalry is an escalating crisis: as wild fish grow ever more valuable, the once clear line between fishing for fun and fishing for profit started to vanish.

EVEN IF AMERICANS find dominion in the harvest of their fish, rising demand poses a new threat. Amateur clients, foreign fleets, and global markets could jeopardize any policy confined to national waters. As after the war, when Senator Magnuson had to step up and pass his landmark law, US waters have become the scene of distressing cloak and dagger stories.

In the summer of 2012, an eight-man bachelor party spent hours on a charter vessel, whooping it up in the salty Pacific air, returning sunburnt to Santa Cruz, California. As they loaded up in the parking lot, a stranger approached, inquiring about their luck. Any yellowfin tuna? They shook their heads. But when they opened their coolers to show off the sixteen big Chinook salmon they had brought in, the stranger looked over the speckled, silvery beauties and offered the revelers $1,000 cash on the spot. He would pack the fish in ice, he explained, and FedEx them to contacts in Asia. There, left whole, their retail value would be $3,000; fileted, they would roll into $6,000 worth of restaurant-grade sushi in Tokyo.

Other transactions simply cut out the middlemen. In 2014, for instance, near a Sitka, Alaska fishing lodge, Captain Kevin Mulligan took a call from six potential overseas clients inquiring about a "package deal." Mulligan, a former commercial harvester, had sold his halibut catch shares and reinvested them in a pilot's license and upgraded his cabin into what he thought would be a more profitable recreational charter operation. One five-day deal, he told them, would cost $3,600 a head. It would deliver staggering beauty, a once-in-a-lifetime experience, cozy comfort surrounded by rugged mountains and virgin forests, delicious food, the thrill of a monster on the line in exclusive wilderness, and...

Yeah, about the fish, the caller interrupted, how many pounds might they catch?

It's hard to guarantee, replied Mulligan, but I feel confident you'll reel in all five species of salmon, plus halibut, black cod, lingcod. All wild and healthy and...

And we can take all that back with us?

Mulligan liked that question less the more he got it. He could hear someone punching keys on the other end, calculating. Well, he said, we like to keep it in two small boxes to take out with you, a variety package of...

That's it?

Well, see, the point is to relax, said Mulligan. Unwind in a place few people ever see. It's all about that unforgettable experience, not the meat. We're seeking an ethic of catch and release in many cases, because...

Okay, the intermediary cut him off. Thank you. Click.

By the time Mulligan circled back, the international clients had already booked with a rival who let them return home with all the halibut they caught. For those six guys, coming from anywhere on earth, the ability to keep 1,800 pounds of prime meat—at fifteen dollars a pound retail, worth $27,000—would more than justify any trip. Mulligan's principled ethics didn't improve the health of the fishery. Halibut stocks rebuilt by commercial catch shares could still get skimmed by anglers looking to export cheap meat.

Marketing recreationally caught fish was only sometimes explicitly illegal. In theory, you own it; you can do what you want with it. Agencies treated anglers' domestic sales taxes and regulations as a different category from commercial revenues. Most ignored trade and tariffs. "It's not just Alaska," said Mulligan. In international airports from Sitka to Cabo San Lucas to Miami and Portland, Maine, "you see big catering boxes stacked up in the luggage area, filled with meat, ready for export, worldwide."

Buddy himself kept bumping into various forms of our increasingly globalized existence. Off Texas, in federal waters, he ran into rickety foreign vessels that might earn enough from a single haul of red snapper to feed the captain's family for an entire year. Back on shore, Katie's Seafood dealt with imports and exports from all over the world. Partly out of self-interest, partly out of a desire to give back to the ocean from which he had taken so much, Buddy set out to meet this increasingly voracious world on its own terms, by sharing experience he'd earned in his.

Part V

GLOBAL

Chapter Sixteen
BRIDGING THE GULF

After years of hard work Buddy might have felt tempted to coast. The alliances he'd helped forge among harvesters, researchers, enforcement agents, environmentalists, chefs, and charter captains—and the spread of catch shares uniting them—helped advance America's fishing renaissance. Under the new direction, the number of US fish populations that were exhausted had shrunk from ninety-two to twenty-one, with fifty completely rebuilt. Fishing jobs had increased 23 percent, and revenues were up 30 percent. But resting on laurels wasn't an option, and not just because of the recreational sector. Foreign vessels in US waters were once again catching America's fish.

Far from patriotic, wild fish often defect from US waters. Fish gotta swim, and some go long distance, and fast. But this ancient genetic trait has been exacerbated by climate change, as warmer surface waters forced fish to gradually migrate toward polar regions or into deeper waters. Washington halibut swim into and out of Canadian waters; Alaska pollock migrate into colder latitudes, where some become Russian pollock and spark geopolitical tensions. Others wander two hundred nautical miles offshore and risk death from high seas vessels. All that's fair game. Yet America's recovering fish populations tempt foreign harvesters to prowl and sometimes cross into US waters, impacting local fish populations (and vice-versa). Poachers, like pirates, lack loyalty to any flag. Working across invisible saltwater borders, the long-term recovery of snapper, grouper and tilefish would depend not only on US efforts, but also on collaborative decisions by three Gulf neighbors: Mexico, Belize, and Cuba.

That interdependence begins with the Gulf's ecology. The Gulf Stream moves its living contents around at up to two yards per second. The powerful Loop Current rises north from the warm West Caribbean waters and barrier reef off Belize, bumps into Texas, absorbs the Mississippi River, then heads east out to the Atlantic through the 103-mile-wide Florida Straits that separate America from Cuba.

Our interdependency is also political. On paper, the United Nations Law of the Sea established lines of jurisdiction that kept US fishermen out of the exclusive waters of these three neighbors, and vice versa. But it doesn't always work out like that. In broad daylight at 12:30 p.m. on January 26, 2015, for example, a US Coast Guard helicopter team observed several men in a Mexican outboard watercraft, or *lancha,* fishing twenty-two miles north of the maritime boundary and thirty-one miles off the Texas coast. Authorities dispatched a boat from South Padre Island to intercept it and, after a thirty-two-minute high speed chase, arrested the poachers, who had hastily dumped evidence overboard but still had in their hull six sharks, seven eels, and 428 pounds of their primary target—red snapper.

Following such incidents, the Coast Guard had confiscated the poachers' vessel and turned over the crew to Customs and Border Protection for repatriation to Mexico. But the cross-border poachers, most of them desperately poor and financed by drug (narco-) cartels—had kept coming back: knowing that on a good day they could earn a month's wages. Their numbers had tapered off in the 1990s, with too few snapper to justify the cost of the diesel to find them. But after 2014 the combination of cheap oil, market demand, and fast-recovering snapper populations brought Mexican *lanchas* back to American fishing grounds. In one week of February 2018, the US Coast Guard seized two lanchas holding a combined 2,800 pounds of snapper with a retail value of $30,000. Years of crackdowns, and even international port agreements, had done little to deter or slow incursions. By September 2024, the US Coast Guard was still busy seizing nine hundred pounds of illegal red snapper from lanchas, intercepting five boats and arresting twenty-three Mexican fishermen. Even more snapper might be ghost-fished by illegal gear that poachers hastily abandon when pursued, to hide evidence of their crimes. One three-mile gill net found by Texas fish wardens held three thousand juvenile sharks, described by one as "an entire generation's worth." Officials estimated that one of every twenty snapper caught in US waters were taken by Mexican poachers, and illegal fishing had for many years accounted for 40 percent of Mexico's overall catch. Senators in Gulf states have worked to crack down on fishing cartels, and to determine whether red snapper appearing in Mexican markets had been caught in US waters.

What Buddy witnessed off Texas left him conflicted. He could empathize with any husband and father cutting corners to feed his family. He'd done enough of it himself in derby days, and back then might have shrugged or turned a blind eye. But now that poached snapper and grouper came right out of the quotas held by guys like him, he felt, "each foreign crew hurts the value of our program, hurts sales and takes jobs." He and fellow shareholders began speaking out. At an April 2015 Gulf Coast Leadership Conference in Johns Pass, Florida, grouper fisherman Jason DeLaCruz warned about all the "foreign pirates sneaking into our waters to steal our fish, which undercuts our conservation efforts and detracts from fishing related businesses around the Gulf." Noting that lanchas sometimes even sold American fish back to American consumers at a cut-rate price (reflecting their avoided compliance costs and lower wages), he complained of the unfair competition that posed for law-abiding captains and regulated seafood markets like Buddy's. "The playing field is not level in the Gulf, and our fishermen are being undercut."

The threat appeared to be escalating, with limited options for stopping it. Despite muscular efforts to track, stop, and destroy illegal vessels, the Coast Guard's high speed chases were losing the battle: in fiscal year 2017, for each lancha the US Coast Guard caught, it detected four more vessels that sneaked back across the border to unload the day's catch. Each boat might steal hundreds to thousands of fish at a time. Each year those poachers collectively made "over

1,100 incursions into US waters taking upwards of 760,000 pounds of red snapper alone." For several million dollars' worth of fish, it appeared that Mexican syndicates were quite willing to sacrifice tens of thousands of dollars in confiscated boats, abandoned gear, and deported crews.

Gulf snapper poaching was a textbook example of the illegal, unreported, and unregulated (IUU) fishing increasingly visible around the world. Though by definition hard to measure, authorities estimated this pervasive problem may claim as much as a third of the global catch for valuable species, diverting up to a ton of seafood every second, with an annual value of $24 billion.

The US saw IUU fishing as more than a matter of sovereignty. It poses national security risk, due to its impacts on individuals, communities, economies, institutions, and governments. And the US government had ramped up port inspections and crackdowns on foreign vessels. In 2017 the Coast Guard sought to recruit four thousand more officers. NOAA officially called out the worst transgressor, "squarely placing responsibility on Mexico for its failure to act as a responsible flag State to control its nationals and vessels," according to spokesman John Ewald. The transgressions led to embargo threats on the half billion dollars' worth of seafood the US imports from Mexico actions that would cripple those law-abiding fishermen who can do little to stop poachers protected by armed mercenaries.

When an estimated fifth to a third of wild-caught seafood US imports were illegal, and worth more than $2.4 billion, it stood to reason that neither a trade war nor ever-costlier border enforcement will solve the problem. What can? Buddy's own experience taught him the most durable solution was to fix the disincentives that drove men to piracy in the first place—slow as that might be. So he began to share ideas with Mexican and other foreign fishermen on how to rescue their own stocks and fishing communities.

Buddy knew the limits of trying to export America's experience. He also wasn't famous for his tactful vocabulary. But the evangelist in him was ready to try. At 10:00 a.m. on November 4, 2013, Ambassador Buddy found himself out in front of Katie's Seafood, shaking hands and talking (through translators) with fishermen and fisheries managers from Mexico, Cuba and several Caribbean nations. All parties had realistic expectations (fishermen could never, for example, single-handedly resolve narco-funded poaching). Yet that meeting became the first catch share fishing exchange, one that also took Caribbean fishermen to wharves in New England and California. Decked out in his finest jeans, green Gulf Wild t-shirt, and a camouflage baseball cap, Buddy told them his story. He described the whack-a-mole regulations, why the catch share referendum was "the best vote I ever lost," and how he transformed from the Gulf's "biggest pirate into its biggest steward." Inside Katie's Seafood he pointed out the current high sticker prices, recalled the derby gluts, and explained how tagging fish had improved both governance and market value. They laughed at his self-effacing stories, scribbled notes, drew parallels to their own situations, took photos with flip-phones, and marveled at the traceability program.

After they left, Buddy chewed over his doubts. He knew these Gulf harvesters each faced their own distinctive challenges in governance and accountability. Some of Mexico's fishermen were on the verge of being shut down over an endangered porpoise. Belize, colonized by Scottish and English buccaneers, had long suffered from foreign and domestic piracy. Cuba had for seven decades under Fidel Castro restricted private property. He figured it would take decades for any of them to establish clearly defined rights, transparency, and recovery plans. What he didn't know is that these neighboring countries had already begun to secure the foundations of progressive national fishery reforms. In a few years, they might even return and offer Buddy a few lessons to learn from.

WEDGED BETWEEN TWO oceans, Mexico's extensive coast-lines host the western hemisphere's fourth largest fishing industry, and one of its richest marine biodiversity hotspots. It's also a target for destructive, cross-border incursions. The upper Gulf of California (Sea of Cortez) is home to totoaba, among the world's largest croaker fish. Chinese workers—initially brought in as railway labor—had been quietly buying up the totoaba for their swim bladders, or *buche*. When dried, Asia's traditional medicine markets reportedly pay brokers between $10,000 and $30,000 for a single dried totoaba *buche,* which retails in China for $100,000 for a single kilogram. Those gold rush prices push *narco* poachers to overwhelm local governance. Setting massive gillnets, their small motorized *pangas* deplete the endangered totoaba and accidentally drown remnants of the world's smallest porpoise, the endemic, and near-extinct, *vaquita.*

Outnumbered and outgunned, coastal communities had tried in vain to avoid disaster. A decade and a half ago, Mexican authorities created the Upper Gulf Biosphere Reserve, and in 2015 started offering millions to compensate displaced fishermen. They beefed up enforcement in the Reserve's no-take zones, sending dozens of police officers to patrol beaches and dismantle poacher camps. Still, nearly every other day, officials and activists pull illegal gillnets out of the water. In 2017, with perhaps thirty vaquita remaining on Earth, a massive, last-ditch effort by international scientists and environmental activists brought in drones, cameras, and night vision binoculars to try to herd *vaquita* into pens for captive breeding.

Curvina golfina was another species of croaker or drum, so-called for the repetitive thumping noise it makes by vibrating its internal swim bladder. For millennia, curvina have spawned in the upper Gulf of California from February through May, when life-stimulating nutrients from winter runoff of the Colorado River combine with tidal currents in the Delta to generate feeding frenzies and massive spawning aggregations. But that Easter season timing set them up for trouble, as curvina became a favorite fish for Lent. During that six-week period, curvina made up the bulk of all fish sold in Mexico City. Between 2002 and 2010, native Cucapá villagers, plus fishermen from outside ports, responded to that spike in demand by hauling in nearly 6,000 metric tons of curvina in just a few months. Scientists and local stakeholders warned overfishing would crash the fishery. Worse, much of the harvest went to waste.

Fishermen eager to make a quick sale gutted the fish on the hot beach or dirty street, degrading its quality and value. Market gluts further pushed down prices to a few cents per pound, less than a recycled plastic bottle. Unable to give fish away, some fishermen dumped curvina just trying to stabilize prices.

A turning point came in 2010. A partnership of fishermen, scientists and advocates set out to design a catch share for the curvina fishery. Within two years, Mexican authorities had established the fishery's first science-based Total Allowable Catch; it then vested 737 individual vessels with curvina-specific shares and permits in exchange for strict counting by officials on shore.

Dramatic transformations followed. Fishermen slowed down. They began timing their trips to maximize value, rather than volume. Employment stabilized under the new system, and channeled curvina rodeos toward productive outcomes. After years combusting a half-gallon of fuel to catch two pounds of curvina, they now burned a tenth as much. To help fish recover, landings were reduced by a quarter; nevertheless, over five years prices increased 67 percent to about seventy cents per kilogram. Between reduced fuel use and rising curvina prices, fishermen profits in 2016 were 26 percent higher than they'd been before catch shares.

Governance improved measurably. Three out of five harvesters demanded better enforcement. The number of port monitors expanded from sixteen to fifty-two, enabling near complete coverage. And under 24/7 satellite monitoring and real-time information sharing, fishermen could prove they went nowhere near vaquita. Once harvesters hit their total catch, they voluntarily stopped fishing and formally asked authorities to end the annual curvina season early. "Having a more ordered fishery through catch shares has helped us to be better managers of our resources and to look for new ways to add value to it," said a local fishmonger, Miriam Pérez. "As a community, we are learning to be responsible for the resource, so our children could keep benefiting from it."

Poaching remained an external threat, not only to US but even more so to Mexico's responsible fishing stewards. Yet, much as red snapper reform did in the US, the exemplary model of curvina catch shares inspired reform among Mexico's fisheries both small and large. Local harvesters of geoduck clams, oysters, and swimming crab began to design their own rights-based fishing systems. Another exemplary fishery emerged after Puerto Peñasco shrimp trawlers also scooped up Mexican hake (also known as Pacific whiting) in their nets to sell on the side. But as demand from Russia and the US soared, so did the value of this harvest. Soon targeted by intent, hake landings doubled, and fishermen grew guarded against the biological and economic losses they'd seen in open access fishing. To forestall any slide toward collapse, harvesters set out, north, to see if catch shares could work for them.

In 2013, following Buddy's meeting with them in Galveston, twenty hake fishermen and managers flew to Newport, Oregon, where proud West Coast trawlers showed Mexican ambassadors how they, too, could heal the Pacific shared by both nations. Sara Skamser of Foulweather Trawl talked of securely defined shares, the step-by-step processes and challenges of allocation, and the gear modifications that could reduce bycatch. The Mexican fishermen came away with a working model. "We want to be better—not just better whiting fishermen, but a better whiting industry to avoid running out of this valuable resource," said Mateo Lopez Leon, a trawler of shrimp and hake. "We want to preserve the biomass, and the only way is through a catch share program. We need to learn so we have a product that will be with us now and in the future."

Mexico has emphasized its Pacific coast, where its biggest fisheries and value concentrate. On the Atlantic, where it hopes to reform shared grouper and snapper fisheries, Mexico has looked north to Buddy's catch share example. Yet it also builds on precedents emerging just across its southern border: from the culturally diverse and ecologically rich country of Belize.

SMALLER THAN NEW Hampshire, with a quarter of that state's population, Belize boasts the western hemisphere's largest barrier reef, an astonishingly rich source of biodiversity, food, jobs and income.

Yet that reef was also at risk. Regulatory institutions struggled for traction. Poverty and malnutrition affected nearly a quarter of the population. Crime levels were among the world's highest. There's also that historical legacy.

Unlike such tropical reef fishing nations as Fiji and Samoa, Belize has no customary tenure systems on which to build. To the contrary, its maze-like coastline was settled (if that's the word) by privateers and mutineers. European outlaws—British Buccaneers, French corsairs, Dutch freebooters—formed what became known as a "Baymen aristocracy," earning fortunes smuggling slaves and contraband or overharvesting indigenous logwood forests. That culture of exploitation and maritime marauding endured into the twenty-first century. While Belize had since 1982 set aside marine protected areas, poachers still hammered reefs and sea floors within and outside them.

One perpetrator of that lethal reef overfishing was a father of three named Yonardo Cus. With his stocky build and broad, dark Amerindian features, Yonardo was proud of his pure Ketchi Maya blood, of being the "last true native" in his town of Punta Gorda. He grew up playing amidst the fallen stones of ancient Mayan ruins in San Miguel village, where upland forests full of mahogany and tropical cedar were themselves being stripped by logging and clearing for marijuana crops and subsistence farms. But from age seven onward, Yonardo wanted only to fish: "As a kid I fished in the river, now I fish in the sea, I have always liked fishing." His family moved to Punta Gorda for employment and better education opportunities, and this meant Yonardo would now be fishing at sea.

Now in his late forties, fishing remained his passion. On an already warm dawn on April 4, 2014, on the southern edge of town near a graveyard, Yonardo shouldered a two-stroke, eight-horse-power motor and inched down a steep cutback to his boat. He only got "the machine" a few years ago, he explained, as he mounted it on the stern. "Before, I was not saving any money because I was a drunk." Yonardo sobered up and over the next seven years saved up earnings from fishing and washing windows and mowing lawns at tourist lodges, then borrowed enough to make the leap from wooden hull and sail to fiberglass and outboard. Sailing had been free but risky. When winds died offshore, he said, "the sea is so calm and the sun is so hot that with only my paddle, it beats me so hard. I cry when I'm out there in the sun, drifting with the current. I *cry.*"

The motor allowed him to escape the doldrums but made him "lazy." Where he used to rise at 1:30 a.m., he now will "only wake at 3:00 a.m., sometimes not even fishing until 4:00 or 5:00 a.m." As he puttered across the bay, Yonardo laid out his homemade gear: a spare oar that he found floating by the shore and now doubles as a bait-cutting board; a driftwood knob he'd refashioned into a fish-stunning club; a knife he made by grinding a piece of steel and inserting it hot into a ¾ inch PVC pipe handle; an anchor he made of twisted and welded construction rebar; a wooden gaffe into which he'd spiked and bent a metal hook; and an artificial lure he made out of frayed rope to resemble a more expensive one that (he says) only works half as well. "People say I'm cheap," said Yonardo, as he climbed into a black plastic garbage bag, with holes cut out for head and arms, to protect his shirt and pants from the mess of mullet bait he was about to gather.

As Yonardo stood with his casting net, he recalled the teachers that had showed him the ways of the sea. An old Guatemalan taught him to hold the cast net in his armpit, rather than his teeth as the men from his own village did, before spiraling out a release for maximum spread and reach. Another showed him how to cut mullet bait into a shape that, when mounted upside down on the hook and trolled through the water, made the flesh twitch like fins. Later, he described how "Mister Keith" Sambala, and "Mister Felix" Arzu had taught him secret lessons about many of the five hundred species found in these waters: how to look for and follow the pelicans, how fish responded to the phases of the moon, or read the tidal action near the river mouth where the lunkers dwelled. His friend "Mister Martin" Reyes, a Garifuna descendent of shipwrecked slaves, showed him how it was possible to listen to vibrations through the end of his wooden paddle to know—even at night, and no matter the depth—whether the habitat below consisted of mud, reef, rock or grass floor: a no-cost fish-finder. "One of my teachers, he died," said Yonardo, "but he left me the lessons he had learned and so he helps me still."

Yonardo anchored one end of his mullet bait net, stretched it against the current, and then curled it inward in a circle. He then crossed inside and pounded his paddle on the gunwale to startle a half dozen mullet into the mesh wall. "No one ever taught me this," he said, smiling. "I learned it as a boy in the river."

Over the next few hours, while Yonardo described bird life and barracuda behavior, dolphins jumped out of the silvery water off the bow and manatee crossed beneath the hull, giving the impression that Yonardo was speaking out loud to them—and would have even if no one had been in the boat to hear him. He smiled and agreed. "I love to fish because every day is different and you don't know what will happen," he proclaimed, as hand over hand he pulled up lines loaded with one or two big snapper. No one challenged him, but he repeated his affirmation, shouting, "I love, love, *love* to fish. I LOVE it!"

Over time, however, Yonardo had loved his fish nearly to death. Day after day, he and other Punta Gorda fishermen removed too many crustaceans, lobsters, finfish, sharks, conch—any edible food—in a classic tragedy of the nearshore commons that did indeed bring near ruin to all.

Development circles traffic in a tired old saying: "give a man a fish and he'll eat for a day; teach a man to fish and he'll feed his family for a lifetime." Yonardo, "Mr. Martin" Reyes and other small-scale fishermen in Belize need not rely on any foreign experts for fishing instructions; they had taught each other to harvest, if anything, *too* effectively. What they needed was to teach each other how *not* to fish: to reward self-restraint in shallow waters among the mangroves and reefs, to self-enforce limits where governments could not. So rather than having strangers "give a man a fish," Elinor Ostrom had shown how when coastal communities secure for each other clearly defined access rights to the nearshore fishing grounds, they feed their families for generations.

Given the lawlessness that had prevailed in his local waters, Yonardo had little context for making sense of this approach. When visitors began writing on whiteboards and using terms like managed access, or territorial use rights for fishing (TURF), he and his fellow fishermen shook their heads, rolled their eyes, crossed their arms, and sighed. "They thought, 'Oh, no. Here comes the latest round of foreign intervention in our lives'," recalled Nic Requena, a Belizean conservation advocate. Yonardo had already endured the designation of marine protected reserves and a World Heritage Site, restrictions on gear, and bans on all fishing during spawning aggregations. Whatever their ecological value, those reforms had been seen by villagers as a kind of robbery of their food and livelihood. "They were all well-meaning," said Requena, "but at some point, fatigue sets in. And so, in the first meetings and workshops the fishermen all naturally resisted what they thought was yet another top-down solution."

What differed now was how fishermen could take ownership of the solution—from the bottom up.

Yonardo, Reyes and a few dozen other seasoned fishermen met to identify threats to their livelihood. Their first instinct was to blame foreigners, and not without cause: Jamaicans, Hondurans, and Guatemalans, having denuded their own shores, did frequently show up in the still relatively healthy waters off southern Belize. But Yonardo knew that he and other Belizeans had also contributed to the depletion. Spiny lobster was one of the biggest casualties: in the first decade of the new millennium, the lobster haul for many fishermen plunged from two hundred to twenty per day. Overall, reef fish populations and queen conch declined by a third. Men like Yonardo in small cobbled-together vessels were forced to burn four-dollars-a-gallon gas racing each other farther offshore, to dive deeper, take more risks and still land less food and earn less income.

By the time Requena showed up, they were ready to try anything. "Twenty of us that wanted an [exclusive managed access] reserve for ourselves finally came together and signed a paper," said Reyes. It took countless meetings to design a pilot recovery plan and get it approved by the national government, then many more months for scientists to gather enough data. But by 2011, the Port Honduras Marine Reserve Managed Access pilot was born: designating waters from Monkey River to beyond the Rio Grande, extending approximately 8 kilometers out to sea for the exclusive use of 136 artisanal fishermen. "It meant only traditional fishermen from here were allowed to fish in our area," Reyes explained, "vetted by a committee [of fishermen and officials], who decided who gets a license." In exchange, those fishermen agreed to report their catch data or to monitor illegal fishing as custodians and stewards, extending the eyes and ears of underfunded officials.

By providing data and supporting patrols Yonardo, Reyes and their Punta Gorda neighbors helped cut illegal fishing 60 percent during the pilot. "In two years' time we've seen a lot more fish," says Reyes. "Black snapper, drummer fish, red silk snapper, croaker." The pilots still need to be realized at scale, with rigorous enforcement and catch logs submitted nationwide. Yet after seeing that the licensing and verification process was working, fishermen who once opposed even small marine protected areas now petitioned for managed access to cover more of their waters and often with larger no-take reserves within. Three-quarters reported seeing both bigger harvests and less illegal fishing. And when they did spot foreign poachers, they had a motive and mechanism to report it and were believed when they did. On his way back to port one day, Yonardo passed a fishing boat he didn't recognize fifty yards away. Studying the size and shape of the boat, along with the number of fishermen on board, he thought, "That's not right. They're not supposed to be there." He didn't confront them immediately. That might identify him as "a snitch," and invite violent retaliation. Instead he waited until they were out of sight to call in a descriptive report to local rangers.

To support their fast-evolving political institution, Yonardo and the others formed a fishing association—with members, dues, regular meetings, and opportunities to supplement their fishing incomes with access to loans and training in on-shore skills. "We wanted to build strength within the fishermen," said Reyes.

Yonardo felt stronger as a fisherman and a provider. Before sitting down to a supper of rice, beans and a spicy stew made from part of the day's catch, he showed off certificates taped on the cinderblock wall, earned by his sons and daughters in school—his pride complicated by the knowledge that they planned to pursue fields far from his own. His eldest son Edwin wants to teach; middle daughter Myra to be a nurse and Yonardo Jr., to be a chef. Their father worried that if none took over his trade everything he'd built and learned over a lifetime would end in Punta Gorda with him, Belize's last Amerindian fisherman. At the thought his mood turned melancholy. "My brothers and my family, none of them want to go into fishing," he said quietly. "It makes me sad they don't. I'm willing to teach anyone. Alone it is nice, but sometimes I want to cry, I *cry*, because I'm wishing I was training someone for what I do."

What Yonardo didn't realize is that his words and example were already helping to train the entire country.

Slowly, then quickly, early success stories from Punta Gorda rippled north up the coast and across the country. Three years after the launch of Yonardo's pilot, the government of Belize committed to engage all three thousand fishermen to put in place managed access catch shares across the nation. By 2021, Belize's strategic expansion of no-take zones, combined with community-driven catch shares and advanced enforcement technology, had stabilized populations of key commercial species like spiny lobster and queen conch.

For years, fishermen had felt pushed around by scientists. Naturally, some pushed back. Now they began working closely with marine biologists, sharing all they knew, confident that it wouldn't backfire in arbitrary limits. Belize became a test ground for swift, low-cost methods for conducting fish stock assessments. By 2017, more than 90 percent of fishermen were submitting their catch data: eager to support more accurate stock assessments, catch limits, harvest controls and performance measures to guide adaptive management of their reef fisheries. In the years that followed, fishermen pressured their resource-constrained government to strengthen science-based decision making and to improve enforcement on the water. Belize's fishermen had been activated as conservation advocates.

It wasn't long before regional officials and NGOs began to visit Belize. Hondurans, Salvadorians, Guatemalans and Mexicans came to see how fishing worked in a similar neighboring culture, ecosystem and economy, and could transform their own. Yonardo's impact extended even beyond Mesoamerica.

As others emulated its model, Belize, backed by fishermen, passed a modern fisheries law in 2020 that in rapid succession expanded its Biodiversity Protection (no-take) Zones from 3 percent to 11.7 percent to 20.5 percent of the nation's territorial waters, and has committed to achieving 30 percent protection with funding support by the Blue Bond, with further expansion underway. A new program, Fragments of Hope, has been re-seeding Belize's barrier reef with genetically robust, diverse and resilient corals, seeking to rebuild areas that have been, or would soon be, bleached. Rather than wait for global interventions, local actions—anchored by fishermen with a secure stake in the fishery—were providing a global model for resilience solutions. At a June 6, 2017, U.N. Oceans Conference, Belize Minister of Fisheries Omar Figueroa, two fishermen, and NGO partners jointly offered Belize's recovery as one to be replicated in tropical waters worldwide.

While Belize's conservation gains were hard-earned and far from finished, the nation's transformation has put fishermen at the heart of fisheries management and ecosystem protection. "We know that our seas face real and urgent dangers," said Leobihildo Tamai, a small-scale fisherman who alongside Yonardo pioneered Belize's new social contract. "But we also know that managed access works because it counters global threats with homegrown resilience, under the care of local stewards whose own survival depends on restoring diverse reef health, biodiversity, prosperity and hope."

CATCHING FISH IN Cuba is a singular story. It picks up where *The*

Old Man and the Sea left off.

Following the 1959 Revolution, Cuba divided its fisheries in two. The most valuable came under state ownership and control, collaborating with the USSR to jointly harvest the Atlantic. To seal the deal, Soviets funded a massive port with refrigeration plants, warehouses, floating docks, subsidized fuel storage, and wharves long enough to accommodate 130 large fishing vessels at a time. By 1980, a Cuban-operated distant-water fleet was regularly harvesting 230,000 metric tons of seafood. The Soviets also helped build four state enterprises in seven ports, which employ fourteen thousand Cuban fishermen, biologists, processing staff, managers, and other technicians.

In the other half, some eighteen thousand smaller scale fishermen work near shore, sailing out of 160 small docks fringing the island. These private fishermen cast lines for lane snapper and other reef fish or may dive (illegally) for lobster. They sail small wooden boats inherited from parents and grandparents and (if they are lucky) outboard motors, most built before 1959. But for half a century they couldn't legally practice their trade.

The 1991 dissolution of the Soviet Union triggered ripple effects offshore. Loss of the petroleum-based line of credit meant Cuba's distant-water fleet stayed home, crowding pressure on nearshore waters. By 1998, overwhelmed national government officials in Havana decentralized political authority to local managers who could monitor and protect nearshore harvesting and processing. The move allowed "much more control by the fleet," according to University of Florida resource economist Chuck Adams, enabling it to "concentrate on the production of high-valued species such as spiny lobster, shrimp, reef fish, tunas, sponges." Another big step came in 2009 when Cuba let all private fishermen sell to state markets, legally. Yet seafood consumption was increasingly reserved for the millions of Europeans and Canadian visitors who began pouring in, drawn by the island's frozen-in-time glamor, stunningly healthy reefs and adrenaline-pumping shark dives. Tourism replaced Soviet support as Cuba's growth engine. Cubans reliant on their book of ration coupons (*la libreta*, which covered consumptive items from rice and coffee to cigarettes), saw their own access to seafood dwindling. Outside of hotels and restaurants with foreign clientele, unauthorized sale of spiny lobster or shrimp caused seizures and fines. But in a two-tiered economy that prizes foreign exchange, many Cubans take the risk.

Other problems arose from the nearshore waters. Cuba has better reported and monitored catch data, but illegal fishing remained a growing problem. Complicating matters, Cuba's marine scientists had for decades been knee-capped by the US trade embargo, or *bloqueo*. Researchers with masks and snorkels could document levels of biodiversity and reef health, but lacked basic access to underwater cameras, sample drills, or satellite data visualizations from Google Earth. While sharks, manatees, snapper, tuna and coral larvae could move freely back and forth between Cuban and US waters, research vessels and fishing officials could not. Beyond export species the overall health of Cuban fish stocks was hard to pin down. But based on landing trends, managers estimated that 20 percent of the country's fish population was "fully exploited," 74 percent including the most valuable species were "over-exploited," and 5 percent were "collapsed."

The pain was felt even in the most remote parts of the country. In 2013, at the end of a dirt road 340 miles from Havana, villagers in Playa Florida gathered at the elementary school to express their fears. One lamented that she and her husband were fishing longer hours but coming home with fewer fish. Another said that he used to catch many, diverse, healthy fish but now caught only the least valuable ones. "Some of the big fish are simply gone," he said. Locals employed by state-owned vessels said that they, too, were making less money as Gulf shrimp harvests declined. Many also spoke of sea level rise, which they saw eroding shorelines and jeopardizing the town's bustling summer tourism trade.

Hope was emerging from unlikely quarters. In 2007, citizens of Cuba, Mexico and the US had formed a "Tri-national Initiative for Marine Science and Conservation in the Gulf of Mexico & Western

Caribbean." Three years later, representatives of all three countries met in Sarasota, Florida, to launch a coordinated effort of reforms to protect sharks and other shared marine resources. More than one hundred shark species (a fifth of all species worldwide) swim in and around Cuban waters. Decimated in other nations, these magnificent prehistoric predators, including Oceanic white tip and Longfin mako still thrive in abundance here. Tri-national scientists began co-identifying and co-monitoring their movements: first comparing notes, then training each other to collect and share data. That joint research led to a series of ecological and diplomatic breakthroughs when in 2015 the data became the basis for Cuba's first national plan for shark conservation, including the Caribbean's first outright ban on "finning." While not a traditional practice in Cuba, in that horrific practice crews hoist a hooked shark to the surface, lop off its fins to dry and sell to Asian markets, then release the still live but mutilated shark to writhe into the depths to die a slow, tortured death. In February 2015, a joint team of Cuban and American marine scientists tagged a Longfin mako shark off the coast of Havana and tracked its five-month, 5,500-mile trek to New Jersey and back. "The amazing journey of a single shark shows why conservation of migratory species cannot be the responsibility of a single country acting alone," said Caribbean expert Dan Whittle. That spring, Discovery featured Cuba in its massively popular Shark Week: chronicling the first-ever use of remote-tracking tags on sharks in Cuba—perhaps the only US/Cuban documentaries jointly produced since the Castro revolution in 1959.

A second alliance, SOS Pesca, focused on ending community-scale overfishing. The Cuban government worked with researchers, fishery managers and environmental advocates to help the fishing villages of Playa Florida and Guayabal (pop. 4,200) design pilot projects giving fishermen a more direct role in the conservation of critical coastal and marine habitats. Much like Buddy had been, Cuban fishermen began as skeptics, wary of both government and outsiders. Yet after many months of seeing their questions, answers, goals and perspectives integrated into a plan, they began to see the now well-documented potential of co-management. Cuba's coastal communities gained confidence and momentum for rights-based approaches. They also developed alternative livelihoods—such as harvesting and processing oysters—to help shift pressure from vulnerable species to mariculture. After four years of moving from isolated suspicion to collaborative stewardship, a meeting in Playa Florida celebrated their new level of trust: in each other as stewards, and in the sea's potential to reward resource husbandry. One fisherman approached an American researcher. He had seven children, he said, many of them had once been looking to escape to the city. Now all of them wanted to fish for a living. "Fishing's what we do," he said. "It's our future."

As relations thawed, diplomats built on the informal foundation laid by American and Cuban harvesters, scientists and fishery managers. Stakeholders gathered at the 2009 MarCuba Conference and, pivotally, in 2011 when a high-level US delegation visited Cuba to share lessons learned about the risks of offshore drilling with Cuban officials. That delegation helped bring the US and Cuba to the negotiating table in 2017 to sign an agreement [jointly] to prevent, contain and clean up oil and other toxic spills in the Gulf.

In 2023 fishermen and officials from both Cuba and the US embarked on a "floating workshop" or *Bojeo a Cuba* to circumnavigate the island. Interspersed with research, fishing, eating and drinking (despite the availability of cold beer, Ambassador Buddy had a family conflict and couldn't make it) the expedition assessed the status of coral reefs and large predators, and explored the influence of human and natural factors, including climate change, on that status.

All the while, Cubans continued to embark on a series of exchanges to the US. They came to learn more about catch shares. They visited Buddy (and Katie's Seafood). They explored how to measure fish populations in the absence of reliable and extensive data. And they returned home with Americans to complete a national vulnerability assessment of their finfish fisheries. In a fresh light, with a broader perspective, Cuba's top officials appreciated how the Playa Florida experiment offered one of the most effective ways to end local overharvesting.

By July 2015, a decade and a half of close and productive ocean diplomacy brought about the normalizing relations of the two nations. That, in turn, fueled more cooperation in the water. The US and Cuba signed a formal agreement to protect the vital marine life in the Gulf waters they share. In 2016, both countries signed watershed accords: to cooperate on environmental protection broadly, to jointly protect marine protected areas, and to establish the joint Research Initiative for a Sustainable Cuba. By 2017, Cuban policy placed conservation and sustainability on equal footing with production, with science-based catch limits and measures to reduce illegal fishing. All this preparation set the stage for Cuba's comprehensive new Fisheries Law, which took effect in 2020. Beyond enshrining provisions to curtail illegal fishing, boost scientific collaboration, train a professional cadre in marine conservation, and rebuild fish populations, the Law for the first time formally recognized and regulated—through a licensing and management framework—the rights of those eighteen thousand private fishermen to operate in the open and sell their catch without a state contract.

Setbacks and hiccups would inevitably arise. In the US, a new administrations took a different direction and changed the US posture to Cuba. That shift exposed the limits to what informal exchanges could achieve. Internationally shared waters ultimately needed bilateral or multilateral fishing laws and rules, scientific monitoring, enforcement and the continuous feedback needed to support adaptive management. Yet ongoing contact among fishing ambassadors like Buddy, plus the rise and seepage of social media, had enabled new conversations, data sharing and online collaboration. This was an exciting and essential evolution, since humans are the only species that recognize borders. In the Gulf Stream, damage to fish in any country's exclusive economic zone drifts into the next. Conversely, recovery in our neighbors' waters benefits us all. "A lot of the species that commercial and recreational fishermen in Florida depend on—snappers and groupers especially—begin their life in Cuba," reasoned Whittle. "The currents carry the larvae on ocean currents through the Florida Straits into southeast Florida. So, by protecting the habitats in Cuba, you are helping to rebuild fish populations in the US."

Gulf countries were not the only ones, however, whose future would shape Buddy's. Seafood harvests and appetites all over the world would affect what happens in American waters and markets. Because most fish now traversed vast seas not by the power of their own fins. They traveled on ice, in the holds of airplanes and trans-oceanic freighters.

Chapter Seventeen

OCEANIC TRANSFORMATION

On May 25, 2015, Buddy boarded a flight in Houston bound for Narita International Airport in Tokyo, Japan. Landing on the far side of the Pacific, jetlagged from the six-thousand-mile flight and fifteen-hour time difference, he was handed a disembarkation card. The form asked whether his visit was business or pleasure. Buddy paused. For him, fishing had always combined both.

He wouldn't be earning money or cutting deals here. But he did hope to sell an alternative vision for managing fisheries in Japan and the entire Asia Pacific region. His growing experience in international forums made clear the skepticism about fishing rights. Eighteen months earlier, in St. John's, Newfoundland, he'd joined a sustainability panel at the World Seafood Congress and told the story of recovery in the Gulf. During the question-and-answer period, a delegate groused that the panel seemed one-sided; why had no critics been invited to speak? "They did invite one," Buddy answered, without missing a beat. "And you're looking at him. I don't think you'll find anyone more hard opposed to catch shares than me. I just knew it was a bad idea. And I'm up here today to explain why it turned out I was wrong, and how it could work in other parts of the ocean."

Japan marked a new and elevated stage of diplomatic outreach for Ambassador Buddy. It was not only the farthest he'd gone to share his story; Japan also exemplified the high stakes for global oceans of getting fishing policy, incentives and investment decisions just right. Japan is one of the oldest and most storied fishing nations, origin of those 23,000-year-old excavated hooks. Along extensive coastlines encircling almost seven thousand islands, Japan's 129,000 fishermen capture 3.2 percent of the world's seafood. Its population, though just 2 percent of the world, consumes 6 percent of its fish—eating 22 kg per capita. Even for someone as cocky as Buddy, the notion that a Galveston captain would have something to teach Japan about working the sea was more than a little intimidating. But he did offer unique insight into how a fishing country recovers from unprecedented calamity at sea.

On Friday March 11, 2011, Japan had suffered the fourth most powerful earthquake the world had seen since modern record-keeping began a century earlier. The 9.1 magnitude undersea tremor struck 40 miles offshore from Tōhoku, 18 miles below the surface of the western Pacific. The seismic motion itself did little damage but the tsunami it triggered caused inconceivable death and destruction. Rising 133 feet (roughly as high as a ten-story building), the wave smashed into the coast and kept moving six miles inland where it killed 15,894 people, displaced 230,000, and damaged more than a million structures causing $235 billion in losses. It also left a dark legacy. Disabling and then causing the radioactive meltdown of three generators at the Fukushima Daiichi Nuclear Power Plant in Ōkuma, the "triple disaster" forced immediate evacuation of 470,000 people and continued to leak radioactive waste and water. An amount estimated to represent almost 40 percent of Chernobyl's radioactive material entered the sea, where strong ocean currents spread it in a contaminated plume far into the Pacific toward North America.

Japanese harvesters suffered immediately. Along the coast 28,000 fishing vessels were destroyed by the catastrophe, along with 319 fishing ports. The government (rightly) halted all fishing operations around Fukushima until the radioactivity returned to safe levels. Trouble was, it proved surprisingly hard for anyone to define what would be safe: either for the fishermen or for seafood consumers. Fish stocks expanded from lack of harvest pressure in the wake of Fukushima, yet as fears of the unknown played on fears of the unseen, even a consumer-friendly, okay-to-eat stamp of approval from scientists and ecologists wasn't sufficient to restore confidence. Long after the country had plugged the leaks and rebuilt the ports, reputational damage continued to depress the region's seafood markets for seventy-three species of fish. It was that double-blow of economic and physical injury to harvesters—who'd played no part in causing the catastrophe—that spurred the Japanese government to invite Buddy to Tokyo, to share how they dealt with the devastation caused when big industrial energy facilities go wrong.

Buddy arrived hoping to offer a breath of fresh hope. The immaculate streets and polite behavior of people in Tokyo made a strong first impression. The Japanese in turn seemed to take an immediate liking to the sunburned Texan. People delighted by Buddy's beard and swagger posed for pictures with him on the sidewalk, calling him Buddy-San. More importantly, the fishermen of Tohoku listened carefully to his message, in particular how public fears of contaminated fish could be turned from a crisis into an opportunity. "We came wanting to share our story and hoped the Japanese could find something in it that struck a bell," said Buddy.

First, the BP oil spill had opened a window for reform, by reducing harvest pressure. "That soon resulted in larger and more abundant fish," Buddy explained, "after they'd been left alone for a little while." He then described how Gulf Wild had restored market confidence that fish from a once-toxic sea was safe to buy: the tags and serial numbers enabled customers to trace each fish at any point of sale in the value chain back to who caught it, where, in what vessel; transparent test data provided to customers showed both water and fish to be clean.

Sounds good, Buddy's hosts nodded, but expensive. Many Japanese fishermen had been struggling to break even before the quake. How, they wondered, could they bear new added accountability expenses? "Yes, the transition involves real upfront costs," Buddy replied, but those are quickly repaid by increased revenues. He showed how the Gulf catch share helped with recovery in three ways. It put both fish and fishermen on more stable footing from which they could better rebound. It facilitated the traceability program. And it allowed fishermen inside the zone of contamination to continue earning income by leasing their shares to those outside. "They may look different and speak differently," said Buddy of his meetings with Japan's fishermen and officials. "But in terms of their needs and hopes they're really not much different than we are. Like us, they often felt frustrated with government officials, people who seemed more worried about getting re-elected than solving fishing problems. But I also saw the same real, genuine desire to change, on the part of the scientific community and by fishermen."

The idea of catch shares has cultural roots in Pacific Island nations. Japan's traditional fisheries had, for Elinor Ostrom, exemplified community-based resource management codes. Local cooperatives here have held user access rights since the early 1700s, when Shōgun era villagers banded together to prevent outside encroachment in their fishing grounds. In 1901, the Meiji Fisheries Law granted official recognition to many of those "fishing societies." Japan's postwar government struggled to formalize local tenure and co-management within Fishery Cooperative Associations (FCAs) covering twelve different species of mollusks, finfish, and crustaceans. Since the 1980s, many of those individual cooperatives have faltered. Without hard scientific catch management, there are few incentives to coordinate marketing efforts, raise membership standards, or create and enforce no-take zones. Yet under clearly defined shares Japan's coastal cooperatives (a fourth of Japan's harvest) could increase their 1.3 million metric ton harvest and earn much more than today's $4.3 billion. Japan had begun exploring gains from integrating a rights-based policy approach across the offshore and industrial fleets still regulated by centralized restrictions that result in competitive overfishing, declining harvests and shrinking exports. In recent years, this once proudly self-sufficient fishing powerhouse had, like the EU and US, grown dependent on imported seafood. Listening to Buddy and considering the accumulating evidence from North America and other catch-share countries, Japanese scientists, fishermen and managers began to wonder if Fukushima might in fact be their chance to build on their own deep traditions and expand fishing rights on a scale that would rival the US.

Indeed, in 2018 Japan passed its landmark Fishery Reform Act. Implemented in 2020, the Act set out to expand assessments to cover all commercial fishery stocks, boost the percentage of harvests under strict science-based catch limits, mandate recovery plans for overfished stocks, and establish a system of individual vessel quotas for offshore fisheries. As with the Magnuson-Stevens Act across the Pacific in the US, full transition to sustainable science-based management might take decades, but the legislation and early implementation efforts would be a pivotal step forward for Japan and the region.

SIMILAR QUESTIONS ABOUT rights-based fishing were being raised in the European Union. There, twenty-three coastal countries collectively control the world's largest portion of the ocean. Europe's total seafood consumption is second only to China's. More than 100,000 large fishing vessels ply EU waters—from the northeast Atlantic and Baltic to the Mediterranean and Black seas—to harvest two hundred different stocks of wild seafood worth half a trillion dollars. Despite that value and Europe's reputation as environmental stewards, however, 45 percent of the continent's fish populations like herring, mackerel and cod are overexploited.

Until recently, a big part of the problem was that extensive rules steered fishermen to discard massive amounts—by many estimates, up to half—of unwanted, unprofitable, or undersized fish, dead or alive. In 2023, Europe reformed its Common Fisheries Policy, in which all vessels are required to land every fish they catch to reduce discarding of unwanted bycatch. To overcome ongoing challenges to this "landing obligation" such as undocumented discards, Europe, like the US, might scale up the adoption of remote cameras and sensors, the electronic monitoring that could help enforce compliance. That same year, Europe's Fisheries and Oceans Pact sought to boost resilience in the sector though the landing obligation, sustainable practices, and encourage cleaner energy sources in the fisheries sector.

Some innovative countries chose to go further than necessary, earlier than required. Early on, Iceland set an example as it put in place catch shares for the entire fleet. In the process they ended overfishing, replenished their territorial waters, and increased value for a sector that, in Iceland, employs 7 percent of the population and provides 12.5 percent of GDP. A similar approach was embraced by Sweden, which has a comparatively small fishing industry yet a disproportionate influence on EU policy. In response to the EU discards ban, Swedish fishermen replaced weekly "use it or lose it" limits with flexible annual allocations, adopted more precise and selective habitat-friendly gear, and allowed whitefish and prawn (nephrops) harvesters to negotiate outcomes. "We can trade quota among ourselves," said Peter Ronelöv Olsson, a thirty-five-year veteran prawn fisherman and head of the Swedish Fish Producers' Organization. "That means if I catch too much of one species, I don't have to dump it as there's a mechanism to get quota to cover it." Parts of Scotland's fisheries, had also graduated to a rights-based approach, with spill-over benefits into EU waters despite its Brexit from the continent. In Lithuania, the Fisheries Ministry recently initiated a catch share in the Baltic Sea to adapt to climate-driven changes in the mix of such stocks as cod, herring and sprat.

Ultimately, however, the transformation of European fishing would likely depend on Spain.

Often seen as the EU's bad boy or wild card, Spain was by any measure—per capita seafood consumption, million tons catch volume, three hundred fishing ports, fleet size, landing value, and employment of 46,000 harvesters—a fishing powerhouse, both for the continent and in its own right, worldwide. The Iberian Peninsula forms a unique fishing keystone. It links Atlantic and Mediterranean waters and, by extension, the northern and southern European fishing economies that depend on them. Spain's two largest categories of fishing vessels—a distant-water fleet, which plies open ocean beyond the EEZ; and industrial fleets that course within it for days at a time—had strong political ties with federal agencies in Madrid. Both explored how catch shares can drive more efficient fishing to boost revenues and reduce costs.

Yet for those same reasons, catch shares had generated skepticism among Spain's third, hard-to-define category of widely dispersed small-scale fishermen. This fleet included men like Juan Ramon, who inherited his trade from generations of ancestors in the Canary Islands. Like him, they typically worked alone or in pairs, on shore or from the back of their own boats, taking day trips close to shore, harvesting with traps or hand lines, and selling in traditional, local, dockside marketplaces. Suspicious of any management established by powerful interests and politicians in Madrid, Ramon feared catch shares might edge people like him out of traditional fishing grounds, and initially responded with a refrain: "The ocean is for all of us!"

Beyond pressure from national fleets, they had to worry about local illegal fishing. Squeezed in the middle by asymmetric rivals, small-scale fishermen saw a future of diminishing returns. "That we won't be able to fish will be a world a little bit destroyed, that there will be no opportunities to fish for a living, that there won't be a future, won't be nature," said Ramon, shaking his head. "I would not want to see a world like that."

Spain's small-scale fleet shared with its counterparts in Portugal, Italy, Greece and the Balkans the challenges of weak monitoring, missing science, and lax outside enforcement. That combination translated to estimates that more than 85 percent of Mediterranean fish populations were being overexploited, tarnishing Spain's reputation. So despite their diminutive classification, small-scale fishers rightly forged a network that was "too big to ignore." Collectively, men like Ramon land more than a quarter of the EU catch value, represent nearly half its fishermen, and own four out of five of its active fishing vessels. As such, local fishing communities would help define the country's future maritime recovery under secure access rights.

As it turned out, Spanish fishermen always have. Starting with medieval monarchs through modern democratic governments, officials in Madrid have devolved autonomy to self-organizing fishing

guilds, known as "*cofradias*." In exchange for loyalty, these fra-
ternities had the dual role of self-governing their fishing practices
while keeping watch for enemies all along the nooks and crannies
of Spain's intricate coastline. Evolving over a thousand years, 229
cofradias had played a pivotal role in the control of informal nearshore access rights and fish markets on shore. As such, groups like
World Wide Fund for Nature (WWF) sought out these cornerstones
of local governance as partners. The idea was to formalize more
durable institutions, empower fishermen as stewards, and lock in
higher value, security, and numbers for whatever species they catch.
If European small-scale fishing hinged on co-management in Spain,
and the fate of Spanish coastlines depended on *cofradias*, the most
pivotal found in the Canary Islands and, specifically, on the oldest
and most biodiverse island of Fuerteventura.

Fuerteventura took its name from strong dry winds blowing off
Africa, just 62 miles eastward. For decades, younger generations
were lost to Europe. But starting in the 1980s the island's economy
had risen with the influx of tourists. Hungry visitors sought local
seafood at waterfront restaurants, boosting prices for the daily catch.
Yet booming demand also attracted unscrupulous outsiders, selling
covertly at the back door, and undermining the ecological and economic integrity of the island's fisheries. Overwhelmed by asymmet-
rical incursions by strangers, traditional fishing guilds lacked formal structure, political recognition or essential resources to resist.
That's when WWF's Beatriz Ayala showed up in the capital Puerto
del Rosario, reaching out to harvesters as part of a national learning
network for nearshore fisheries. As heads of the island's three *cofradias*, Fito Carballo, Juan Placeres, and Juan Ramon were ready to
listen, share their experiences, and give rights-based management a
closer look.

They discovered that to a large extent they already held, within
their customary guild, the basic ingredients for custom designing
catch shares for their fishing grounds. They organized small meetings with a trusted group of traditional fishermen, who together
could compile how much of which species had been caught off

which bays or rocky outcrops. As artisanal harvesters they could be selective, targeting different species at various depths, in unique locations, with specific bait or gear. On Monday a fisher like Juan Ramon might fish for dusky or Yellowbelly grouper; on Tuesday, Pink dentex or Atlantic wreckfish; on Wednesday Moroccan white sea bream; on Thursday *vieja*, or parrotfish; Friday Red porgy or Blacktail comber; and on Saturday he might harvest *pulpo* or octopus.

Estimates of past catches by Juan Ramon and Fito laid a rough foundation for a longer-term systemic vision of recovery and process for governance. Their fears and hopes helped shape contours of tighter rules, scientific assessments, co-monitoring licenses and cracking down on illegal activity. Through adaptive management the cofradias chose to go beyond traditional EU mandates to set up customized rules, establish no-take zones, and eliminate traps within what they knew to be the most sensitive nursing grounds. This bottom-up approach was a revelation to Fuerteventura's fishermen. Still, some asked whether it could work, gain wider support and link laterally with other cofradias.

A few examples from Spain's coastal edges offered Juan Ramon grounds for encouragement. In Galicia, WWF could showcase how, decades earlier, it had helped cofradias secure territorial access rights around a particularly delectable crustacean that had suffered from overfishing but was protected then restored. Swimming to shore and then descending from cliffs from the end of long ropes, these shellfish hunters bounced from rock ledge to ledge right at the intertidal surf zone. Dodging incoming big waves, they would scoot across, up and down slopes all to pry loose a few pounds of *percebes*, or goose barnacle. This traditional culinary delicacy tastes like a cross between abalone and oyster; prices go up at the holidays as celebratory diners pop off the head and suck out the insides.

At the other edge of Spain is Catalunya's *sonso* or sand eel fishery. The traditional, small-scale fishery was considered as much art as science, but in 2006, it risked being shut down when EU legislation banned any towed gear that could run roughshod over shallow coastal zones. Over the next few years, the local cofradia there stressed how the selective *sonso* seine net was only used in early mornings on sandy seafloors and were prepared to prove it. By 2012, as part of a co-management plan, the local *cofradia* agreed to take precautions to reduce harvest and fund scientific research documenting the health of the fishery and light impact of their gears, in exchange for more flexibility in their activities.

Small-scale fishers from both regions reported that after initially accepting lower catches, they had earned more and seen steady recovery. Back on Fuerteventura, Fito Carballo, Juan Ramon and their colleagues in the island's *cofradias*, begun exploring ways to differentiate their catch from illegal and unregulated harvests. One leading idea, inspired in large part by what they've heard of Gulf Wild on the other side of the Atlantic, was a way to tag their catch so that hotels and restaurants could trace seafood back through responsible stewards to their source. With technical support from WWF and other partners, and formal backing from Madrid, Juan Ramon saw such a bottom-up model as catching on fast, spreading value and accountability all along the coast, and offering a model for both small- and large-scale fleets. "We need to walk side by side, ending wasteful practices of industrial fishing fleets and of irresponsible fishing, and make a joint proposal to Europe, and to the world."

IN RECENT YEARS, trade, philanthropic, development and conservation entities shifted their focus to that global scale, recognizing the vulnerability of the three billion people who depend today on fish for animal protein, and the still greater numbers who will need fish as world population grows to 8.5 billion and beyond. Number 14 of the seventeen United Nations Sustainable Development Goals (SDGs), adopted in 2015, focused on "life below water," recognizing seafood as a cornerstone to feeding humanity. That SDG (along with linked goals, like SDG2) called on member states by 2030 to "manage and protect marine and coastal ecosystems...effectively regulate harvesting...end overfishing...restore fish stocks in the shortest time possible...[and] produce maximum sustainable yield." Achieving all that in the next five years might seem impossibly ambitious, but a path to that stable future does exist.

A first step was to reduce the waste that is now the single biggest cause of global hunger. Each year, 1.3 billion tons of food, roughly a third of the world's total supply, is lost to post-harvest rot and damage. In open access seas—where fishermen had to dump fish of the wrong size or species, or that exceed their trip limit—up to 50 percent of harvested seafood never makes it from hook to plate. Twenty-five years ago, fishermen annually discarded twenty-seven million tons of fish (the bulk of which likely died), to feed a quarter of the humans who eat seafood. But the spread of smarter fisheries management, including catch shares, helped dramatically cut that waste to less than a third, or between nine and seven million tonnes. Alaskan pollock also provided a model for "nose-to-tail" use of every bit of a fish, from eyes and bones to bladders and oil.

Still more promising, new evidence showed how fishermen can both increase harvests enough to feed an additional six hundred million people at today's per capita consumption rate and increase the global population of live fish in the sea. In groundbreaking research, scientists and economists from the University of California Santa Barbara and the University of Washington teamed up to create a new "upside" bio-economic model that gives the most holistic view to date of the potential in our oceans if nations move to catch shares. While previous studies aggregated trends from a few isolated fisheries, the upside model team built a comprehensive database of 4,373 fisheries worldwide, representing 77 percent of global catch. The researchers found that, compared to business as usual, managed fisheries could within ten years harvest seventeen million more metric tons of wild fish (a 23 percent increase) and annually generate $90 billion more profits (up 315 percent)—even as they more than doubled the fish in the sea (increasing biomass by 782 million metric tons or 112 percent), with all the corollary benefits to marine ecosystems.

What would it take globally to galvanize enough fisherfolk to turn the tide? In countries representing seven percent of global catch (Canada, Iceland, Norway, Namibia, South Africa, Australia and New Zealand) the reforms are largely complete. From Japan to Chile, pivotal countries now have key building blocks of change. Progress within each continues to mount as each seafood harvester shares their experience elsewhere, as each fishery learns from another, generating momentum that could move the overfished ocean past a global tipping point toward recovery.

IN THE WESTERN Hemisphere, several countries had made progress on reform, together setting hundreds of species on the road to recovery. The EU also continued its continent-wide progress toward improved management. But the most critical countries lay in Asia, where 60 percent of the world's fish were caught and consumed.

Buddy got a taste of the intensity of Asia's offshore fishing on that 2015 trip to Tokyo. On his last morning, he woke before 2:00 a.m., put on his baseball cap, and made his personal pilgrimage to the Mecca of every seafood vendor and fisherman on earth: the Tsukiji fish market.

First built in 1935, Tsukiji (pronounced SKEE-gee) soon became the world's largest of its kind, annually selling about 660,000 tons of fish worth $4 billion. Its markets offered nearly every form of edible seafood from around the Pacific, 500 species ranging from snails, urchins and octopus to sea cucumber, shad roe, lionfish and live eels. It was most famous for its auctions of giant Bluefin tuna, a population of three regional species, all of them fished down over a century to just a tiny fraction of their original numbers. (Pacific Bluefin tuna are at 2.6 of their historic size and vulnerable, while its cousins in the South Pacific and Atlantic are classified as critically endangered by IUCN yet still being caught). Largely unmanaged in the open ocean, these torpedo-shaped, warm-blooded animals are shipped to Tokyo from as far away as South Africa and Western Australia and put up in auctions that draw more than 30,000 tourists a year. "I got there early and so got in the first group to see what's going on," Buddy grew excited again at the memory, his voice breathless as a boy's. Listening to the rush of Japanese, he didn't have a clue what was going on but watched in fascination as clusters of Tokyo's famed sushi chefs and retailers examined the flesh of each of these long-lived and marvelous animals, capable of swimming forty-seven miles an hour and diving more than 4,000 feet. When the bidding began, voices rose to a shout. Prices for a 500-pound fish usually settle in the mid five-figure range, but some fish have sold for hundreds of thousands of dollars. Not long ago a single Atlantic Bluefin set a record, claiming $1.7 million.

Tuna, like shark and swordfish, is a "highly migratory species." A young tuna might embark on a journey of more than 5,000 miles, then spend its life ranging across the Pacific, Atlantic, Indian, or Southern oceans. These high seas global commons fall under the 1982 United Nations Convention on the Law of the Sea. The Convention describes fishing "freedoms," "duties," and "obligations," but its laws neither set nor enforce any limits, accountability measures or other rules.

There were, however, precedents for catch shares for highly migratory species. Australia and New Zealand's systems covered tuna species in their territorial waters. Croatia, France, Italy, and Spain had quota programs for Bluefin in the Mediterranean, as did the US Bluefin bycatch quota system. A smaller Japanese-run fish market in Honolulu, Hawaii offered another intriguing prototype, in which a limited number of ethnically-diverse longliners coordinated sustainable fishing of bigeye and yellowtail tuna, both within and outside of US waters.

It is neither 500-pound tuna nor shark, however, that will sate the hunger of the planet's fastest growing populations. An estimated 25 to 60 percent of the wild fish that humans eat are caught by small-scale fishermen. In the Asia-Pacific region, people depend on uncharismatic species like hilsa, Japanese anchovy, or blue swimming crabs, in which management strategies may, in turn, depend on reforms, rights, incentives and enforcement efforts that engage the fishermen of these species themselves.

EVEN IN COUNTRIES where governments were historically weak,

brutal or dysfunctional, local leadership can have far-reaching benefits. Indonesia, South Pacific Islands, and the Philippines archipelago may lay claim to the title of "the Amazon of the sea," a Coral Triangle endowed with more species of fish and corals than any place else on earth, and declared by scientists to be the world's "center of marine biodiversity." This rich marine life was both an essential source of food and the lure for tourism.

Yet for many coastal communities, stability remained precarious, and prosperity elusive. Despite having designated 1,200 of its most diverse and productive habitats marine protected areas, for example, the government in Manila had been unable to prevent the overfishing crisis that has crashed ten of the country's thirteen primary fishing grounds and undermined reef habitats. Tens of millions of Filipino families depend for half their protein on 1.6 million small-scale fishing families in 873 coastal communities; some, driven by desperation for food or income, resort to the most brutally wasteful way of harvesting seafood: dynamite (or blast, or explosive) fishing.

The lethal technique was casually imported from the West. It began in World War II by American soldiers, was reintroduced by research expeditions, and was only later picked up by hungry locals who procure dynamite from soldiers, or improvised bombs of combustible fuel. A dozen empty beer bottles, a bag of fertilizer and a disposable lighter: it's hard to think of this as fishing gear. But as a bank concentrates money, coral attracted fish, so blowing up a stretch of reef is in the short run highly effective. Perversely, the most productive fishers are driven to destroy the best reef habitat: grazed by schooling grouper, croakers, sweetlips, sturgeon, butterfly fish and parrotfish. They may drop three to fifteen bombs per hour, ideally detonating below the surface and close to the coral, stunning or killing life (including humans) within the blast radius. Fish that float to the surface get scooped up by hand or dip nets. Four out of every five sink to the seafloor, where if no one dives down to retrieve them, they rot alongside the now lifeless rubble of shattered coral.

In the Philippines, some estimate that blast fishing accounted for a quarter of all landings, degrading three-quarters of the country's reefs. While the country's Bureau of Fisheries and Aquatic Resources has tried to crack down on the long-illegal practice, in 2012 declaring an "all-out war," officials estimated roughly ten thousand detonations took place each day. Many go unprosecuted; scuba divers have recorded blasting within hearing distance of a police station. For obvious reasons, fishers rarely admit to the practice. If caught red—or due to short and unpredictable fuses, one—handed, most claim ignorance of the law. One exception was Manoi Berting.

Manoi grew up near Tinambac, a municipality of 60,000 inhabitants in the province of Camarines Sur, a six-hour bus ride from Manila. Still wiry, in his sixties, dressed in cargo shorts, T-shirt, and a baseball cap, Manoi is old enough to remember when the sea still yielded sufficient food for everyone—but also when the strangers began showing up to explode their reef. He's honest enough to admit that he joined in, personally causing much of the wreckage left for the next generation, which has seen the average fisherman's daily catch decline from 40 kg in the 1940s to 3 kg today. Manoi deeply regretted that legacy. But with ten hungry children to feed, he asked visitors, "Wouldn't you have done the same?"

For years, Manoi's only experience with environmentalists was Westerners showing up to denounce him and his community for the blast fishing. But when conservationists from Rare listened to him as part of their Fish Forever program, he saw a change afoot. They began seeking to understand the locals' frustrations and priorities, their view of the nearshore reefs and what had happened over time and why. In return, he learned about people in similar circumstances who had benefited from systems of fishing rights—developing their own local designs and fish recovery zones based on their villages' knowledge, needs and timetables. After years of intense study and negotiations that often became contentious and messy, in 2015, two local governments, Tinambac and Cantilan, approved TURF-reserves designed by and for fishing communities. Other Filipino TURFs soon followed, affecting the lives of nearly two thousand households that depend on fishing for their livelihoods and daily sustenance.

As in Belize, these communities began sharing their experience: island to island, then nation to nation. Some Filipino fishermen participated in exchanges with Vietnam; others got involved in informal fishing diplomacy with Japan. Community fishing advocate, Emilie Litsinger, who has organized dozens of such interactions over the years, found herself constantly "amazed by the peer-to-peer discussions that take place, regardless of language barriers or cultural differences, and the candor of government officials and fishers describing the challenges they have faced or successes they have worked to achieve. It is incredible to see participants hear about something new or innovative that they could bring back to their communities. The excitement is contagious."

Indeed, decades later, more than 1,400 coastal communities were reportedly involved in Fish Forever TURF-reserves, managing exclusive access areas to ensure sustainable fishing practices and the protection of marine ecosystems. The initiative had contributed to both increased fish biomass and improved livelihoods for around 150,000 fishermen and 1.6 million community members who depend on these resources. Based on early successes in the Philippines, emulated in places like Japan, Vietnam, or Indonesia, the world's fishing nations increasingly recognized the outsized if overlooked role of 108 million workers (half of them women) involved in small-scale fisheries, and established nearshore fishing rights as a cornerstone of global food security and poverty reduction.

AS BUDDY HEADED to the airport, he thought about the crazy adventure awaiting him back home: a new star turn, this time in a reality TV series. Shot for National Geographic, it would revolve around Katie's Seafood market which, small as it was, handled a quarter of all commercially harvested reef fish caught in the Gulf of Mexico on its way to being distributed across America. The show would be called *Big Fish, Texas*, and there was no doubt as to who that "big fish" described. Only now, after threading hour after hour through the noisy, sprawling, swirling maze of streets and buildings of Tsukiji, Buddy felt small. "I was just blown away, and humbled," by the drama and pace of operations in Tokyo's exchange. "I've been to fish markets all over the US, from Fulton to San Francisco, and there's just no comparison at all," he said. "The size and scale of what they do there is phenomenal and eye opening. You've got a couple hundred motorcycles, each with mini-refrigerator boxes on back, all coming and going daily, moving a huge, huge amount of fish."

As he settled into a jumbo jet for his own trans-Pacific migration, Buddy's head was still swimming. He could now see Galveston's place in the world afresh, as a citizen, fisherman, fishmonger, and restaurateur (he'd soon open Katie's Seafood Restaurant next door). He long knew America had a ferocious seafood appetite, but now better appreciated how fast and furiously our globalized economy moved the world's single-most traded food commodity, with exports worth $186 billion, and with half coming from developing countries: seafood. That commerce meant Americans in any city could buy just about any fish caught anywhere. While Buddy would continue to focus on selling local fresh fish caught in the Texas Gulf—redfish, grouper, snapper, tilefish, oysters, shrimp and blue crab—he knew his customers might just as well opt for New England scallops or lobster, or Chilean sea bass.

Katie was exceptional in the high proportion of local fish it carried. Buddy's country had in recent years flipped from being a net exporter of fish before World War II to now importing nearly 90 percent of all the seafood (fish, mollusks, and crustaceans) Americans eat. Most of the shrimp, tilapia, tuna, salmon, groundfish, crab, and squid come from aquaculture and from the harvesters and harbors in China, Thailand, Canada, Indonesia, Vietnam, and Ecuador. US food services and restaurants bypassed Alaska to ship in pollock from Russia, king crab from Iceland, and halibut from Canada. America could meet 100 percent of its seafood demand through imports.

Yet unlike cotton or coal or copper, wild fish are not generic and globally interchangeable; rather, they are living, renewable and locally distinct populations, each adapted to local conditions in a sea that remained far from "level." Nations harvest under vastly different natural, technical, political and economic conditions. Some of their fisheries are stable, a few are recovering, many are rapidly depleting, and all are finite, having hit and declined from a global peak estimated, depending on assumptions, to range between 86 or 130 million metric tons.

Back on Wharf Road, Buddy found himself thinking again about Tsukiji, which he'd learned would be moved to a new location after nearly nine decades; its former site would be redeveloped into what Tokyo's mayor has described as "a culinary theme park." Buddy knew from the ocean that nothing stays the same. In his own life, he found himself fishing less and going to policy meetings more; he tried to spend more time with his wife, and failed, and Katie always smiled and forgave his absences as she always had, and he knew his restless ambitions often bothered her, but he couldn't stop. He noticed his father becoming frail. While they stayed in orbit around the fish operations, his sons kept growing up and older. Nick was now married, and Buddy soon had his first of several grandchildren. Amidst all the turmoil and change, he began to think more about the legacy he would leave behind. "When I was young, I didn't give a damn," he reflected. "If I wanted something, I was just always looking for ways to do it with the least resistance. But as I get older, I want to learn more and think about the things around me."

Chapter Eighteen
A LEGACY BEQUEATHED

On February 3, 2016, National Geographic premiered *Big Fish, Texas*. The reality TV show introduced half a million viewers to the Guindon fishing clan—with volume cranked to eleven. The show created a nickname: "Hurricane Buddy." It edited his interactions with wife, father, brother, and sons to amplify emotions and gestures, and elevate minor disputes into existential conflicts. Amid snarling electric guitars, the narrator growled how in the "cutthroat" world of the Gulf, fishermen are forced to "battle the odds, other fishermen, even mother nature herself!"

Big Fish producers wrestled with the same problem *Deadliest Catch* confronted a decade earlier. From Great Lakes to Alaska to New England and the Gulf, catch shares had sapped a fair bit of the old, competitive theatrical tension from the fisherman's life. Though Buddy spoke of "loving the danger," and "never knowing what you're going to get," by then fishermen could sit out even rumors of a storm. Under catch shares, no commercial vessel battled his neighbor. Wharf Road had no rivals, cutthroat or otherwise. And with biomass estimates being approximately three times higher than previous projections, when a crew heads off to catch five tons, there's not a whole lot of suspense whether they will, in fact, return that day with five tons of large, fresh, healthy fish.

There was still drama, but of a subtler kind: strategic, political, unfolding beneath the surface. While proud of the sea change, Buddy remained far from complacent. He'd watched seemingly endless snapper, grouper and tilefish crash before and knew they could again. For this *Semper Fi* Marine, and other vigilant harvesters, catch shares had shifted the dramatic tension to whether America's seas would be rebuilt to last, taking on new threats bearing down on the legacy of wild fishing.

SOME THREATS LAY beyond Buddy's reach. Land-based organic and plastic pollution kept flowing into the Gulf from the Mississippi River basin, starting as far away as Buddy's birth state of Minnesota. In 2017, Texas and Louisiana harvesters suffered the largest hypoxic dead zone in history of the Northern Gulf. As excess phosphorus and nitrogen fertilizer ran off farms and lawns, it spured an algae "bloom" that decomposed into an oxygen-depleting, New Jersey-sized swath that suffocates life at the base of the food chain.

Plastic runoff may prove worse. Wrenching photos show large bags strangling large charismatic animals, yet the real damage is protracted and tiny. It comes as ten million tons of plastic annually flush down rivers out to sea, break down into microscopic particles and fibers, sickening reefs, smothering life, and entering the food chain. Plastic lasts for decades, even centuries. By 2050, researchers warn oceans may hold more plastic than fish. Debris in the Mississippi basin was better managed, but even tire wear and washing machines discharge untreated microfibers into the semi-enclosed Gulf. Buddy's fishing grounds had among the highest concentrations of nutrient and plastic pollution on earth.

Land-based pollutants compound pressure from acidification, bleaching, warming and sea-level rise. Samples from 20 countries in the Gulf and Caribbean indicate reefs may be approaching unstable ecological thresholds or tipping points. These findings were sobering, but hardly fatalistic. Just as doctors urge patients to boost their health through rest, exercise and healthy eating, ocean resilience grows through responsible stewardship. So while Buddy and catch share fishermen couldn't stop these external death threats to the sea, they could help resist the onslaught by replenishing life within it. "Just as fish depend on healthy reefs, reefs depend on healthy fish populations," explained marine scientist Doug Rader. "Some fish eat algae that can otherwise crowd out corals, while other, predatory fish control the populations of snails that can damage corals. It's even possible that some fish might slow coral disease by eating diseased coral tissue. There are dozens of these complex interactions that together keep coral reefs healthy."

BUDDY COULD, IF he chose, fight a more immediate risk: fish farms. To produce animal protein, farmed seafood may offer an equally valid strategy as fishing. But a deep cultural divide has long separated hunter-gatherers like Buddy from those who raise fish like sentient crops in fixed closed pens or floating tethered cages. As wild fish supplies leveled off around 1990, farm-raised fish surged so rapidly that by 2015 aquaculture was meeting more than half of human demand for seafood. By 2030 two of every three fish eaten may be grown. American consumers rely mostly on farmed shrimp, tilapia, and Atlantic salmon, imported from Thailand, China, and Chile, respectively. Scattered salmon and mussel farms dot nearshore coastal waters within statewide jurisdictions, but so far no commercial aquaculture—or in pens offshore, "mariculture"—exists in federal waters. That may change, fast, starting in the heart of Buddy's hunting grounds.

The New Orleans-based Gulf Seafood Institute believes that open-ocean farms in the Gulf represent the future of sustainable seafood. It was not alone. Research suggests that, through deliberate science and careful testing of scalable pilots, the fastest growing seafood sector could potentially feed the world's growing populations. While still relatively small in the US, mariculture expansion began to gain bipartisan support starting in 2005, when President Bush first authorized farms in the Gulf. A decade later the Obama administration approved 20 permits to grow Gulf species such as red drum, cobia, and almaco jack, which if built out could yield 32,000 tons of farmed fish, a mass equal to the region's wild harvest. By 2018, President Trump's Commerce Secretary Wilbur Ross pushed Gulf mariculture to create jobs and erase America's $20 billion "seafood trade deficit."

As mariculture advanced, Buddy raised several perceived risks. One was crossbreeding. Escaped, invasive or genetically modified species that spawn with wild fish can (and often did) weaken the gene pool's resilience. Another threat, habitat loss, came as coastal mangroves or wetlands were cleared for pens. Then there's pollution. Chemicals like antibiotics, fungicides, dyes, PCBs and dioxins accumulate up the food chain and pose risks to human health, while biological pollutants, including excrement, excess feed, parasites and disease spill into the wild. Finally, mariculture may paradoxically increase pressure on the sea, as wild fish often get ground into pellet feed for domesticated carnivores, like salmon. Buddy felt mariculture might degrade his sea, hurt the Gulf Wild label premium, and depress the value of wild fish. To prevent "irreparable harm to the Gulf ecosystems and coastal communities," in 2016 the Shareholders' Alliance challenged the permits in a federal lawsuit. "I'm not afraid of the competition," Buddy emphasized. "What I worry about is the destruction of habitat in the Gulf. What will happen when you concentrate fish here like they do in other oceans? What effect will that have on the natural stocks of fish? I don't believe they have a broad view and are taking enough precautions. My fear is that nobody has really looked at what happens if we make a mistake here."

Against these risks, mariculture offered counterarguments. Propagation of herbivorous fish—tilapia, barramundi, catfish, carp, oysters, and clams—can supplement global seafood diets and alleviate pressure on wild catches. Innovative farmers have begun replacing wild fish meal with feed made from fermented bacteria, yeast, algae, or insect larvae. Others surrounded fish pens with seaweed farms or mollusk filter-feeders to buffer and clean the water.

Ultimately, there is no impact-free lunch. Lab-grown, genetically engineered meat substitutes kept graduating from experimental technology to novelty items. But fish eaten by the rest of world would for decades still come from animals with eyes, gills and fins, harvested wild at sea or born and bred in pens. Ex-fisherman and author Paul Greenberg compared the modern commercial propagation of bass, cod, salmon and tuna with the raising of cattle, pigs, sheep, and poultry. In *Four Fish,* he wrote how the dangers from producing meat (or vegetable protein) on land often exceed any risks from farming fish. "I realized that the interplay of domestication and wildness is one of the most important issues going on with fish today," he argued. "Choosing which fish will be our domesticated seafood will have huge ramifications for our species and for the planet."

Some of Buddy's prominent wild fishing rights allies agreed. Research led by UC Santa Barbara scientist Steven Gaines has underpinned the catch shares revolution. Yet even fixing the entire world's wild fisheries, Gaines reasoned, would still not suffice to meet global hunger for protein. To his own surprise, he discovered in writing a 2017 paper, fish farming might. Gaines found mariculture can feed far more people in far less space at a far lower cost than land-based agriculture. Its ecological footprint can be fifty to one hundred times smaller, needing no irrigation, emitting no carbon and even (if focused on bivalve filter feeders), cleaning marine pollution. Done with care, the expansion of mariculture is projected to be limited by consumer demand or availability of feed ingredients derived from wild fisheries, rather than by climate change, as it can be largely insensitive to changing temperature, oxygenation and salinity."

Buddy's opposition tempered as he learned more. Moving mariculture well out to sea, for instance, could reduce threats to near shore habitat loss, disease or pollution. Regulations could be written, as NOAA did for the Gulf, to protect the purity of wild fish by prohibiting the farming of genetically engineered or non-native species. And the fast-growing species likely to be farmed in Buddy's waters—cobia, Almaco jack, and Red drum—don't compete with snapper or grouper for genetic purity or market price. Ocean advocacy groups increasingly recognize sustainable fish farming as a valuable correlate to sustainable wild fisheries. Michael Rubino, a national seafood consultant, even saw an upside for Buddy's businesses, as fish becomes a bigger part of the American diet: "in the Gulf, there's an opportunity for fishermen and seafood farmers to work together to market a US product."

TO ACHIEVE THE full suite of their original goals, catch share programs would continue to evolve. Climate change introduced extraordinary ecological challenges. New second generation entrants deserved better access to be able to harvest seafood as second generation catch share fishermen. And economic benefits from secure fishing rights, while real, could still rise higher and spread wider. Voices across the spectrum have argued that catch shares can exacerbate inequality and shut out smaller vessels. Liberal academics charged that by "privatizing public resources," catch shares concentrate wealth in elite hands, while Republicans like Florida's Congressman Steve Southerland lamented: "Gone are the days when enterprising young people can buy a boat and set out to make a living for their families. Now they must lease access to the fish they want to catch, paying one of the gifted few for the privilege."

Such attacks gained teeth through litigation and legislation. West Coast opponents sued to block catch share management on the grounds that some fishermen would no longer be "free to harvest the seas," having been "locked out" as "the government excluded" small hook and line fishermen. To prove social damage, critics highlighted demographic change: seafood harvesters grew fewer in number and older, heralding the death of fishing villages. Yet those trends started generations before anyone conceived of catch shares. They were equally common in regions like the southeast coast, where catch shares didn't take off. The real driver of change in the fishing sector was technological. Advanced fish-harvesting technologies, from longline hooks to hydraulic winches to hyper-fast engines, required less labor, more capital, and fueled the overfishing that was always the surest way to drive men off the water—forever. New England had documented fleet consolidation since at least the 1860s, as fished-out waters supported fewer and fewer vessels at sea, with the most notorious taking place thirty years before catch shares.

Rather than push out struggling fishermen or bar new ones from entering, catch shares continued to evolve to meet the needs of its community. That disputed West Coast groundfish catch share, for instance, set aside a 10 percent quota intended for adaptive management. Potential beneficiaries submitting a formal proposal could include local families, processors, users of certain gear types, and Indigenous Peoples, regardless of their fishing history. Noting these reserves and provisions, the judge rejected claims that fishermen had been excluded or harmed, and dismissed the lawsuit. There were, as always, opportunities to improve. But the door to adaptive, community-oriented fishing remained wide open.

In the Gulf, Buddy had grown used to being blamed, a poster boy for social inequality. But critics who called him a sea lord (never to his face, often sniping in anonymous blog comments) rarely considered his pre-catch share risks and struggles. He took on debt. Rose before dawn. Bicycled to the docks. Ripped his face up. Abandoned his family for days on end. Sacrificed weddings and christenings while racing in dangerous seas. It was that legacy of sweat equity and real investments that had been converted into shares. Even then, he'd caught more than 8 percent of all the snapper but received a much smaller quota share.

What about aspiring fishermen? The Magnuson-Stevens Act had allowed catch share systems to set aside up to 25 percent of cost recovery funds—a share of royalties to ease transition to a new system. But the Gulf Council had prioritized rebuilding snapper populations; only after the fishery regained density and value could fishermen start making room for new kids on the dock.

Appreciating how hard it is to break in, some fishermen who brought out the welcome wagon were late entrants themselves. For years William "Bubba" Cochrane had worked as a deckhand saving enough in 2006 to buy his own vessel. He too, like Buddy, voted against catch shares, since as a newbie he'd get almost no quota. Nonetheless, he learned how to engage the new market. When they cut the snapper catch limit in half, then in half again, and the quota dropped to ten dollars a pound, Bubba figured its value couldn't go much lower. He mortgaged his home to finance a $1.3 million purchase of 130,000 pounds of shares, an investment that has since quadrupled in value. An outsider, William L. "Tres" Atkins III came to Galveston in 2006 with big ambitions and modest means. He scraped together a permitted boat and started to fish when snapper populations, and prices per pound, hit an historic low. Like Bubba, he took advantage of those low prices to first lease and then buy shares, building out a fleet and wholesale seafood businesses to rival Buddy's.

Some new entrants deployed fresh, even radical, tactics. Jason DeLaCruz came late to the Florida grouper fishery, and at the smallest possible scale. Diving with scuba gear and a spear gun, he hunted individual fish for the adrenaline rush, swimming quickly to the surface with his impaled prize before a shark could trace the blood trail to its source. Over seasons of *Deadliest Catch,* Jason watched Alaska's fisheries grow less deadly and more stable under catch shares. Even when catch limits were low, he saw how each share held it's long term value. "There's a point in most guys' lives when they see a chance to get in and exploit a niche and make it big," he said. "You often only get one chance. It usually comes in your thirties. And I decided that reef fish would be the ticket for me and my business partner [Matt Joswig], our shot to do that." With their combined life savings ($500,000) in hand, he began searching up and down the coast until he could find and buy thirteen grouper permits holding, in aggregate, a quarter of a million pounds of shares. He would later deploy longline gear, but still saw the Gulf like a spearfisherman constrained by air supply: thinking hard about where groupers go, when they feed, how they swim—and what people want from them. He believed consumers might pay more to know that life and death saga of the fish they were about to eat—the sizzle of a story that improves a filet's taste—a legacy he brought to the Gulf Wild traceability system.

Many coming into fisheries via catch shares were both young and educated. Stevie Fitz grew up in Boston crewing on vessels harvesting groundfish in the waters north of Cape Cod. But as the chilly Atlantic got crowded, he lit out to become a deckhand for his uncle Fitz, who fished for Dungeness crab, Pacific sanddabs, Petrale sole and Chilipepper rockfish in California's Half Moon Bay. Uncle Fitz, a rare commercial fisherman in the United States using Scottish seine gear, taught Stevie how to use the light nets, which without all the heavy steel cables, wood and steel doors that weigh down standard trawl nets don't drag, scrape and churn the seafloor habitat. Seining catches fewer fish but protects their quality, which Fitz's customers value most. It took time to master, but Stevie learned to retrieve his nets gently and slowly, curling them to guide fish into the lightweight mesh. Knowing his uncle was eyeing retirement, he began to save up to buy both his boat and upgraded equipment that would avoid bycatch, "to start my own business, preserve my strong family fishing heritage, and bring a higher quality and sustainable product to the dock." With his eco-friendly fishing technique, he succeeded on all fronts. Though he arrived just as the groundfish fishery transitioned to catch shares, and was allocated no shares, Stevie's unique skills and mindset enabled him to secure financing and break in.

The list of young entrepreneurs using catch shares to break into fishing continues to grow. Owen Hackleman worked on whale watching and sport-fishing boats to pay for a marine science degree at Cal Poly, where he tagged fish for a professor's academic research. He began fishing commercially with his dad but then bought his own vessel with the help of the California Fisheries Fund, leasing quota to build up his business. He used sustainable gear to catch shortspine thornyheads and other rockfish, focusing primarily on the high value live fish market in Vietnamese restaurants. On the Atlantic, Ryan Nolan worked as a deckhand while saving up to buy a boat and shares to dredge Cape Cod scallops. Bypassing processors, he had his crews harvest, shuck, rinse and package scallops at sea, a labor-intensive effort that has paid off. In the years after introduction of the Atlantic scallops catch share in 2010, scallops doubled in value, from six dollars to twelve dollars per pound, while allowable catch rose 30 percent to 47 million pounds. Shane Cantrell, also a marine sciences graduate (from Texas A&M), worked as a federal fishery observer, then monitored impacts from the BP Deepwater Horizon spill. Seeing how catch shares had made both fishermen and the Gulf more resilient, he decided he "had to get in." It was not a move, he conceded, for the faint of heart. He'd need more than three tons of quota to break even. At thirty-eight dollars a pound, that share would set him back a quarter million dollars. So he began leasing shares until he could afford to buy. "Quota is great for turning around the fishery," he said, "but it's really friggin' expensive for young guys like me ... with worse odds than opening a restaurant."

Buddy (who would soon, in fact, struggle to open a restaurant) couldn't agree more. So he, Bubba, Jason, Tres and other shareholders saw that it would be to their own benefit—economically, ecologically, and politically—to make it easier for responsible outsiders like Cantrell to acquire shares. New entrants would provide a hedge against long term stagnation or deterioration of share value: if the established guys wanted the option of cashing out down the road, they had to attract and equip more fishermen with the capacity to buy in. And if banks (leery of the revocability of catch shares) wouldn't offer low-interest loans, harvesters would step in themselves. The result? Buddy's nonprofit, the Shareholders' Alliance, set up a separate entity: a community trust or quota bank in which members bought up thirty-five tons of snapper quota for the Alliance to loan to the next generation of catch share fishermen who needed it. "It's a way for new entrants to get out in the market, make contacts, and find new sources of revenue," Buddy said. "It took six months to get together a group of shareholders who could put up a certain amount of quota, but it's been interesting to see how people come up with new ideas, figure out what will work, and are willing to step up and sacrifice income to make it work."

The Gulf guys followed New England's blueprint to "guide, fund and sustain America's small-boat fishing traditions" through a permit bank system that loans out quota on credit—leveling the financial playing field for new or small fishers vying against larger industrial fleets. Under Cape Cod's Paul Parker, those early efforts grew into national initiatives known as Catch Together and its financial backbone, Catch Invest. Both help small-scale local fishers and communities purchase and retain access to fishing quotas, which might otherwise be bought by large corporations. By doing so, sustainable rights-based fishing practices could reinvest profits back into the communities and build local capacity to manage ocean resources more effectively.

A second model was the California Fisheries Fund, which had similarly diversified the West Coast groundfish fishery. Alaska had applied a third, equally effective strategy: allocating a portion of pollock, an inherently capital-intensive fishery, to what had historically been non-pollock fishing communities. Some of those communities leveraged that equity to gain first jobs and ultimately vessels, growing their collective share from 10 to17 percent. NOAA fisheries economist Dan Holland found in these partnerships a pattern exactly contrary to the exclusionist critique: catch shares were providing a clear path for new entrants. Far from erasing fishing villages, they were fortifying local economies. A secure access right enabled "fishermen to become more diversified by allowing them to buy into fisheries in which they have not historically participated," said Holland, helping "create a more diversified and stable stream of fishing revenue for the community."

Buddy suspected today's fishermen had an *easier* path in than he, back in the day, ever did. Their ability to make incremental investments let them "test the waters" with lower risks of exposure. In the past, permitted boats rarely changed hands. Now, with a sixty-dollar commercial fishing license, just $4.50 lets you lease a pound of red snapper, catch it, and put it up for sale for 50 percent more; outright purchase of that share goes for fifty-five dollars. "Anyone with a business plan can start leasing quota," he explained. "Then, once you have your boat paid for, you can move into buying quota. You start to think: I can get in as a twenty-five-year-old, buy a thousand pounds a year, reinvest half my gross earnings into the business, and build up equity over thirty years."

That was all hypothetical. And these half dozen cases were, admittedly, anecdotes. Joining a catch share fishery would remain as tough as breaking into any rapidly maturing business: newcomers had to find a fresh angle on an old trade. Tres and Bubba married timing with risk tolerance. DeLaCruz customized storytelling. Stevie marketed eco-friendly gear as a value-add. Young eyes could see old problems in a fresh light. Still, just because some fishermen with guts, gumption and skills did manage to get in didn't answer the complaint that just as many, if not more, still couldn't make the leap. As always in food production, no one was guaranteed to be a business owner, even if Buddy and friends did their damnedest to ensure regular infusions of new and innovative blood.

In a time of extreme inequality—and of political hand-outs of federal lands and resources to the special interests that fund campaigns—public debate about access to public resources remained more vital than ever. Fortunately, reforms led by commercial harvesters like Buddy regenerated enough ocean wealth that there were, once more, living assets worth arguing over. By increasing the price, population, harvested size, and spawning capacity of snapper and other species, catch shares have made Wharf Road and its counterparts on other coastlines a place attractive to young strivers seeking their fortunes in America's revived seafood economy. "For most of my professional life the next generation showed no interest in commercial fishing, for very good reasons," said Chris Brown, who has fished out of Point Judith, Rhode Island for 38 years, and was president of the Seafood Harvesters of America. "It offered kids nothing but a lot of hard work for low pay and no security. But now you see them hanging around the docks, asking questions, showing interest. To me that's a good sign. It means we have a future."

BUDDY'S MIND REMAINED focused on that future; his body, on the other hand, was a victim of his past. Six decades of hard living had taken a toll. "He's gained some weight," his brother Kenny said one night. "He's not as fluid on the dock as he used to be." Limping around, Buddy reluctantly conceded it took longer to recover from injuries. So while his market still handled a quarter of the Gulf's fresh fish, this alpha patriarch grew focused on the painful business of "succession planning."

Over time Buddy handed over operations and sales at Katie's

Seafood to his eldest son, Nick. He began coaching his second son, Ricky, to take on communications and outreach, encouraging him to speak at Gulf Council meetings. Offshore, he surrendered the wheelhouse to his third son, Hans. He worked to keep his youngest, Christopher, in school long enough to have choices about his life direction. But Buddy himself still had a hard time letting go.

Though Nick went to business school, the family's first college graduate, the "*Big Fish*" camera found Buddy second-guessing his decisions at every turn. When Nick accepted a fish delivery of less than perfect quality, Buddy blamed his son's "lack of attention," railing about how that "ivory tower crap he learned in college" bypassed what mattered most on the loading docks. When he dragged Nick out on the water to transfer respect for the life force in every snapper, his son just wanted to get back to the office and bring order to the books. "Sometimes I get so passionate about the thing that I have built," Buddy allowed, "that I forget that the people I want to pass it on to don't have the experience I have."

Similar tensions erupted with Ricky, who struggled to launch a website that might win his father's stinting praise. Later, trying to show initiative, Ricky bought shipping boxes that look spiffy on the outside but didn't keep fish cool enough to please his father. When the two of them attended a Gulf Council meeting to speak against reallocating commercial shares to the recreational sector, Ricky acquitted himself well enough, but only when prepped with words provided by his father; the son still had to carve out an identity of his own. Hans, twenty-six, had most closely followed Buddy's career, taking up fishing early and becoming a captain of his own crew at a young age. He walked and talked with a swagger, and Buddy was proud, but pointed out how "he's got a lot of growing up to do." Cast in the shadow of a fishing legend, it seems Hans would try forever to match his father's prowess and earn respect from his deckhands, his family, and especially Buddy himself.

Buddy fought to defend a multi-million-dollar business he could bequeath them. Seeing threats at every turn, he went out of his way, sometimes far out of his way, to confront them. One day, with a camera crew hovering at a distance, he set off in search of recreational vessels fishing outside their season. If he could catch poachers on film, federal authorities could bring misdemeanor charges, carrying penalties of up to a year in jail and a $1,000 fine per violation. "I need to even up the playing field," said the man who was transformed by catch shares from pirate into vigilante law enforcer. "Otherwise, they could reverse the rebuilding process."

To fool outlaw anglers, Buddy zipped out in a small recreational boat, enlisting his son Christopher, then fourteen, and his father Greg, eighty-two, to resemble a family at play. The Guindon men could legally fish under Buddy's commercial quota, but any anglers they came upon would be breaking the law. Buddy got so worked up racing around the Gulf trying to find bad guys, a priority his two passengers didn't share, that his tunnel vision blinded him to dynamics in his own boat.

Greg had hoped to recapture a bit of those long-ago early mornings in Minnesota, when he and little Buddy fished for walleye on Black Lake: fathers and sons on the surface and countless fish below. Instead, he saw Buddy grousing how poaching was "serious business," scanning the horizon, and not helping Christopher improve his cast. Greg looked from his son to his grandson and shook his head. "When Buddy was a teen, I was gone," Greg recalled. "I'd left the family, house, car, business, to pursue my own way, and cried from St Paul all the way to Kansas City. Mistake of the century. So, I want to say 'wake up Buddy! This is time you have with Christopher. Once it's gone it never comes back!'"

Buddy was left confused. "I went out there to catch illegal fishing," he told Katie. "And they went out there to go fishing. For our livelihood and for the good of this country, these fisheries need to be rebuilt. I don't understand why they went with me if that's what they were going to do."

Katie, caught in the middle, reminded Buddy it's not his job to rebuild a fishery single-handedly. When he has his son and dad on board, he needs to take time and enjoy it. When she reminded Buddy how Greg's departure had hurt him while growing up, Buddy protested that he's often around his boys. "You can be there physically," she noted, "but you're not there mentally. Fishing with you is more important to Chris than you realize. This is time you can't get back."

GREGORY A. GUINDON died peacefully at his home in Galveston on December 10, 2015. The church service at Sacred Heart included the usual somber readings from Ecclesiastes: "One generation passeth away, and another generation cometh: but the earth abideth forever." Buddy had been raised Catholic ("the nuns had beaten the catechism into me"), and so recalled John 21:6, in which the voice of a stranger on shore urges professional fishermen getting skunked at sea to "cast your net on the right side of a boat, and ye shall find some. They cast therefore, and now they were not able to draw it for the multitude of fishes." It was, he figured, a fair parable for what catch shares had done. Still, religion was more of a "social thing," he allowed. "For me it's more an understanding that there's a force greater than yourself or anyone. It's the ashes-to-ashes part. I hope there's a hereafter, and if there is that you can go out and fish in it. If there's not, then…hell, I don't want to go!"

Following the church service, family and friends enjoyed shrimp, oysters and red snapper, sharing photos, videos and stories in celebration of Greg's life. When it was his turn to speak, Buddy "tried hard not to be the blubbering mess that I ended up being." They'd had a testy, on-again-off-again relationship, he and his dad. Like Buddy, Greg had never missed an opportunity to browbeat his son with unsolicited "opinions and advice on everything from sales to fishing tactics." An inveterate gambler, he'd gone missing to marry and live with a second wife in Vegas for decades rather than spend time with Buddy, Kenny and their families. Yet it was Greg Guindon who'd instilled in Buddy his deep love of fishing: standing side by side pulling up animals from the depths was the closest bond they'd ever known. That was his father's legacy. "The worst part was how his death affected my children, who didn't really get to know him until the last few years of his life. The younger ones didn't really understand the process of leaving this earth, a process some of us older fishermen have seen too much of."

Buddy took his dad's advice on his next trip with Christopher. They didn't search for outlaws, discuss the market or assess federal legislation. Business and politics could wait. It was just the two, father and son, rocking on the waves off Galveston Island, waiting for that first bite. Buddy looked at Christopher, the anticipation on his face, and recalled how it had been for him with his own dad five decades earlier. Hell, maybe this was the hereafter.

Time had its own loop currents. Its tides took away and gave back. His father, mother, brother Kenny, two of his sisters, and some of his oldest fishing buddies were gone. Buddy himself showed more scars, slower reflexes, and a bit less energy. Still, alongside his sons there were new generations of fishermen rising to replace the ones who left the salt water and whose ashes were scattered upon it. Above all, while still under siege, his beloved Gulf was growing ever more resilient, on its way to teem with life again. It remained a force greater than any one fisherman alone. Flooding and ebbing, the sea was rising up anew to welcome and reward the unbroken chain of innovative stewards who across time chose to wake early, bind a curved hook to a fiber strand, impale a chunk of bait on it, step over to the water's edge and cast it out into the unknown.

ACKNOWLEDGMENTS

Sea Change exemplifies collective action that has unfolded in two stages. One community embarked toward the replenishment of ocean fisheries in North America and abroad; the next helped share the remarkable story of that quiet restoration. We are deeply indebted to both.

We owe gratitude foremost to numerous funding partners who put wind into the sails of fisheries transformation, including Acacia Conservation Fund, William K. Bowes Jr. Foundation, The Campbell Foundation, Stanley Druckenmiller, Philip and Alicia Hammarskjold, Heising–Simons Foundation, Kingfisher Foundation, The David and Lucile Packard Foundation, Quadrivium Foundation, Gary Rappeport, Edward Stern, and Walton Family Foundation. Without them, there would be no story to tell.

Commercial fishing is more than a job: It's a calling, a craft, and a way of life. We have had the extraordinary fortune of working with some of the best. Buddy, Katie, and the entire Guindon family opened their doors and their stories to us. Other Gulf fishing leaders, including Eric Brazer, Shane Cantrell, Bubba Cochrane, Felix Cox, Jason DeLaCruz, Brett Fitzgerald, Scott Hickman, David Krebs, Susan Shipman, Tj Tate, Bryant Thomson, Donnie Waters, and Wayne Werner, brought the challenges and triumphs of their industry to vivid life.

The Pacific coast introduced us to a different set of experiences and voices—Linda Behnken, Geoff Bettencourt, Bob Dooley, Stevie Fitz, Heather Mann, Brent Paine, Joe Pennisi, Brad Pettinger, Charlie Price, Michelle Tarantino Norvell—each contributed their hard-earned wisdom. Conversations with shoreside allies like Scott Coughlin, Jim Gilmore, Sara Skamser, and Arnie Thomson deepened our understanding of the challenges at the water's edge. On Canada's coastline, we gained perspective from Wes Erikson, Howard McElderry, Brian Mose, Shawn Stebbins, and Bruce Turris.

Along the Atlantic coast, Chris Brown, Tom Dempsey, Ben Martens, John Pappalardo, Paul Parker, Maggie Raymond, and Tom Rudolph led by example. Welcoming us on board in the Great Lakes, Charlie Henriksen demonstrated the legacy of the first catch share, while Pete Flaherty provided context on how stakeholders forged abstract concepts into a working system.

Over the years, a remarkable community of EDF staff partnered with fishermen, regulators, researchers, and innovators to help overcome opposition to catch shares and usher in reforms that provide lasting and adaptive benefits for fishing communities and the ocean. We thank Ashley Apel, Pam Baker, Seema Balwani, Jeffrey Barger, Donald Barry, Willow Battista, Alexandra Bauermeister, Kate Bonzon, Sarah Hagedorn Bowman, Merrick Burden, Melissa Carey, Benson Chiles, Denise Choy Stetten, Jenny Couture, Jen Cruz, Erica Cunningham, Chris Cusack, Patty Debenham, Michael Delapa, Eileen Dougherty, Pete Emerson, David Festa, Tim Fitzgerald, Rod Fujita, Monica Goldberg, Tom Grasso, Sepp Haukebo, Phoebe Higgins, Ayelet Hines, Andrew Hutson, Marcie Jones, Robert Jones, Shems Jud, Kendra Karr, Karly Kelso, Kristin Kleisner, Jake Kritzer, Fred Krupp, Jessica Landman, Emilie Litsinger, Owen Liu, Kat Mah, Melissa Mahoney, Gretchen Martin, Kristen McConnell, Barbara McCullough, Sally McGee, Huff McGonigal, David McKinney, Sarah McTee, John Mimikakis, Ted Morton, Matt Mullin, Roxanne Nanninga, Preetha Nooyi, Ryan Ono, Maggie Ostdahl, Heather Paffe, Sarah Poon, Doug Rader, Nancy Raditz, Matt Rand, Diane Regas, Alexis Rife, Pam Ruiter, Nicole Sarto, Harrison Schmidt, Eric Schwaab, Elizabeth Silleck, Nicole Smith, Sarah Smith, Jack Sterne, Kent Strauss, Priya Sundareshan, Helen Takade-Heumacher, Matt Tinning, Johanna Thomas, Whitney Tome, Carlito Turner, Nya Van Leuven, Babs Wallace, Katie Westfall, Dan Whittle, Josh Wiersma, Daniel Willard, Julie Wormser, Candace Wu, Kate Wunderlich, Alex Yarborough, Jeff Young, and many more.

Beyond US waters, collaborations between fishermen and EDF staff spread. In Belize, Yonardo Cus offered a taste of his catch and of the world he works to sustain—and shared his knowledge alongside conservationists Larry Epstein and Nic Requena. In Cuba, we acknowledge the leadership of Lalo Bone, Valerie Miller, and Daylin Munoz Nunez; in Mexico, Juan Manual Calderón, Ciro Calderon, Gabi de la Vega, Scott Edwards, Rodrigo Elizarraras, José Fraire, Grecia Galindo, Dulce Lizarraga, Rafael Ortiz-Rodríguez, Laura Rodriguez Harker, Aristo Stavrinaky, Ana Suarez, Danna Velarde, Cristina Villanueva, Luis Villanueva, and Pedro Zapata; and in Europe and the UK, Aditi Dasgupta, Klaas de Vos, Andrea Giesecke, Erik Lindebow, Jo Pollett, Erin Priddle, and Melanie Siggs.

There was often no clear line between internal and external partners, when all were focused on the same shared outcome. Redstone Strategy Group's initial analysis proved catalytic, thanks to Ivan Barkhorn, Jason Blau, Lee Green, Dietmar Grimm, and Larry Linden. A "kitchen cabinet" gave consistently sage advice, including Dick Allen, Larry Band, Kit Barron, Scott Burns, Michael Clayton, David Crabbe, Mike Dickerson, Barry Gold, Ray Hilborn, Monica Jain, and Dorothy Lowman. In Washington, DC, Patrick Collins, Darrell Connor, Tim Hobbs, and Jim Sartucci helped navigate policy and political changes. Academic partners Dr. Chris Costello, Dr. Steve Gaines, and Dr. Jane Lubchenco helped demonstrate the power of effective solutions. Non-governmental organization collaborators—including Conservation Law Foundation, Marine Conservation Institute, Marine Stewardship Council, Ocean Conservancy, Rare, Seafood Harvesters of America, The Nature Conservancy, Wildlife Conservation Society, and WWF—have advanced science, community support, and innovations for healthy oceans. And we also appreciate the leadership of federal fishery scientists and managers at US National Oceanic and Atmospheric Association Fisheries and of the regional fishery management councils.

The second stage of collective action brought this remarkable story to life in the book you hold.

Creating a work of narrative nonfiction from first spark to published pages often felt like embarking into the ocean itself on a quest to bring value from hook to table. It takes a sturdy vessel, a worthy catch, and an extraordinary crew you can count on through fair and foul weather as conditions invariably change. *Sea Change* would not exist without the generous wisdom, encouragement, and sheer hard work of many individuals (some above, now acting also in an editorial role) and organizations, to whom we extend our deepest gratitude.

This journey began with a simple conversation with Greg Alexander of Acacia Conservation Fund, who pointed out that, while catch shares had come a long way, few understood the profound transformation underway. Greg, along with Fred Nelson, not only provided crucial financial support but also invaluable feedback that helped shape early drafts. Without their belief in this story, it might have remained adrift.

Several exceptional colleagues dedicated their time and expertise to elevate every page: Doug Rader lent his vast scientific knowledge and sharp eye, steering us clear of inaccuracies and sharpening the narrative with clarity and rigor; Michele Lee Amundsen offered the invaluable perspective of an outsider, helping us refine confusing passages and streamline our message; and the brilliant writer and author Miriam Horn brought her editorial magic, polishing our manuscript into something far more graceful and compelling.

A host of EDFers lent their insights, shaping key chapters with their thoughtful questions and updates. Pam Baker, Kate Bonzon, Shems Jud, Valerie Miller, Sarah Poon, Rafael Ortiz-Rodríguez, Jack Sterne, Jeff Young, and Pedro Zapata proved instrumental in enriching the content with their deep knowledge. New perspectives from Brianna Curran, Keith Gaby, Negin Janati and Amy Middleton, illuminated how this story extends far beyond fisheries, touching broader environmental and economic themes. Laura Catalano, Rahel Marsie-Hazen, Eric Pooley, Shawn Regan, Colin Rowan, Tad Segal, Matthew Smelser, and Jonathan Webster played key roles

ACKNOWLEDGMENTS

in guiding the early research and shaping it into stories that would become a cohesive narrative.

A special thanks to our first literary agent, Kim Witherspoon, and her team at Inkwell, who saw potential in this project and guided us through the early stages with steady hands and sharp instincts. Kirsten Johanna Allen and Will Neville-Rehbehn at Torrey House Press were the perfect partners to take this story beyond the shoreline, helping us shape a vision that connects human and natural communities in harmony. The dedicated team, including Gray Buck-Cockayne, Eryon Greenburg, Miah Hardy, Scout Invie, Kathleen Metcalf, Lark Washburn, and June Wisteria poured their expertise and energy into ensuring *Sea Change* found its audience and purpose.

Of course, writing a book is an all-consuming endeavor, one that seeps into family dinners, road trips, and the quiet moments before sleep. We are forever grateful to our spouses, Eric Annis and Vanessa Lemaire, for their patience, encouragement, and unwavering belief in the value of this work—even when it meant enduring long stretches of absent-minded stares and late-night revisions. Finally, with hope for the future, we dedicate this book to our children.

ENDNOTES

PREFACE

world's most nutrient-rich protein: Leschin-Hoar, Clare, "1 in 10 People May Face Malnutrition as Fish Catches Decline." *The Salt*, June 30, 2016.

who depend on seafood to live: Golden, C., Allison, E., Cheung, W., et al., "Nutrition: Fall in fish catch threatens human health." *Nature* 534, 317–320 (2016); Bennett, Abigail, Patil, Pawan, Kleisner, Kristin, Rader, Doug, Virdin, John, and Basurto, Xavier, "Contribution of Fisheries to Food and Nutrition Security: Current Knowledge, Policy, and Research." NI Report 18-02, Duke University, 2018.

ecosystems, particularly coral reefs: World Bank Group. *Blue Economy.* Accessed October 1, 2024, https://www.worldbank.org/en/topic/oceans-fisheries-and-coastal-economies; The Nature Conservancy. *A Healthy Ocean Depends on Sustainably Managed Fisheries.* January 2021.

solve interconnected crises—to nourish: Arnarson, Atli,, "8 Signs and Symptoms of Protein Deficiency." *Healthline, June 25, 2024*; Semba, R. D., "The Rise and Fall of Protein Malnutrition in Global Health." *Ann Nutr Metab.,* 69(2): 79-88. August 30, 2016.

INTRODUCTION | SETTING THE HOOK

longer than anyone on earth: Okinawa Research Center for Longevity Science. *Okinawa Centenarian Study.* Accessed October 8, 2024.

an ancient gene pool: "Okinawa Exploration Backgrounds," *Blue Zones*, March 20, 2014.

a seafood-rich diet: Michael Booth, "The Okinawa diet: could it help you live to 100?" *The Guardian*, June 19 2013.

world's oldest fishhooks: Lyons, Kate, "World's oldest fish-hooks found on Okinawa, Japan." *The Guardian*, September 18, 2016.

singular and consequential inventions: Ewalt, David M., "No. 19: The Fish Hook." *Forbes.* Accessed October 3, 2024.

understanding of how we evolved: Fujita, Masaki, Yamasaki, Shinji, Katagiri, Chiaki, et al., "Advanced maritime adaptation in the western Pacific coastal region extends back to 35,000–30,000 years," *Proceedings of the National Academy of Sciences,* Vol. 113 (40). October 4, 2016.

to inhabit offshore islands: Corbyn, Z., "Archaeologists land world's oldest fish hook." *Nature,* November 24, 2011.

catching and eating more fish: Allen, John S., "Was Seafood Brainfood in Human Evolution?" *Psychology Today,* January 21, 2010.

larger, more complex brains: Moseman, Andrew, "Did dining on seafood help early humans grow these big brains?" *Discover Magazine,* June 2, 2010.

fossil shell and bone trash: Corbyn, Z., "Archaeologists land world's oldest fish hook," *Nature,* November 24, 2011.

gleaned animals from coastal shallows: Minkel, J. R., "Earliest Known Seafood Dinner Discovered," *Scientific American,* October 17, 2017.

seafood provided an evolutionary edge: Callaway, Ewen. "Seafood gave us the edge on Neanderthals," *New Scientist,* August 12, 2009.

perfect protein: Sharpless, Andy, "The Perfect Protein," Oceana.org, 2013.

harvesting power of fishermen: NOAA Fisheries. *Fishing Gear: Bottom Longlines.* Accessed October 3, 2024, https://www.fisheries.noaa.gov/national/bycatch/fishing-gear-bottom-longlines

depths with pinpoint accuracy: Bailey, K. M., "An empty donut hole: the great collapse of a North American fishery." *Ecology and Society* 16(2): 28, 2011.

37 million strong in four million vessels: Food and Agriculture Organization of the United Nations. *General facts regarding world fisheries.* May 2010.

catching trillions of fish: Greenberg, Paul, and Worm, Boris, "When Humans declared war on fish," *The New York Times,* May 8, 2015.

in a bleak global cascade: Shikakuma, Shinichiro, "Coastal Fisheries Co-Management in Okinawa, Samoa and the Philippines with Fish Aggregating Devices as Sources of Alternative Income." *Senri Ethnological Studies,* 67, 197-214, February 2005.

devastation continues to worsen: Costello, Christopher, Ovando, Daniel, Clavelle, Tyler, et al, "Proceedings of the National Academy of Sciences." *PNAS*, 113(18): 5125-5129, May 2016; Cressey, D. Fisheries: Eyes on the ocean. *Nature* 519, 280–282, 2015.

world's fisheries are in dire straits today: Edgar, Graham, "Investigation reveals global fisheries are in far worse shape than we thought—and many have already collapsed," *The Conversation,* August 31, 2024.

without radical management changes: Costello, C., Ovando, D., Clavelle, T., Strauss, C., Hilborn, R., Melnychuk, M., et al., "Global fishery prospects under contrasting management regimes." *Proceedings of the National Academy of Sciences of the United States of America*, 113(18), 5125-5129. March 28, 2016.

for income and food, to recover: United Nations. *World population projected to reach 9.8 billion in 2050, and 11.2 billion in 2100.* June 21, 2017.

or cellular cultivation: Boylan, Camille, "The future of farming, hydroponics," PSCI, November 9, 2020; Barzee, Tyler, El Mashad, Hamed M., Cao, Lin, *et al.*, "Cell-cultivated food production and processing: A review." *Food Bioengineering*, 1(1): 4-25, March 2022.

for-hire fishing guides alike: Abbott, Joshua K., and Willard, Daniel, "Rights-based management for recreational for-hire fisheries: Evidence from a policy trial," *Fisheries Research* 196, 106–116. December 2017.

formerly depleted fish stocks: NOAA Fisheries. *Status of Stocks 2023.* Accessed October 4, 2024, https://www.fisheries.noaa.gov/national/sustainable-fisheries/status-stocks-2023; Broderick, Matt, "NOAA Fisheries Releases 2023 Status of Stocks," July 22, 2024; Grimm, Dietmar, Barkhorn, Ivan, Festa, David, Bonzon, Kate, Boomhower, Judd, Hovland, Valerie, and Blau, Jason, "Assessing catch shares' effects evidence from Federal United States and associated British Columbian fisheries." *Marine Policy*, 36(3), 644-657. 2012.

a neighboring country's EEZ: "The United States is an Ocean Nation." Map of the US Exclusive Economic Zone. Accessed October 8, 2024, http://www.gc.noaa.gov/documents/2011/012711_gcil_maritime_eez_map.pdf

coast to coast to coast: NOAA Fisheries. *Status of Stocks 2023.* Dec. 31, 2023.

second to Alaska in productivity: "Gulf of Mexico." Environmental Defense Fund. May 29, 2015.

fastest in the country: "2020 Fisheries of the United States." NOAA Fisheries. May 2022.

imports 79 percent of its seafood: Davis, Christopher G. and Rexroad, Caird E., "US Seafood Imports Expand as Domestic Aquaculture Industry Repositions Itself." May 22, 2024; "US Aquaculture." NOAA Fisheries. Accessed October 8, 2024, https://www.fisheries.noaa.gov/national/aquaculture/us-aquaculture; Gunther, Marc, "Q&A with Paul Greenberg: Seafood is not software." The Guardian. July 17, 2014; "Sustainable Seafood: Seafood Communities," NOAA Fisheries. Accessed October 8, 2024, https://www.fishwatch.gov/sustainable-seafood/the-global-picture.

CHAPTER ONE | LANDLOCKED ORIGINS

gathering along the lakeshores: Tarlach, Gemma, "How the Great Lakes Formed—And the Mystery of Who Watched It Happen." *Atlas Obscura*, January 11, 2024.

fishhooks, and harpoon points: "Ancient Michigan," *Ancient American Net Roots*, March 31, 2012.

speared fish through the ice: "Fishing in the Western Great Lakes," *Native American Net Roots,* May 15, 2012.

removed only enough to subsist: Krech, Shepard III, *The Ecological Indian: Myth and History.* WW Norton & CO. 1999.

History offers a different thesis: Anderson, Terry, "Conservation Native American style." PERC. July 1, 1996.

surplus their families could not eat: Bogue, Margaret Beattie, *Fishing the Great Lakes: An Environmental History,* 1783–1933. University of Wisconsin Press, 2000.

at least among native tribes: Ewers Anderson, Kristen, "Communal tenure and the governance of common property resources in Asia," Food and Agriculture Organization of the United Nations. April 2011.

largest inland commercial fisheries: Welcomme RL, Cowx IG, Coates D, Béné C, Funge-Smith S, Halls A, Lorenzen K. "Inland capture fisheries." *Philos Trans R Soc Lond B Biol Sci.* 365(1554):2881-96. September 2010.

haunt the next two centuries: Malthus, Thomas, "An essay on the principle of population," 1798.

resources to satisfy hunger: Dunn, Peter M., "Thomas Malthus (1766-1834): Population growth and birth control," University of Bristol. 1998.

disease, war, and collapse: "Malthus, The False Prophet" *The Economist*, May 15, 2008.

extirpated by the agency of man: Kolbert, Elizabeth, "The Scales Fall," *The New Yorker*, July 26, 2010.

license fees: Michigan Department of Natural Resources. *History of state-licensed Great Lakes commercial fishing.* Accessed October 11, 2024, https://www.michigan.gov/dnr/managing-resources/fisheries/business/commercial/history-of-state-licensed-great-lakes-commercial-fishing.

ancient and universal roots: Canales, Mary K. RN PhD, "Othering :Toward an understanding of difference." *Advances in Nursing Science*, 22(4): 16-31, June 2000.

communities who depend on it: Forty years earlier, Danish economist Jens Warming was the first to advance this analysis: that property rights, game theory, and externalities shape fishery outcome; see: Topp, Niels-Henrik, "The Impact of Open Access to Fishing Grounds," *History of Political Economy.*, 40 (4): 671–688, 2008.

you want to catch them: Jensen, Trygvie, *Wooden Boats and Iron Men.* 2007.

to make business decisions: Allen, R. (n.d.), "What is overfishing? Examples & Solutions to prevent." Our Endangered World. January 23, 2024.

wasn't smooth, neat, or pretty: Bonzon, Kate, "Wisconsin Great Lakes ITQ Program: Stability and profitability in a changing ecosystem." Environmental Defense Fund. June 8, 2010.

since 1968 to 1.6 million pounds: Egan, Dan, "In Lake Michigan, resilient whitefish, fishermen fight for a comeback." Milwaukee Journal Sentinel. August 16, 2011; Bardwell, Neely, "From waters to table: The story of the Great Lakes whitefish." *Great Lakes Now.* June 27, 2024.

in a century: Bergquist, Lee, "A century later, whitefish are turning up in Wisconsin rivers." Milwaukee Journal Sentinel. November 27, 2017.

CHAPTER TWO | COLD WAR EXCLUSION

unbelievable during the Cold War: Hitz, Charles R., "1970 Operation of the Soviet Trawl Fleet off the Washington and Oregon Coasts during 1966 and 1967." Carmel Finley. October 15, 2012.

transform commercial fishing in the US: Follansbee, Joe, "A part of NW fishing science could be lost." Cascade PBS. December 1, 2013.

putting the nation's fish at risk: "Peril Discerned in Soviet Fishing," *The New York Times*, January 23, 1964; Finley, C., "So why were those Soviet boats fishing off Washington?" October 19. 2012.

US Exclusive Economic Zone (EEZ): Reagan, Ronald, "Statement on United States Ocean policy." The American Presidency Project. March 10, 1983.

Hawaiian Islands in the Pacific: "What is the EEZ?" NOAA Fisheries. Accessed October 8, 2024, https://oceanservice.noaa.gov/facts/eez.html.

each state in the region: "Fishery Management Councils." NOAA Fisheries. Accessed October 11, 2024, https://www.fisheries.noaa.gov/southeast/funding-and-financial-services/fishery-management-councils; "Council Process and Organization." Magnuson-Stevens Fishery Conservation and Management Act." October 2022.

about commerce and geopolitics: Ted Morton, "U.S. Ocean Fishing Law

Forged by Cold War Politic," PEW Charitable Trusts, July 2015.

this could get interesting.: Jeffrey D. Hartman, *"US Coast Guard Academy: Hartman USCG (Retired),"* Arcadia Publishing, 2020.

adopts for its own use: NOAA Fisheries. *What is the law of the sea?* Accessed October 8, 2024, https://oceanservice.noaa.gov/facts/lawofsea.html; Nandan, S. N., "The Exclusive Economic zone: A Historical Perspective." Accessed October 8, 2024, http://www.fao.org/docrep/s5280T/s5280t0p.htm.

take over more of the fishing role: Christie, Donna R., "Regulation of international joint ventures in the fishery conservation zone." Accessed October 8, 2024, http://digitalcommons.law.uga.edu/cgi/viewcontent.cgi?article=1975&context=gjicl.

CHAPTER THREE | PARTING THE (SALT)WATERS

with the smell of fish.: Biank Fasig, Lisa, "McDonald's fare a highlight of storied career," *Cincinnati Business Courier*, March 6, 2006.

still peaks during Lent: Smith, K. Annabelle, "The fishy history of the Mconald's Filet-O-Fish sandwich," *Smithsonian Magazine*, 2013.

proved undesirable and unreliable: McDonalds. *McDonald's Filet-O-Fish Journey.* February 26, 2016.

pollock from the sea: Food and Agriculture Organization of the UN. *The State of World Fisheries and Aquaculture 2024 – Blue Transformation in action.* 2024.

billion dollars a year: Bailey, Kevin M., *Billion Dollar Fish*, University of Chicago Press, 2021.

enough to pay off loans: Criddle, Keith R., "Adaptation and maladaptation: factors that influence the resilience of four Alaskan fisheries governed by durable entitlements," *ICES Journal of Marine Science*, 69(7): 1168-1179, September 2012.

CHAPTER FOUR | BECOMING THE HIGHLINER

16.9 million to 5.1 million pounds: McQuaid, John, "Managers maneuver at cliff's edge," *New Orleans Times-Picayune.* March 26, 1996.

older they get, the more fertile: Louisiana Fisheries. *Red Snapper FAQ's: Biology and Life History.* Accessed October 8, 2024, http://www.seagrantfish.lsu.edu/faqs/redsnapper/biology.htm.

down to 2.6 percent: NOAA Fisheries. *Gulf of Mexico recreational red* *snapper management.* Accessed October 8, 2024, http://sero.nmfs. noaa.gov/sustainable_fisheries/gulf_fisheries/red_snapper/overview/ status/index.html.

1994 and they kept growing: "Oceans of Trouble: Are the world's fisheries doomed?" *New Orleans Times-Picayune*, September 9, 2015.

valuable for sale as meat: Batsleer, J., Hamon, K. G., Van Overzee, H. M. J., *et al.*, "High-grading and over-quota discarding in mixed fisheries," *Rev Fish Biol Fisheries* 25, 715–736, 2015.

trip length, boat size, or hours logged: SouthEast Data, Assessment, and Review. *Stock Assessment of Red Snapper in the Gulf of Mexico.* December 3, 2009; NOAA Fisheries. *History of Management of Gulf of Mexico Red Snapper.* Accessed October 17, 2024, https://www. fisheries.noaa.gov/southeast/sustainable-fisheries/history-management-gulf-mexico-red-snapper.

transporting snapper across state lines: Jacobsen, Rowan, "The Gumbo Chronicles," March 9, 2012; McQuaid, John, "Gulf on the brink," *New Orleans Times-Picayune*, March 25, 1996.

spawning potential kept falling: Cowan, J.H., Grimes, C.B., Patterson, W.F., et al. "Red snapper management in the Gulf of Mexico: science-or faith-based?" *Rev Fish Biol Fisheries* 21, 187–204. 2011.

CHAPTER FIVE | RECALCULATED RISKS

steelworkers, and bush pilots: Pfieffer, Lisa, and Gratz, Trevor, "The effects of rights-based fisheries management on risk taking and fishing safety," *Economic Sciences*, 113(10): 2615-2620. February 16, 2016; Janocha, Jill, "Facts of the catch: occupational injuries; illnesses; and fatalities to fishing workers 2003-2009," *Beyond the Numbers*, 1(9). August 2012; "The Deadliest Jobs In America, In One Graphic," *Planet Money*, January 23, 2013.

weather conditions to avoid: Lambert, Debra L., Thunberg, Eric M., Felthoven, Ron G., Lincoln, Jennifer M., and Patrick, Wesley S., "Guidance on fishing vessel risk assessments and accounting for safety at sea in fishery management design," NOAA Fisheries, August 2015.

secondary concerns, like safety: Novotney, Amy, "The psychology of scarcity," *Monitor on Psychology*. 45(2): 28, February 2014.

destroying oceanic wealth: "Crab rationalization program frequently asked questions and small entity compliance guide." NOAA Fisheries. October 15, 2018; Woodley, Christopher J. MMA., Lincoln, Jennifer M. PhD., and Medlicott, Charles, "Improving Commercial Fishing Vessel Safety Through Collaboration," *Efforts on the Home Front*, 2010.

pounds of fish—became "inconsequential": Environmental Defense Fund. *US Alaska halibut and sablefish fixed gear individual fishing quota program.* Accessed October 11, 2024, https://fisherysolutionscenter.edf.org/united-states-alaska-halibut-and-sablefish-fixed-gear-individual-fishing-quota-program-0; Fina, Mark, "Evolution of Catch Share Management: Lessons from Catch Share Management in the North Pacific," *Fisheries*, 36(4), April 2011.

to one or two each year: Dietmar, Grimm, Barkhorn, Ivan, Festa, David, *et al.*, "Assessing catch shares' effects evidence from Federal United States and associated British Columbia fisheries," Environmental Defense Fund. November 24, 2011.

didn't fully work: Jenkins, Matt, "The most cooked-up catch," *High Country News*, July 27, 2019.

lowered and lifted each day: Kozak, Linda Consultant, "House Natural Resources Committee Oversight Hearings," Crab Group of Independent Harvesters, pp 137, 2010.

incentives provided by catch shares: Pfieffer, Lisa, and Gratz, Trevor, "The effects of rights based fisheries management on risk taking and fishing safety," *Economic Sciences*, 113(10): 2615-2620, February 16, 2016.

safer without the race: Knapp, Gunnar, "Effects of IFQ Management on Fishing Safety: Survey Responses of Alaska Halibut Fishermen, Institute of Social and Economic Research," University of Alaska Anchorage, 1999

work-related fishing fatalities: Brooks, J., "Alaska's fishing fatalities are dropping no matter how you mix numbers," *Juneau Empire*, October 19, 2015.

CHAPTER SIX | THE NATURE OF DISSENT

this new animal, catch shares: Baker, Pamela, Emerson, Peter M., and Cox, Felix G., "Managing the Gulf of Mexico Commercial Red Snapper Fishery," Hathi Trust. Accessed October 2024

other environmental groups: Verini, James, "The Devil's Advocate," *The New Republic*, September 24, 2007.

more efficient irrigation: Eilperin, Juliet, "Thomas J Graff, 65; helped transform US water policy," *Washington Post*, November 14, 2009.

cheaper than anyone imagined possible: Gerdes, Justin, "Cap and Trade Curbed Acid Rain: 7 Reasons Why It Can Do The Same For Climate Change," *Forbes*, February 14, 2012.

NOTES

1990s on catch shares: R.M. Fujita, D. Hopkins, Z. Willey, "Creating incentives to curb overfishing," *Oceanographic Literature Review*, 1997; Economics Research International. *Research Article Bioeconomics of Commercial Marine Fisheries of Bay of Bengal: Status and Direction.* April 2014.

shift effort to maximize economic yield: "The Gordon Schaefer Model." Cited: Habib, Ahasan, Hadayet, Ullah, and Nguyen, Duy Ngoc, "Research Article Bioeconomics of Commercial Marine Fisheries of Bay of Bengal: Status and Direction," Economics Research International, April 2014.

not a lack of ownership: Macinko, Seth, and Bromley, Daniel, "Property and fisheries for the twenty-first century: Seeking coherence from legal and economic doctrine." *Vermont Law Review* 28(3), January 2004; Macinko, Seth, and Bromley, Daniel, "Who Owns America's Fisheries?" *Island Press*, January 2002.

confusions, contrivances, and deceits: Bromley, Daniel W., "Abdicating Responsibility: The deceits of fisheries policy," *Fisheries*, 34(4), 2009.

basis of investigative articles: Rust, Suzanne, "System turns US fishing rights into commodity, squeezes small fishermen," *Reveal*. March 12, 2013.

videos: Shuman, Brooke, and Mascorro, Anthony, "Our camera footage got raided. You won't believe why," More Perfect Union, November 14, 2023.

full-length books: Van Der Voo, L., *The Fish Market*, St Martin's Press, 2016.

without compensation: Leal, Donald R., "Saving fisheries with free markets," Property and Environment Research Center, February 2006.

necessity be self-enforcing: FAO Fisheries. *Case studies in fisheries self governance.* Accessed Oct. 8, 2024, http://www.fao.org/3/a-a1497e.pdf.

a more sinister ideology: Adler, Jonathan H., "Duke Environmental Law and Policy Forum." Vol XXIII(253), Spring 2013.

brings ruin to all: Hardin, Garrett, "The Tragedy of the Commons," *Science*; Garrett Hardin, *Society*, December 13, 1968.

remove stones and gravel...or catch fish: Ridley, Matt, *The Origins of Virtue: Human Instincts and the Evolution of Cooperation*, Penguin, October 30, 1997.

informal fishing areas in the US and overseas: Ostrom, Elino, *Governing the Commons,* Cambridge University Press, October 2015.

broader range of benefits: Brinson, Ayeisha A., and Thunberg, Eric M., "Performance of federally managed catch share fisheries in the United States," *Fisheries Research*, 179, 213-223, July 2016.

reality is more subtle: Yandle, Tracy, and Crosson, Scott, "Whatever Happened to the Wreckfish Fishery? An Evaluation of the Oldest Finfish ITQ Program in the United States." *Marine Resource Economics* 30 (2): 193-217. April 2015.

wield excessive power: Tinning, Matt, "Rotten gets it wrong about New England and catch shares," Environmental Defense Fund. January 10, 2018.

community fishing infrastructure intact: "California Groundfish Project," Nature.org. Accessed October 4, 2024, https://www.nature.org/en-us/about-us/where-we-work/united-states/california/stories-in-california/california-groundfish-project.

economy and the consumer: Hauter, Wenonah, "Catch shares: A dangerous weapon in 'war' on environment," *The Hill*, June 16, 2011.

and then discard the rest: Sumaila, U. Rashid, "A Cautionary Note on Individual Transferable Quotas" *Ecology and Society*, 15(3): 36, 2010.

nutritious omega-3 fatty acids: Global Health Watch. *What is Omega-3, and how much do I need?* Accessed October 8, 2024, http://www.gb-healthwatch.com/Nutrient-Omega3-Overview.php.

negative social impacts: Sumaila, U. Rashid, "A Cautionary Note on Individual Transferable Quotas," *Ecology and Society*, 15(3): 36, 2010.

denigration of catch shares: Raines, Ben, "Kingpins of the Gulf make millions off red snapper harvest without ever going fishing," AL.com, January 24, 2016.

are entirely lease-dependent: Ropicki, Andrew, Willard, Daniel, and Larkin, Sherry L., "Proposed policy changes to the Gulf of Mexico red snapper IFQ program: Evaluating differential impacts by participant type," *Ocean and Coastal Management*, 152(1): 48-56, February 2018.

more lucrative positions: Abbott, Joshua, Garber-Yonts, Brian, and Wilen, James E., "Employment and remuneration effects of IFQs in the Bering Sea/Aleutian Islands crab fisheries," Arizona State University, 2010.

true kingpins of the Gulf: "How a rogue environmental group transformed American Fisheries." Alabama.com. October 5, 2016; Shuman, Brooke, and Mascorro, Anthony, "Our camera footage got raided, you won't believe why?" More Perfect Union, November 14, 2023; Van Der Voo, Lee, *The Fish Market* St. Martin's Press. 2016; Rust, Suzanne, "System turns US fishing rights into commodity, squeezes small fishermen." *Reveal.* March 12, 2013.

creating divisions within larger tribes: Johnson, Kirk, and Van Der Voo, Lee, "Spoils of the sea elude many in an Alaska antipoverty plan," *The New York Times.* June 19, 2013.

CHAPTER SEVEN | THE RENAISSANCE BEGINS

reinforcing efforts to fish clean: Dropkin, Alex, "The Gulf's Red Snapper fishery makes a comeback," *Texas Observer,* September 24, 2014.

available to them next year: Agar, Juan J., Stephen, Jessica A., Strelcheck, Andy, and Diagne, Assane, "The Gulf of Mexico Red Snapper IFQ Program: The First Five Years," *Marine Resource Economics,* 29(2): 177-198. June 2014.

economic value of the fishing industry: "Gulf of Mexico Reef Fish Shareholders Alliance," Shareholdersalliance.org. Accessed October 15, 2024, https://shareholdersalliance.org.

might also turn things around here: NOAA Fisheries. *Southeast.* Accessed October 8, 2024, http://sero.nmfs.noaa.gov/operations_management_ information_services/constituency_services_branch/freedom_of_information_act/common_foia/IFQShareholders.htm.

CHAPTER EIGHT | SPARKING INNOVATION

quarter-million square miles of the Northern Gulf: Donn, Jeff, and Weiss, Mitch, "Gulf awash in 27,000 abandoned wells," NBC News. July 7, 2010; Wray, Richard, "Abandoned oil wells make Gulf of Mexico environmental minefield," *The Guardian* July 7, 2010; Gewin, Virginia, "Is the United States ready for offshore aquaculture?" April 20, 2017.

voracious carnivore likes to eat: Schwartzkopf, Brittany D., Langland, Todd A., and Cowan, James H. Jr., "Habitat Selection Important for Red Snapper Feeding Ecology in the Northwestern Gulf of Mexico." *Marine and Coastal Fisheries,* 9(1): 373-387, 2017.

fish will leave the area: Lallo, Ed, "Rigs to Reef Builds Needed Habitat for Gulf Seafood." Gulf Seafood Foundation. Accessed October 5, 2024, http://gulfseafoodnews.com/2013/11/25/rigs-to-reefs-habitat-rigs-to-reef.

fish that breed in the Gulf: Dell' Amore, Christine, "Gulf Oil Spill 'Not Over': Dolphins, Turtles Dying in Record Numbers." *National Geographic.* April 9, 2014.

persistent volatile compounds: Major, D., Derbes, R. S., Wang, H., and Roy-Engel, A. M., "Effects of corexit oil dispersants and the WAF of dispersed oil on DNA damage and repair in cultured human bronchial airway cells, BEAS-2B." *Gene Rep.* 22-30, June 2016.

not yet been fully analyzed: Rader, Douglas N.,"Gulf spill reveals environmental blind spot." Austin American Statesman. April 10, 2011.

including on animal DNA: "Gulf spill oil dispersants associated with health symptoms in cleanup workers." National Institutes of Health. September 17, 2019; Khatchadourian, Raffi. "The Gulf War: Were there any heroes in the BP oil disaster?" *New Yorker.* March 14, 2011.

remained closed two years later: "Southeast Fisheries Management." NOAA Fisheries. Accessed October 5, 2024, http://sero.nmfs.noaa.gov/deepwater_horizon/closure_info/index.html.

hide from predators: Stiles, Margot L., Stockbridge, Julie, Lande, Michelle, and Hirshfield, Michael F., "Impacts of Bottom Trawling on Fisheries, Tourism, and the Marine Environment." Oceana. May 2010.

a complex set of risks: Kuriyamaa, Peter T., Branch, Trevor A., Bellman, Marlene A., Rutherford, Kate, "Catch shares have not led to catch-quota balancing in two North American multispecies travel fisheries," *Marine Policy*, 71, 60-70. September 2016.

unintentional killing of juvenile snapper: Gallaway, Benny J., Cole, John G., "Reduction of Juvenile Red Snapper Bycatch in the U.S. Gulf of Mexico Shrimp Trawl Fishery," *North American Journal of Fisheries Management*, 19(2): 342-355, January 8, 2011.

manage the content of their harvest: "Smart Catch." SmartCatch. Accessed October 5, 2024, https://smart-catch.com/about.

market segmentation or future trading: Monterey Bay Fisheries Trust. *California Farm Link - working to support the next generation of fishermen.* Accessed October 5, 2024; California Farm Link. *The Resilerator - A comprehensive 10 week course designed for farmers, ranchers, and fishers with 2+ years of experience.* Accessed October 8, 2024, https://www.californiafarmlink.org/courses/the-resilerator.

often farm-raised freshwater tilapia: Marko, Peter, "Facing an epidemic of mislabeled seafood," *Los Angeles Times*, December 8, 2014.

with EDF's scientific support: "Eurofins Analytical Laboratories, Inc - Central Analytical Laboratories." Eurofins. Accessed October 2024, https://www.eurofinsus.com/centralanalytical.

heavy metals, and dispersants: Fitzgerald, Tim, "Environmental Defense Fund Partners with Gulf Fishermen to launch Gulf Wild Seafood Assurance Program," Environmental Defense Fund. March 25, 2011.

and one hundred fishermen: Schwartz, Ariel, "Gulf Wild Cuts Down On Seafood Fraud By Tagging Fish." *Fast Company.* June 14, 2011.

the fish he could afford: Lallo, Ed, "A Gulf fisherman's looks don't always tell the whole story," Gulf Seafood Foundation. Accessed Oct. 8, 2024,

http://gulfseafoodnews.com/2013/11/30/gulf-fishermans-looks-dont-always-tell-whole-story.

any buyer to find my fish: Gulf Wild. *Transparensea.* Accessed October 15, 2024, https://gulfwild.com/Main/Programs/TransparenSea.

see where the fish was caught: "H-E-B Wild Caught Fresh Whole American Red Snapper." H-E-B.com. Accessed October 9, 2024, https://www.heb.com/product-detail/fish-market-whole-large-american-red-snapper/373324.

premium price for his product: Schwartz, Ariel, "Gulf wild cuts down on seafood fraud by tagging fish," *Fast Company,* June 14, 2011.

CHAPTER NINE | AT SEA ADAPTATION

excess carbon sinks into the sea: Wilson, Lindsay, "Global carbon emissions and sinks since 1750." Shrink that footprint.com. Accessed October 9, 2024, http://shrinkthatfootprint.com/carbon-emissions-and-sinks.

global average: National Centers for Environmental Information. *The Gulf of Mexico is getting warmer: New study quantifies 50 - warming trend.* Accessed October 5, 2024, https://www.ncei.noaa.gov/news/gulf-mexico-getting-warmer; Kearby, Ric, "Gulf of Mexico has reached alarmingly high temperatures," Climate Adaption Center, Aug. 23, 2024.

reach as high as 90°F: "Gulf of Mexico water temperature." SeaTemperature.org. Accessed October 5, 2024, https://www.seatemperature.org/north-america/united-states/gulf-mexico-temp.htm; Furness, Dyllan, "Estuaries in South Florida are warming faster than the Gulf of Mexico and global ocean." USF College of Marine Science. August 7, 2024.

linked to stronger hurricanes: Niiler, Eric, "How climate change fueled hurricane harvey." *Wired.* August 29, 2017.

single deadliest weather event: Little, Becky. "How the Galveston hurricane of 1900 became the deadliest US natural disaster," History.com. Accessed Oct. 2014, https://www.history.com/articles/how-the-galveston-hurricane-of-1900-became-the-deadliest-u-s-natural-disaster

any other US coastal city: Union of Concerned Scientists. *Infographic: Sea Level Rise and Global Warming.* April 2013.

Combined with rising tides: "Sea Level Rise Viewer." NOAA Fisheries. Accessed October 5, 2024, https://coast.noaa.gov/slr.

nurseries vital for ocean life: Glamore, W. C., Rayner, D. S., and Rahman, P. F., "Estuaries and climate change," Water Research Laboratory, University of New South Wales, .

increasing erosion and run-off: Kistner, Rocky, "There's An Environmental Disaster Unfolding In The Gulf of Mexico," *Huffington Post.* July 11, 2019.

spawn the next generation: NOAA. *Gulf of Mexico 'dead zone' is the largest ever measured.* August 2, 2017.

must learn to adapt: Fujita, Rod, "At the Brink: Ocean Tipping Points." Environmental Defense Fund. March 6, 2015

made to other fishermen: Etheridge, Lindsey, "Consolidating the BP Oil Spill Litigation." 9: 3 SandBar 7. August 2010.

those little herbivores do: Lancaster University. *Fish lightly to keep snapper on the reef.* January 12, 2017; Nicholas A. J. et al. "Human disruption of coral reef trophic structure," *Current Biology*, 27 (2): 231-36. January 23, 2017.

ravages of a more acidic sea: Wright, Pam, "Ocean acidification threatens Alaska's Red King Crab." November 7, 2017.

to have a healthy reef fishery: Waters, Donald. A., "Hearing on the Environmental and Economic Impacts of Ocean Acidification." Statement to Congressional Subcommittee on Oceans, Atmosphere, Fisheries and Coast Guard. April 22, 2010.

CHAPTER TEN | MARITIME MITIGATION

half a ton of fuel: Tyedmers, Peter H., Watson, Reg., and Pauly, Daniel, "Fueling Global Fishing Fleets." *Ambio, A Journal of the Human Environment*, 34(8): 636-37. December 2005.

by 2006: US Energy Information Administration. *Diesel fuel retail price falls below $2.00 per gallon for first time since 2005.* February 17, 2016.

per pound of fish landed grew six-fold: Mitchell, C., Cleveland, J., "Resource scarcity, energy use and environmental impact: A case study of the New Bedford Massachusetts USA Fisheries," *Environmental Management*, Vol. 17:3. May 1993,

as much fuel per fish: Gardiner, Peter, Virdin, John, and Van Santen, Gert, "Saving fish and fisheries: towards sustainable and equitable governance of the global fishing sector." World Bank Group. May 1, 2004.

more diesel and more power: World Bank Group. *Global Fisheries Sunken Billions.* February 14, 2017.

deterioration of aquatic ecosystems: Dean, Cornelia, "Fishing Industry's Fuel Efficiency Gets Worse as Ocean Stocks Get Thinner," *The New York Times.* December 20, 2005 *return to small, artisanal fishing:* Tyedmers, Peter H., Watson, Reg., and Pauly, Daniel, "Fueling Global Fishing Fleets," *Ambio, A Journal of the Human Environment*, 34(8): 636-37. December 2005.

per unit of fish as traps: European Commision. *Energy Efficiency for Fisheries.* Accessed October 15, 2024, https://sustainable-fisheries.ec.europa.eu/socio-and-economic-analysis/studies/energy-efficiency_en.

larger, more powerful fleets: Jacquet, Jennifer, and Pauly, Daniel, "Funding Priorities: Big Barriers to Small-Scale Fisheries." *Conservation Biology* 22(4):832-35. 2008; Cavraro, Francesco, Anelli Monti, Marco, Caccin, Alberto, et al. "Is the small scale fishery more sustainable in terms of GHG emissions? A case study analysis from the Central Mediterranean Sea." *Marine Policy*, 148. February 2023.

sixty-four dollars a barrel, they ate up half: Muir, James F., "Fuel and energy use in the fisheries sector," FAO Circular. 2015.

to fill up: Davie, Sarah, Minto, Coilin, Officer, Rick, Lordan, Colm., and Jackson, Emmet, "Modeling fuel consumption of fishing vessels for predictive use," *ICES J. of Marine Science*, 72(2): 708-719, Jan./Feb. 2015.

as the entire aviation industry: National Geographic Pristine Seas, "Team uncovers new marine source of carbon emissions into atmosphere." Phys Org. January 18, 2024; Atwood, Trisha B., Romanou, Anastasia, DeVries, Tim, et al. "Atmospheric CO2 emissions and ocean acidification from bottom-trawling." Frontiers in Marine Science 10, 2023; Sala, E., Mayorga, J., Bradley, D., et al. "Protecting the global ocean for biodiversity, food and climate," *Nature*, 592: 397–402, 2021.

nations are racing to catch up: Heine, Hilda, and Figueres, Christiana, "Polluters on the High Seas," *The New York Times.* April 6, 2018.

more and more energy-inefficient: Dean, Cornelia, "Fishing industry's fuel efficiency gets worse as ocean stocks get thinner," *The New York Times*, December 20, 2005.

country added thirty million people: "Tanzania alarm over expected population boom," *The East African*, January 1, 2013.

countries subsidize fuel for fishing: Bradsher, Keith, "Fuel Subsidies Overseas Take a Toll on US," *The New York Times.* July 28, 2008.

inflicting long-term damage: Moerenhout, Tom, "Support for fuel consumption for fisheries." IISD. December 19, 2019; "Fisheries subsidies agreement: What's the big deal?" PEW. May 10, 2023; "A shameful failure to tackle overfishing." *The Economist.* December 19, 2017.

financial support for fossil fuel: Mason, Jeff, and Ennis, Darren, "G20 agrees on phase-out of fossil fuel subsidies despite climate crisis." *Reuters*. September 26, 2009.

increased subsidies: Koop, Fermin, "G20 stalls on fossil fuel subsidies despite calls for climate action," Dialogue Earth, June 28, 2019.

0.1 pound of carbon to one pound of wild pollock: Corbeley, Andy, "This Beloved Alaskan Fish has the Lowest Carbon Footprint of Any Major Protein in the World," Good News Network. July 28, 2021.

less carbon per pound of protein than tofu: Tyedmers, Peter H., Watson, Reg., and Pauly, Daniel, "Fueling Global Fishing Fleets." *Ambio, A Journal of the Human Environment*, 34(8): 636-37. December 2005.

reduce spending to fatten profits: Juarez, Alexia, "How a community based fishery program is bringing sustainability to Mexico's Upper Gulf of California." Environmental Defense Fund. April 20, 2021.

recharged by hydropower or the sun: Jackson, Lisa, "Net zero heroes: Hybrid and electric commercial fishing vessels set out to cut the industry's carbon emissions," Global Seafood Alliance, December 22, 2022.

CHAPTER ELEVEN | FEDERAL COHESION

possibilities for more such programs: "International Affairs." NOAA Fisheries. Accessed October 5, 2024, http://www.nmfs.noaa.gov/ia/slider_stories/2016/03/msa_amended_2007_.pdf; "Fact Sheet: Magnuson-Stevens Fishery Conservation and Management Reauthorization Act." White House Archives. January 12, 2007.

jobs up and down the coasts: "Status of the Stocks: Record-Low Number of Stocks On Overfishing List In 2023." NOAA Fisheries. May 02, 2024.

were just an "ownership fetish.": Bromley, Daniel, "Abdicating responsibility: the deceits of fisheries policy." *Fisheries magazine*, 34(4), 2009.

slow, stop, and even reverse overfishing: Costello, C., Gaines, S., and Lynham, J., "Can Catch Shares Prevent Fisheries Collapse?" *Science*, 321(5896): 1678-1681. September 19, 2008.

fixer-upper: Foulsham, George,"New study to UCSB, Hawaii scientists offer solution to global fisheries collapse." *The Current*. September 18, 2008.

governance structures: "Working group, matching property rights institutions with fishery characteristics." NCEAS. January 2007.

comprehensive national ocean policy: "Catch Shares." NOAA Fisheries. Accessed October 15, 2024, https://www.fisheries.noaa.gov/national/sustainable-fisheries/catch-shares.

thorny questions: "United States Fisheries Policy." Resources. July 20, 2015.

Councils over representation: Okey, Thomas A., "Membership of the eight Regional Fishery Management Councils in the United States: are special interests over-represented?" *Marine Policy*, 27(3): 193–206. May 2003.

rank: Rogalski, William R., "The Unique Federalism of the Regional Councils Under the Fishery Conservation and Management Act of 1976," Hein Online, 1976.

performance: Eagle, Josh, Newkirk, Sarah, and Thompson, Barton, *Taking Stock: Of The Regional Fishery Management Councils (Pew Ocean Science Series) 2nd Edition*, Island Press, November 2003.

and priorities: Rosenberg, Andrew A., Swasey, Jill H., and Bowman, Margaret, "Rebuilding US Fisheries: Progress and Problems," *Frontiers in Ecology and the Environment*, 4(6): 303-308. August 2006.

falsified quotas, and deliberate mislabeling: "Recap of the Carlos Rafael case." *The Standard-Times/South Coast Today.* Accessed October 18, 2024, https://www.southcoasttoday.com/story/news/2017/09/25/recap-carlos-rafael-case/17269130007.

I'm scared to death: Russel, Jenna, "Last of their Kind," *The Boston Globe*, June 16, 2013.

their famously bitter rivalry: Ferling, John. *Jefferson and Hamilton: The Rivalry That Forged a Nation*, Bloomsbury Press, January 2014.

given an unrestricted commercial environment: Kulrlansky, Mark. Cod: *A biography of the fish that changed the world.* Vintage. May 6, 1999.

fishermen destroyed: Jefferson, Thomas, ed. Boyd, Julian P., *The Papers of Thomas Jefferson*, Princeton University Press, 1974.

nursery of seamen and a source of naval power: "Editorial Note: Report on the Fisheries." *Founders Online.* National Archives. Cited: The Papers of Thomas Jefferson, 19(24): 140-172. January–31 March 1791, ed. Boyd, Julian. P. Princeton University Press.

build more ships: Dahl, Darren, "Why The Founding Fathers Believed In Broad-Based Employee Ownership." *Forbes.* Feb. 1, 2017.

from the fishery's overall productivity: Michie, Jonathan, Blasi, Joseph R., Borzaga, Carlo, *The Oxford Handbook of Mutual and Co-Owned Business*, Chapter 8.1, p 114, OUP Oxford, March 30, 2017.

code guiding all fishing fleets: Acheson, James M., "Anthropology of Fishing." *Annual Review of Anthropology*, 10, 275-316. 1981.

performance depended on shared incentives: Blasi, Joseph, R. Freeman and D. Kruse, *The Citizen's Share: Reducing Inequality in the 21st Century,* Yale University Press, New Haven, 2014

cod populations in the Gulf of Maine since 1980: Zielinski, Sarah, "Why Smarter Fishing Practices Aren't Saving Maine Cod From Collapse, " *Smithsonian,* October 29, 2015

had nothing left to catch: Steele, D. H., Andersen, R., and Green, J. M., "The Managed Commercial Annihilation of Northern Cod." *Newfoundland & Labrador Studies,* 8(1): 34-68. 1992.

to best meet local needs: "NOAA Policy Encourages Catch Shares to End Overfishing and Rebuild Fisheries." NOAA Research. November 4, 2010.

swayed by her ties to EDF: Gaines, Richard, "Distorting Catch Share Criticism." Gloucester Daily Times. September 8, 2009; Mass. fishing activist vows new petition on catch shares." *Bangor Daily News.* Nov. 24, 2011.

CHAPTER TWELVE | SCIENTIFIC CREDIBILITY

comprehensive, ecosystem-based framework: Office of Press Secretary, White House, "National Policy of the Oceans, Our Coasts and the Great Lakes." June 12, 2009.

science to underpin those decisions: "Executive Directors Report." Council Coordination Comm. Meeting, Boston, Mass. May 19, 2009.

swimming around out there: "Glossary: Measuring the effects of catch shares." Measuring the effects of catch shares. Accessed October 15, 2024, http://www.catchshareindicators.org/glossary.

compromised due to "industry capture": "Interview with Daniel Pauly: The Present and the Future of World and US Fisheries." American Fisheries Society. July 13, 2015.

at least for his state constituents: Rainer, David, "Alabama Marine Resources Director Makes Point With "Show and Tell" Red Snapper Event." *The Outdoor Wire,* Aug 31, 2015.

conditions for harvested species: Clements, Katherine M., "Fish don't wear watches but their ears tell their tales: Unveiling age through otoliths." The Log. June 12, 2024; Zhang, Sarah, "Fish-ear bones offer clues to health of ocean, species." *The Seattle Times.* July 21, 2013.

experiment with new electronic technologies: "Southeast Fisheries Science Center Facilities." NOAA Fisheries. Accessed October 7, 2024, http://www.galvestonlab.sefsc.noaa.gov/stories/2017/Foster/index.html.

Fisheries Research, in 2017: "Southeast Fisheries Science Center Facilities." NOAA Fisheries. Accessed October 7, 2024, http://www.galvestonlab.sefsc.noaa.gov/publications/pdf/979.pdf.

collapse of the Pacific sardine fishery: "West Coast South West Science." NOAA Fisheries. Accessed October 7, 2024, https://swfsc.noaa.gov/publications/CR/1990/9067.PDF.

have been off-limits to fishing: Guy, Allyson, "Can this California fisherman build the perfect net?" April 26, 2017.

beginning of something huge: LaScala-Gruenewald, Diana, "Monterey Fisherman Develops New, Eco-Friendly Trawl Gear." *Monterey County Now*, Aug 22, 2013.

CHAPTER THIRTEEN | SMART BOAT TRANSPARENCY

Despite strict confidentiality requirements: "Enforcement." NOAA Fisheries. Accessed October 7, 2024, http://www.nmfs.noaa.gov/ole/about/our_programs/vessel_monitoring.html.

VMS rules were clarified: The Federal Register. *Vessel Monitoring Systems; Approved Mobile Transmitting Units and Communications Service Providers for Use in the Fisheries of the Western and Central Pacific.* Accessed October 4, 2024, https://www.federalregister.gov/documents/2010/10/15/2010-26071/vessel-monitoring-systems-approved-mobile-transmitting-units-and-communications-service-providers.

most electronically monitored fishing nation: Aloysius, T. M., Van Helmond, Lars O., Mortensen, Kristian S., et al. "Electronic monitoring in fisheries: Lessons from global experiences and future opportunities." EM4FISH. November 2019; "The Governance of Electronic Monitoring (EM) Systems for Industrial Tuna Fisheries." WWF. August 16, 2024; "Electronic Monitoring: A Key Tool for Global Fisheries." Pew. Sep. 20, 2019.

mapping system shared by the fleet: "California Groundfish Project." The Nature Conservancy. Accessed October 7, 2024, https://www.nature.org/en-us/about-us/where-we-work/united-states/california/stories-in-california/california-groundfish-project; "Partnership Preserves Livelihoods and Fish Stocks," *The New York Times*. November 27, 2011.

monitor nearshore seafood harvesting: "Wildlife Conservation Society Helps Safeguard Belize's Barrier Reef with Conservation Drones." Wildlife Conservation Society. July 22, 2014.

assess average catches per vessel: "SmartPass: Oregon Using Cameras, Artificial Intelligence To Capture Fisheries Effort To Improve Management." Columbia Basin Bulletin. February 26, 2021; "Smart Pass White Paper." Environmental Defense Fund. Accessed October 7, 2024, https://fisherysolutionscenter.edf.org/resources/smartpass-white-paper.

national fisheries monitoring programs: "Revolutionizing Ocean Monitoring and Analysis." Global Fishing Watch. Accessed October 4, 2024, http://globalfishingwatch.org; "Six pilot projects making fishing more sustainable." Environmental Defense Fund. Accessed October 4, 2024, https://www.edf.org/oceans/these-six-pilot-projects-are-making-fishing-more-sustainable.

tracking devices, and fishing licenses: "OceanMind." *OceanMind.* Accessed October 15, 2024, https://www.oceanmind.global.

about 20,000 years: "National Observer Program FY 2012 Annual Report." National Marine Fisheries Service. March 2013; Skalley, Courtney. "Fisheries Observer in the Bering Sea: A day in the life." Washington School of Marine and Environmental Affairs. November 29, 2023; "NOAA Fisheries Announces Preliminary 2024 At-Sea Monitoring Coverage Target for Groundfish Sector Fishery." NOAA Fisheries. February 20, 2024.

smart boat" technology: "Smart Boats and Networked Fisheries." Environmental Defense Fund. Accessed October 7, 2024, https://www.edf.org/sites/default/files/documents/SmartBoatVision.March2019.web_.pdf.

protect vital, teeming, ocean conservancies: "Commercial Vessel Monitoring Systems for Gulf Reef Fish." NOAA Fisheries. Accessed October 15, 2024, https://www.fisheries.noaa.gov/southeast/sustainable-fisheries/commercial-vessel-monitoring-systems-vms-gulf-reef-fish.

CHAPTER FOURTEEN | BOTTOM-UP CONSERVANCIES

his Hawaiian bodysurfing childhood: Yong, Ed, "Obama: The Ocean President," *The Atlantic*, January 2017.

executive overreach: Lazo, Alejandro, "Obama Heralds Creation of World's Largest Marine Reserve off Hawaii," *The Wall Street Journal*, September 1, 2016.

massive scale of his efforts: Goad, Jessica, and Goldfuss, Christy, "President Obama Needs to Establish a Conservation Legacy in Addition to a Drilling Legacy," Cap20, January 10, 2013.

new marine sanctuaries: Harvey, Chelsea, "Obama just announced the first new marine sanctuaries in 15 years," *Washington Post*, October 5, 2015.

marine monuments: Vasilogambros, Matt, "The Atlantic Ocean's First National Monument," *The Atlantic*, Sept 15, 2016.

waters under federal protection: Hirschfeld-Davis, Julie, "Obama Creates Atlantic Ocean's First Marine Monument," *The New York Times*, September 15, 2016.

a fourteen-thousand-fold increase: Marine Protected Areas of the US. *Benefits of a national system of marine protected areas.* Accessed October 7, 2024, https://dlnr.hawaii.gov/dar/files/2014/04/MPApub.pdf.

excessive "commercial pressure": Waghorn, Terry, "Can we eat our fish and protect them too?" *Forbes*, February 21, 2012.

any living or nonliving marine resource: Lubchenco, Jane *et al.*, "Plugging a hole in the ocean: The emerging science of marine reserves," *Ecological Applications*, 13(1): S3–S7, 2003.

increase by half to "30 by 2030": Kareiva, Peter, "Conservation Biology: Beyond Marine Protected Areas," *Current Biology,* 16 (14), July 2006; Marine Conservation Institute. *World Resoundingly Agrees to Protect 30% of the Planet by 2030, Now Comes the Hard Part.* December 21, 2022; Gibbens, Sarah, "Biden Commits to Ambitious 30x30 Conservation Target," *National Geographic*, January 27, 2021.

blanket 16 percent of the planet's surface: "October 2023 update of the WDPA and WD-OECM," Protected Planet, October 5, 2023.

such as fishing and mining: International Union for Conservation of Nature. *Marine Protected Areas and Climate Change: Issue Brief.* 2017; Marine Conservation Society. *Marine Protection Atlas.* Accessed October 21, 2024, https://mpatlas.org/mpaguide/#-8.44669,24.14891@0.82.

conservation refugees: Dowie, Mark, *Conservation Refugees: The Hundred-Year Conflict between Global Conservation and Native Peoples*, MIT Press, 2009.

under some form of MPAs: Fujita, Rod, "The business of marine reserves: Achieving financially sustainable ocean conservation," Environmental Defense Fund, May 1, 2013.

spawning aggregation sites: NOAA Fisheries. *Gulf of Mexico seasonal and/or area closures and marine protected areas.* Accessed October 18, 2024, https://www.fisheries.noaa.gov/resource/map/gulf-mexico-seasonal-and-or-area-closures-and-marine-protected-areas-0.

Buddy's prime fishing grounds: Pendleton, Linwood, Crowder, Larry, Dunn, Daniel, *et al.*, "Marine Protection in the Gulf of Mexico. Current Policy, Future Options, and Ecosystem Outcomes," Duke Nicholas Institute, October 2010.

Hope Spots: YaleEnvironment interviews Sylvia Earle. "A Blueprint for Restoring the World's Oceans," Yale Environment 360, October 12, 2009.

whales, rays, sharks, sea turtles: "NOAA proposes expanded Flower Garden Banks National Marine Sanctuary," *Offshore*, June 10, 2016.

would restrict his fishing freedom: NOAA. *DEIS for sanctuary expansion.* Accessed October 16, 2024, http://flowergarden.noaa.gov/management/expansiondeis.html.

networks linked by fish migration corridors: Roberts, Callum. M., O'Leary, Bethan. C., McCauley, Douglas. J. *et al.* "Marine reserves can mitigate and promote adaptation to climate change." *Environmental Sciences*, 114(24): 6167-6175. June 5, 2017.

marine mammal, reptile, and fish species: Ford, Matt, "The world's biggest marine refuge: 442,000 square miles, 7,000 species, 5 sunken aircraft carriers," *The Atlantic*, August 26, 2016.

east of the Falklands: "Protected Planet," Protected Planet. Accessed October 2024, http://www.protectedplanet.net.

size of two Texases: New Zealand Ministry of Foreign Affairs and Trade. *Ross Sea region marine protected area.* Accessed October 18, 2024, https://www.mfat.govt.nz/en/environment/antarctica-and-the-southern-ocean/ross-sea-region-marine-protected-area.

no-take reserve: Service, Shannon, "Palau's plans to ban commercial fishing could set precedent for tuna industry," *The Guardian*, March 26, 2014.

10 percent of the ocean: "WCS Community Fisheries Program," Wildlife Conservation Society. Accessed October 4, 2024, https://www.wcs.org/our-work/solutions/oceans-and-fisheries; "Only Four Percent of the Ocean is protected, Research Shows," *Science Daily*, October 26, 2015.

has no extractive activities: "Marine Protected Areas," Marine Protected Areas. Accessed October 4, 2024; Davis, John, "Why we should be optimistic about the future of MPA finance: Interview with Amílcar Guzmán Valladares and Viviana Luján Gallegos of Wolfs Company," Open Communications for the Ocean, March 11, 2021.

marine life would increase rapidly": Dreifus, Claudia, "In half earth, E. O. Wilson calls for a grand retreat," *The New York Times.* Feb. 29, 2016.

the next five years: Einhorn, Catrin, "US plan to protect oceans has a problem, some say: too much fishing," *The New York Times*, April 30, 2024.

reef fishermen found that in two: Nowak, Rachel, "Barrier Reef 'no take ' zones see leap in fish numbers," *New Scientist*, June 23, 2008.

interest from no-fishing areas: North Carolina State University. *Applied Ecology*. Accessed October 7, 2024, https://appliedecology.cals.ncsu. edu/absci/wp-content/uploads/Review-of-the-Benefits-of-No-Take-Zones_Final.pdf.

do away with trawl fishing altogether: Oceana. *Safeguarding Sensitive Seafloor Habitats*. Accessed October 4, 2024, https://usa.oceana.org/ our-campaigns/essential_fish_habitat/campaign; "Oceana calls for Spanish trawling ban," *World Fishing & Aquaculture*, August 13, 2014.

It really got confusing: Barcott, Bruce, The Unfulfilled Promise of the World's Marine Protected Areas" Yale Environment 360, June 16, 2011.

fences off 8.5 percent of its waters: Rising, James, Heal, Geoffrey, "Global benefits of marine protected areas," National Bureau of Economic Research, March 2014.

benefits of any spillover: Milman, Oliver, "Most protected marine areas fail to properly guard aquatic life: study" *The Guardian*, February 6, 2014.

MPAs never exist in a vacuum: Christie, Patrick, "Marine Protected Areas as Biological Successes and Social Failures in Southeast Asia," American Fisheries Society Symposium, 42:155–164, 2004

have fallen short of their goals: Coleman, Felicia, Baker, Pamela, and Koenig, Christopher, "A Review of Gulf of Mexico Marine Protected Areas: Successes, Failures, and Lessons Learned," *Fisheries*, 29(2): 10-21, January 9, 2011.

protection for exploited species: Coleman, Felicia, Baker, Pamela, and Koenig, Christopher, "A review of Gulf of Mexico Marine Protected Areas: Successes, Failures, and Lessons Learned," *Fisheries*, 29(2): 10-21, January 9, 2011.

size alone matters little: Edgar, G., Stuart-Smith, R., Willis, T. *et al.*, "Global conservation outcomes depend on marine protected areas with five key features," *Nature*, 506, 216–220, February 5, 2014.

net negative impact on the sea: Hilborn, R., "Policy: Marine biodiversity needs more than protection," *Nature*, 535, 224–226, July 13, 2016.

showed up in her nets: NOAA Fisheries. *West Coast Groundfish*. Accessed October 7, 2024, http://www.westcoast.fisheries.noaa.gov/fisheries/ groundfish_catch_shares.

depleted species declared rebuilt: Bernton, Hal, "Two rockfish species make a comeback as conservation limits pay off," *The Seattle Times*, June 24, 2017; Jud, Shems, "Two more rockfish species declared 're-built,'" Environmental Defense Fund, July 13, 2017.

deep-water area the size of Norway: Schmalz, David, "Collaboration between Fishermen and Environmental Groups Results in a Win-Win for Everyone," Monterey Bay Fisheries Trust, May 2, 2018; Jud, Shems, "EDF and fishermen help secure 140,000 square miles of new ocean protections," Environmental Defense Fund, April 10, 2018; Shems, Jud, "West coast fishermen are having their fish and protecting habitat too," Environmental Defense Fund, April 13, 2018.

would have taken months to zone: Dooley, Bob, "Voices from the waterfront," NOAA Fisheries, December 3, 2012.

territorial use right for fishing, or TURF: Afflerbach, Jamie, Lester, Sarah, Dougherty, Dawn, and Poon, Sarah, "A global survey of "TURF-reserves," *Global Ecology and Conservation* 2, 97-106, December 2014.

called a TURF-reserve: Rife, Alexis, "Community based fishery management delivers individual and collective benefits in Belize," Environmental Defense Fund, April 18, 2014.

they are now expanding: Environmental Defense Fund. *Environmental Defense Fund Solutions* 44(3). 2013.

support of conservation groups like Rare: Environmental Defense Fund Oceans. *Cabinet of Belize approves catch shares in Belize's network of marine protected areas.* December 13, 2010.

these sacred, off-limits reserves: CRISP. *Aleipata marine protected area management plan.* January 2008.

highly replicable and scalable approach: Bernstein, Lenny, "Well funded program tries new approach to tackle overfishing in developing world," *The Washington Post*, February 23, 2014.

partners in ocean protection: Christian, Bonnie, "Fishermen and conservationists work together to improve Californian fisheries," *Huffington Post*, December 7, 2017.

Oceans Policy executive order: Malakoff, David, "Trump's new oceans policy washes away Obama's emphasis on conservation and climate," *Science*, June 19, 2018.

CHAPTER FIFTEEN | A SHARED DOMINION

seven million pounds: NOAA Fisheries. *NOAA announces the 2018 Gulf of*

Mexico red snapper recreational seasons and clarifies permit regula-tions for vessels fishing in federal waters. April 18, 2018.

pastimes endures for future generations: Lubchenco, Jane, "American Sportfishing Association 2009 Summit," October 27, 2009.

exert influence on their behalf: "American Saltwater Guides Association," American Saltwater Guides Association. Accessed October 16, 2024, https://www.saltwaterguidesassociation.com; US Fish and Wildlife Service. *2022 National Survey of Fishing, Hunting and Wildlife-Asso-ciated Recreation.* Accessed October 18, 2024, https://www.fws.gov/sites/default/files/documents/Final_2022-National-Survey_101223-ac-cessible-single-page.pdf.

against their commercial counterparts: Carter, Alexandra, and Conathan, Michael, "The rise of the recreational fishing lobby," Cap20. March 19, 2018.

making money off of a public resource: Yeoman, Barry, "The Gulf War: The Battle Over Gulf Red Snapper," *Texas Monthly*, June 2016.

hardening into place after 1990: Cowan, J.H., Grimes, C.B., Patterson, W.F. et al. "Red snapper management in the Gulf of Mexico: science-or faith-based?" *Rev Fish Biol Fisheries*, 21, 187–204, June 2011.

49 percent to recreational interests: Gulf of Mexico Fishery Management Council. *Reef fish amendment 28 red snapper allocation and recre-ational accountability measures.* May 16, 2014.

three distinct sets of rules and fees: NOAA Fisheries. *History of man-agement of Gulf of Mexico Red Snapper.* Accessed October 16, 2024, https://www.fisheries.noaa.gov/southeast/sustainable-fisheries/histo-ry-management-gulf-mexico-red-snapper.

openly acknowledged that agenda: Conery, Rob, "The Gamefish Debate," *On The Water*, July 27, 2016.

gift them to anglers instead: Southwick Associates for the American Sport-fishing Association. *The Economic Gains from Reallocating Specific Saltwater Fisheries.* May 12, 2015.

$68 billion in sales and 472,000 jobs: NOAA. *Economic impact of U.S. commercial, recreational fishing remains strong.* December 13, 2018.

versus a few hundred commercial rigs: American Sportfishing Associa-tion. *NMMA releases 2010 US recreational boat registration statistics report.* October 3, 2011.

thousands of public and private docks: American Sportfishing Associa-tion. Economic Contributions of Recreational Fishing By US States and Congressional Districts Released. March 8, 2023; "By the numbers: Recreational fishing in the US," *Coastal Angler & The Angler Magazine*, March 23, 2023; "It's official: Gulf of Mexico states take the helm of private recreational red snapper seasons," HuntingLife.com, February 10, 2020; NOAA. *Establish a Vermillion Snapper MSY proxy and adjust the stock annual catch limit.* July 2017.

150,000 tons of fish from the water: "Recreational Fishing Data" NOAA Fisheries. Accessed October 4, 2024, https://www.fisheries.noaa.gov/topic/recreational-fishing-data; "New report of the economic contributions by recreational fishing released." The Billfish Foundation. March 13, 2023.

more accurate, credible, and timely data: "Recreational electronic reporting at a glance." NOAA Fisheries. Accessed October 7, 2024, https://www.fisheries.noaa.gov/recreational-fishing-data/recreational-electronic-reporting-glance; Lubchenco, Jane. "American Sportfishing Association 2009 Summit." October 27, 2009.

weeks or as it turned out, days: Binns, Holly. "New Rules for Gulf of Mexico Red Snapper Can Bolster Recovery." Pew Charitable Trusts. August 28, 2019.

huge losses through dead discards: "Fishery Bulletin." NOAA Fisheries. Accessed October 7, 2024, https://www.st.nmfs.noaa.gov/spo/FishBull/1124/campbell.pdf.

chance she dies an unrecorded death: Thompson, Melissa, Van Wassenbergh, Sarah, Rogers, Sean, Seamone, Scott, and Higham, Timothy, "Angling-induced injuries have a negative impact on suction feeding performance and hydrodynamics in marine shiner perch, Cymatogaster aggregata," *Journal of Experimental Biology*, 221(19) October 9, 2018.

and what happened to them: Coleman, Felicia, Figueira, Will, Ueland, Jeffrey, and Crowder, Larry, "The Impact of United States Recreational Fisheries on Marine Fish Populations," *Science* 305(5692): 1958-1960, September 24, 2004; Bartholomew, A., and Bohnsack, J. A., "A Review of Catch-and-Release Angling Mortality with Implications for No-take Reserves," *Rev Fish Biol Fisheries* 15, 129–154 (2005).

pared it to just seventy-two hours: Golden, Devin, "Federal gulf red snapper season set for three days," *Sport Fishing*, May 3, 2017.

25 percent more than their limit: Bren School of Management. *The Snapper Saga: An Assessment of Sector Separation on the Gulf of Mexico Recreational Red Snapper.* March 22, 2013.

in a twenty-eight-day derby: Committee on Oversight and Accountability. *Examining the management of Red Snapper fishing in the Gulf of Mexico.* May 2017; Horn, Miriam, *Rancher Farmer Fisherman,* pp 281-82, W. W. Norton and Company, October 2016.

67 percent over limit: Diagne, Assane, Crabtree, Roy, and Hood, Peter, "Final framework action to the fishery management plan for the reef fish resources of the Gulf of Mexico," NOAA. 2015.

achieved by commercial sector reforms: "Southeast," NOAA Fisheries. Accessed October 7, 2024, http://sero.nmfs.noaa.gov/sustainable_fisheries/gulf_fisheries/reef_fish/2013/am28/documents/pdfs/gulf_reef_am28_feis.pdf.

to keep fresh, local seafood on the menu: "Seafood Harvesters of America," Seafood Harvesters of America. Accessed October 7, 2024, http://www.seafoodharvesters.org.

That one, he won: Environmental Defense Fund. *Federal court rules gulf recreational red snapper management broken.* March 27, 2014.

ordered NOAA to develop a better plan: "Court rules gulf red snapper management illegal, lack of accountability in recreational sector cited as harmful to all," Alabama.com, April 7, 2014.

Florida Congressman Steve Southerland: Tinning, Matt, "Out with the tide: Lessons from Steve Southerland's shock electoral defeat," Environmental Defense Fund, November 5, 2014.

supported by research across the US and Europe: Lewin, W. C., Arlinghaus, R., and Mehner T., "Documented and potential biological impacts of recreational fishing: insights for management and conservation," *Reviews in Fisheries Science,* 14, 305-367, January 18, 2007; Ferter K., Weltersbach, M. S., Strehlow, H. V., *et al.,* "Unexpectedly high catch-and-release rates in European marine recreational fisheries: implications for science and management," *ICES Journal of Marine Science,* 70, 1319-1329, July 21, 2013; Eero, Margit, Strehlow, Harry, Adams, Charles, and Vinther, Morten, "Does recreational catch impact the TAC for commercial fisheries?" *ICES Journal of Marine Science,* 72 (2): 450–457, January 2015.

effects of catch-and-release fishing: Eurekalert. *Study in Science reveals recreational fishing takes a big bite of ocean catch.* August 26, 2024.

to avoid responsibility: "Charter Fisherman's Association," Charter Fisherman's Association. Accessed October 16, 2024, http://joincfa.org.

Fishing Permit Pilot Program: NOAA. *Headboat Collaborative Pilot*

Program Final Report. March 7, 2018; South Atlantic Fishery Management Council. *For-Hire Limited Access for the Snapper Grouper, Coastal Migratory Pelagics, and Dolphin Wahoo Fisheries in the Atlantic.* June 2024.

profits for the recreational fishing sector: Abbott, Joshua, and Willard, Daniel, "Rights-based management for recreational for-hire fisheries," *Fisheries Research*, 196, 106-116, December 2017.

$139 per year of benefits per angler: Abbott, Joshua K., Lloyd-Smith, Patrick, Willard, Daniel, and Adamowicz, Wiktor, "Status-quo management of marine recreational fisheries undermines angler welfare," Proceedings of the National Academy of Sciences, August 20, 2018.

dollars spent on the fishing trip: "iSnapper FAQ," Sportfish Center. Accessed October 16, 2024, https://www.sportfishcenter.org/isnapper/faqs.

data from traditional federal and state programs: Fishing Data Innovation Taskforce. *Improving Net Gains: Data-Driven Innovation for America's Fishing Future.* Page 4, 2017.

And these apps proliferate: "Recreational Electronic Reporting At a Glance" NOAA Fisheries. Accessed October 5, 2024, https://www.fisheries.noaa.gov/recreational-fishing-data/recreational-electronic-reporting-glance.

given location, species, or type of angling: South Atlantic Fishery Management Council. *Seminar series: Electronic self reporting in recreational fisheries.* May 14, 2024.

smartphone apps as a feedback tool: Venturelli, Paul, Hyder, Keiran, and Skov, Christian, "Angler apps as a source of recreational fisheries data: Opportunities, challenges and proposed standards," *Fish and Fisheries* 18 (3): 578–595, 2017.

catch-rate data to fishing managers: Jiorle, Ryan , Ahrens, Robert, and Allen, Michael, "Assessing the Utility of a Smartphone App for Recreational Fishery Catch Data," *Fisheries Magazine* 41(12): 758-766, 2016.

dismissing the need for scientific justification: Major Expansion of Federal Red Snapper Season Announced, *Coastal Angler Magazine,* July 8, 2017.

adapted to the characteristics of each sector: Goldberg, Monica, "There's nothing modern about overfishing," Environmental Defense Fund, April 27, 2017.

CHAPTER SIXTEEN | BRIDGING THE GULF

America's fishing renaissance: NOAA Fisheries. *U.S. fishing generated more than $200 billion in sales in 2015.* May 9, 2017.

with fifty completely rebuilt: NOAA Fisheries. *Status of Stocks 2023.* Accessed October 5, 2024, https://www.fisheries.noaa.gov/national/sustainable-fisheries/status-stocks-2023.

spark geopolitical tensions: Weiss, Kenneth, "US fishing fleet pursues pollock in troubled waters," *Los Angeles Times*, October 19, 2008.

428 pounds of their primary target—red snapper: Defense Visual Information Distribution Service. *Coast Guard interdicts more Mexican fisherman poaching in Gulf of Mexico.* January 26, 2015.

could earn a month's wages: Burnett, John,"A Battle On The Gulf Pits The Coast Guard Against Mexican Red Snapper Poachers," NPR, August 12, 2021; Hill, Katie, "Coast Guard Intercepts 3 Boats off Texas Coast with 2,425 Pounds of Illegally Caught Red Snapper," *Outdoor Life*, August 31, 2022.

arresting twenty-three Mexican fishermen: Ackerman, Allyson, "Coast Guard seizes 900 pounds of illegal red snapper, shark off Texas shore," *Houston Chronicle*, September 30, 2024.

an entire generation's worth: Keys, Lili, "Illegal fishing in gulf grows, anglers call for action," *Lonestar Outdoor News.* September 17, 2014.

40 percent of Mexico's overall catch: Oceana. *Mexico joins the port state measures agreement to address illegal fishing.* March 31, 2023.

had been caught in US waters: "New bill from Sens. Cruz, Tuberville, Britt takes aims at cartels engaged in illegal red snapper fishing," Ted Cruz, March 6, 2024.

regulated seafood markets like Buddy's: NOAA Fisheries. *International Affairs.* Accessed October 16, 2024, http://www.nmfs.noaa.gov/ia/iuu/faqs.html.

fishermen are being undercut: "U.S. Gulf Fishermen Call for Federal Action Against Foreign Illegal Fishing," *PR Newswire*, April 9, 2015.

across the border to unload the day's catch: Gronewold, Nathaniel, "Coast Guard risks rough seas stopping red snapper poachers," *Green Wire.* February 27, 2018.

upwards of 760,000 pounds: "U.S. Gulf Fishermen Call for Federal Action

Against Foreign Illegal Fishing," *PR Newswire*, April 9, 2015.

annual value of twenty-four billion: Pew Research Center. *Ending Illegal Fishing.* Accessed October 16, 2024, http://www.pewtrusts.org/en/projects/ending-illegal-fishing-project.

more than a matter of sovereignty: NOAA Fisheries. *International Affairs.* Accessed October 16, 2024, http://www.nmfs.noaa.gov/ia/iuu/noaa_taskforce_report_final.pdf.

economies, institutions, and governments: Shaver, Amanda, and Yozell, Sally, "Casting a Wider Net: The Security Implications of Illegal, Unreported, and Unregulated Fishing," Stimson Center, February 1, 2018.

recruit four thousand more officers: "U.S. Coast Guard Seeks 4,000 New Recruits," *The Maritime Executive*, July 19, 2017.

US imports from Mexico: Gronewold, Nathaniel, "Coast Guard risks rough seas stopping red snapper poachers," *Green Wire*, February 27, 2018.

seafood US imports are illegal: Oceana. *President BidenNOAA: Stop illegal seafood from entering the US.* Accessed October 16, 2024, https://usa.oceana.org/illegal-fishing-and-transparency-president-biden-and-noaa-stop-illegal-seafood-entering-us; Pramod, Ganapathiraju, Nakamura, Katrina, Pitchera, Tony, and Delagran, Leslie, "Estimates of illegal and unreported fish in seafood imports to the USA,"*Marine Policy*, 48, 102-113, September 2014.

marine biodiversity hotspots: Lara-Lara, Jose Ruben, "Los ecosistemas marinos," *Capital natural de méxico*, 1. Accessed October 16, 2024, http://www2.biodiversidad.gob.mx/pais/pdf/CapNatMex/Vol I/I05_Losecosistemasmar.pdf.

$100,000 for a single kilogram: Joyce, Christopher, "Chinese Taste For Fish Bladder Threatens Rare Porpoise In Mexico," NPR, February 9, 2016; Emerson Smith, Joshua, "$30K fish bladder fuels poaching, trafficking and wildlife crisis," *San Diego Union Tribune*. May 17, 2017; Popescu, Adam, "Cartels, Spies, and the Last Days of the Vaquita." *Outside*, January 31, 2019.

poachers to overwhelm: Malkin, Elisabeth, "Before Vaquitas vanish, a desperate bid to save them," *The New York Times*, February 27, 2017.

endemic, and near extinct: Lara-Lara, Jose Ruben, "Los ecosistemas marinos," Capital natural de méxico, 1. Accessed October 16, 2024.

dumped curvina to stabilize prices: Zapata, Pedro, "Revitalizing the Mexican Corvina Fishery with Sustainable Management," Environmental

NOTES

Defense Fund, February 25, 2013.

26 percent higher than before catch shares: Environmental Defense Fund Mexico. *EDF experiences with gulf curvina in the Upper Gulf of California 2011-2016.* Accessed October 16. 2024, https://blogs.edf.org/edfish/wp-content/blogs.dir/18/files/2017/02/Curvina-season-2016-.pdf.

reform among Mexico's fisheries both small and large: Environmental Defense Fund. *Los mares mexicanos, fuente de orgullo hoy y mañana.* September 3, 2017.

(also known as Pacific whiting) in their nets: "Reconocen a merluza en Carta Nacional Pesquera," El Vigia, June 13, 2013.

could work for them: Rodriguez, Laura, "In Sinaloa, Mexico, Fishermen are rewriting their legacy," Environmental Defense Fund, June 4, 2018.

now and in the future: "The Take on Hake: Pacific whiting fleet shows others how to operate a viable, sustainable fishery," *Fishermen's News,* November 1, 2013.

crime levels: Eipper, John, "Latin America World's Most Violent Region," World Association of International Studies, April 14, 2014.

that historical legacy: UNESCO. *Belize Barrier Reef Reserve System.* Accessed October 16, 2024, http://whc.unesco.org/en/list/764.

reefs and sea floors within and outside them: Bruno, John, "My Depressing Summers in Belize," *The New York Times.* July 6, 2017.

kind of robbery of their food and livelihood: Alves, Catherine, Garcia, Olga Denise, and Kramer, Randall, "Fisher perceptions of Belize's Managed Access program reveal overall support but need for improved enforcement," *Marine Policy*, 143, 105192, September 2022.

136 artisanal fishermen: Belize Fisheries Department. *Port Honduras Marine Reserve Management Plan: 2017-2021.* Accessed October 16, 2024, http://www.fisheries.gov.bz/port-honduras-marine-reserve.

spiny lobster and queen conch: "Case study: Belize – Towards Expansion of No-Take Areas in the MPA System," *The Commonwealth*, June 30, 2021.

low-cost fish stock assessments: FISHE. *What to do when you have no data.* Accessed October 16, 2024, http://fishe.edf.org/what-do-when-you-have-no-data.

with further expansion underway: "Belize's request for sustainable solutions to finance marine protect areas," *The San Pedro Sun*, March 30, 2024.

rebuild areas that have been, or will soon be, bleached: Helgason, Nicole, "Fragments of hope is an example of reef restoration done right," Reef

Builders, February 26, 2016.

replicated in tropical waters: Epstein, Larry, "Bold commitments to sustainable fisheries at the United Nations will help Belize achieve sustainable oceans goals," Environmental Defense Fund, June 14, 2017.

130 large fishing vessels at a time: Ginsburgs, George, and Slusser, Robert M. "A Calendar of Soviet Treaties: 1958-1973," Documentation Office for East European Law, University of Leyden, 1981.

fishermen, biologists, processing staff, managers, and other technicians: Adams, Chuck, "An Overview of the Cuban Commercial Fishing Industry and Implications to the Florida Seafood Industry of Renewed Trade," University of Florida. Accessed October 6, 2024, http://ufdcimages.uflib.ufl.edu/IR/00/00/18/50/00001/FE16200.pdf.

data visualizations: Nelson, Bryn, "Cuba: How politics has become a hurdle for its researchers," *Science News Explores*, August 24, 2017.

"over-exploited," and 5 percent were "collapsed": Baisre, Julio. A., "An overview of Cuban commercial marine fisheries: the last 80 years," *Bulletin of Marine Science*, 94(2), January 2017.

critical coastal and marine habitats: McDonald, Brent, "Crown Jewel of Cuba's Coral Reef," *The New York Times.* July 13 2015.

at the 2009 MarCuba Conference: "Cuba: Havana - Colac Mar Cuba 2009," Mission Blue, October 30, 2009.

risks of offshore drilling with Cuban officials: Peterson, Emily, Whittle, Daniel, and Rader, Douglas, "Bridging the Gulf: Finding Common Ground on Environmental and Safety Preparedness for Offshore Oil and Gas in Cuba," Environmental Defense Fund, 2012.

other toxic spills in the Gulf: Environmental Defence Fund. *US and Cuba Find Common Ground.* Accessed October 6, 2024, https://www.edf.org/us-and-cuba-find-common-ground.

to circumnavigate the island: NOAA Ocean Exploration. *Cuba's Twilight Zone Reefs & Their Regional Connectivity.* Accessed Oct. 6, 2024, http://oceanexplorer.noaa.gov/explorations/17cuba-reefs/welcome.html.

including climate change, on that status: Clynes, Tom, "Historic Cuban voyage searches for clues to coral reef survival," Environmental Defense Fund, September 14, 2023; "Bojeo A Cuba: A circumnavigation expedition around Cuba to explore coastal coral reefs," *Bojeo A Cuba.* Accessed October 6, 2024, https://drive.google.com/file/d/1yXC8m-RkbbDtvtQK6Ac9qeIz7Lub2FeCm/view?usp=drive_link.

assessment of their finfish fisheries: Puga, Rafael, Valle, Servando, Kritzer,

Jacob P. *et al.*, "Vulnerability of nearshore tropical finfish in Cuba: implications for scientific and management planning," *Bulletin Marine Science*, 94(2): 377-92, 2018.

ways to end local overharvesting: Hamilton, Jill, "The Sea That Unites Us," Nicholas School of the Environment, July 28, 2017.

in the Gulf waters they share: Environmental Defense Fund. *US and Cuba sign agreement to protect shared marine life.* November 18, 2015.

without a state contract: Environmental Defense Fund. *Sustainability is on the hook as Cuba adopts new fisheries law.* July 14, 2019; "In new law, Cuba takes official aim at overfishing." *Eco Americas.* July 2019.

CHAPTER SEVENTEEN | OCEANIC TRANSFORMATION

death and destruction: Kazama, Motoki, and Noda, Toshiro, "Damage statistics (Summary of the 2011 off the Pacific Coast of Tohoku Earthquake damage)" *Soils and Foundations* 52 (5): 780-92, October 2012.

toward North America: Funabashi, Y., and Kitazawa, K., "Fukushima in review: A complex disaster, a disastrous response," *Bulletin of the Atomic Scientists*, 68(2), 9-21, March 1, 2012; Tabuchi, Hiroko, "Tank Has Leaked Tons of Contaminated Water at Japan Nuclear Site," *The New York Times*, August 20, 2013.

319 fishing ports: Popescu, Irina, and Ogushi, Toshihiko, "Fisheries in Japan," European Parliament Policy Department, December 2013.

wasn't sufficient to restore confidence: Guy, Alison, "Worried about Fukushima radiation in seafood? Turns out bananas are more radioactive than fish," Oceana, October 25, 2017.

eventy-three species of fish: Wakamatsu, H., Miyata, T. "Reputational damage and the Fukushima disaster: an analysis of seafood in Japan". *Fish Sci* 83, 1049–1057, 2017.

dependent on imported seafood: Popescu, Irina, and Ogushi, Toshihiko, "Fisheries in Japan," European Parliament Policy Department, December 2013.

quotas for offshore fisheries: Tokyo Sustainable Seafood Summit. *Fishery Reform and the Future of Coastal Fishing Communities in Japan.* Accessed October 6, 2024, https://sustainableseafoodnow.com/archive/en/report/tsss2019/1659.

worth half a trillion dollars: European Environment Agency. *Status of Marine Fish and Shellfish Stocks In European Seas.* January 18, 2024.

electronic monitoring to enforce compliance: European Commission. *Landing obligation: First study of implementation and impact on discards.* August 27, 2021; *European Commission. Discarding in Fisheries.* Accessed October 6, 2024, https://ec.europa.eu/fisheries/cfp/fishing_rules/discards_en.

energy sources in the fisheries sector: European Commission. *Discarding in Fisheries.* Accessed October 6, 2024, https://ec.europa.eu/fisheries/cfp/fishing_rules/discards_en.

Early on, Iceland: Priddle, Erin, " How the government can use quotas to build a sustainable future for UK fishing," London School of Economics, May 25, 2018.

12.5 percent of GDP: "An Icelandic Success," *The Economist,* January 3, 2009.

despite its "Brexit": Priddle, Erin, " How the government can use quotas to build a sustainable future for UK fishing," London School of Economics, May 25, 2018.

in its own right worldwide: "Spain is the European leader in the production and consumption of frozen seafood products." FAO. January 6, 2019.

too big to ignore: "Too Big To Ignore" *Too Big To Ignore.* Accessed October 6, 2024, http://toobigtoignore.net.

out of five of its active fishing vessels: European Commission. *Fishers of the Future: A study that examines the future role of fishers in society up to 2050.* Accessed October 6, 2024, https://ec.europa.eu/fisheries/sites/fisheries/files/docs/publications/2016-small-scale-coastal-fleet_en.pdf.

access rights and fish markets on shore: Franquesa, Ramon, "Fishermen Guilds in Spain (Cofradias): Economic Role and Structural Changes," Research Gate. Accessed October 6, 2024, https://www.researchgate.net/publication/265991036_fishermen_guilds_in_spain_cofradias_economic_role_and_structural_changes.

pounds of percebes, or goose barnacle: "Percebeiros in Galicia (Keeping Barnacles)" YouTube.com, Accessed October 6, 2024, https://www.youtube.com/watch?v=0eeceWNb6_I.

more flexibility in their activities: Tudela, Sergi, Lleonart, Jordi, Martin, Paloma, and Demestre, M., "The co-management of the sand eel fishery of Catalonia (NW Mediterranean): The story of a process," *Scientia Marina* 78(S1):87-93, April 2014.

single biggest cause of global hunger: Ehtesham Khaishgi, Amna, "Food waste is main cause of global hunger, says UN agency official," *Arab News*. September 17, 2017.

seafood never makes it from hook to plate: Gustavson, Jenny, and Cederberg, Christel, "Global food losses and food waste: Extent, causes and prevention," Food and Agriculture Organization of the UN, 2011.

of the humans who eat seafood: Alverson, Dayton, Freeberg. Mark, Murawski, Steven, and Pope, J.G. "A global assessment of fisheries bycatch and discards," FAO Fisheries Technical Paper, 1994.

between nine and seven million tonnes: Gilman, E., Perez Roda, A., Huntington, T., Kenelly, S. J. *et al.* "Benchmarking global fisheries discards," *Scientific Reports*, 10(14017), 2020; Food and Agriculture Organization of the United Nations. *Food loss and waste in fish value chains.* Accessed October 17, 2024, https://www.fao.org/flw-in-fish-value-chains/value-chain/capture-fisheries/discards-and-bycatch/en.

population of live fish in the sea: Environmental Defense Fund. *The potential for global fish recovery: How effective fisheries management can increase abundance, yield, and value.* Accessed October 6, 2024, https://www.edf.org/sites/default/files/content/upside-model-report-summary.pdf.

if nations move to catch shares: "New Research: Key Ocean Reforms Drive Huge Economic, Nutrition and Conservation Gains," *Business Wire,* June 4, 2015; David and Lucille Packard Foundation. *Ocean Prosperity Roadmap Infographics.* June 7, 2016.

fraction of their original numbers: Intl. Scientific Committee for Tuna and Tuna-Like Species in the North Pacific Ocean. *Pacific Bluefin Tuna Stock Assessment*, Report of the Pacific Bluefin Tuna Working Group (2016).

journey of five thousand miles: Olson, Danielle, "The Great Migration of Bluefin Tuna," Smithsonian Ocean. Accessed October 6, 2024, http://ocean.si.edu/ocean-news/great-pacific-migration-bluefin-tuna.

accountability measures, or other rules: Bonfil, Ramon, Munro, Gordon, Tor Valtysson, Hreidar, *et al.* "Distant Water Fleets : Ecological, Economic and Social Assessment," Fisheries Centre Research Reports (1998).

within and outside of US waters: Barnes, Michele, Lynhame, John, Kalberg, Kolter, and Leung, PingSun, "Social networks and environmental outcomes," *Social Sciences*, 113(23): 6466-6471, May 23, 2016.

caught by small-scale fishermen: Jentoft, Svein, Chuenpagdee, Ratana,

Barragán Paladines, Maria José, and Franz, Nicole, *The Small-Scale Fisheries Guidelines*, Springer, June 2017.

center of marine biodiversity: Stoyle, George, "The Coral Triangle: Amazon of the Seas," Oceanographic. Accessed October 17, 2024, https://oceanographicmagazine.com/features/exploring-the-coral-triangle-raja-ampat.

and undermined reef habitats: Environmental Defence Fund. *Empowering Fishing Communities Worldwide.* Accessed October 5, 2024, https://www.edf.org/oceans/reforming-fisheries-philippines.

reintroduced by research expeditions: "Dynamite Fishing with Jacques Cousteau" Accessed October 5, 2024, https://www.youtube.com/watch?v=FHrlXY9Gd6c.

a quarter of all landings: Marsh, James B., *Resources & Environment in Asia's Marine Sector,* p. 153, Taylor & Francis, 1992.

degrading three-quarters of the country's reefs: Palma, Mary Ann, Tsamenyi, Martin, and Edeson, William, *Promoting Sustainable Fisheries: The International Legal and Policy Framework to Combat Illegal, Unreported and Unregulated Fishing*, p. 10, Brill, May 2010.

all-out war: "BFAR declares war vs dynamite fishing." *Philippine Daily Inquirer.* February 27, 2012.

ten thousand detonations still take place each day: Guy, Allison, "Local Efforts Put a Dent in Illegal Dynamite Fishing in the Philippines," Oceana. July 8, 2016.

members who depend on these resources: Rare. *Fish Forever in the Philippines.* Accessed October 6, 2024, https://rare.org/program/philippines; Rural 21. *Fish forever - Community led solutions to solve coastal overfishing.* November 24, 2011.

food security and poverty reduction: Food and Agriculture Organization of the United Nations. *Voluntary Guidelines for Securing Sustainable Small-Scale Fisheries.* 2015.

coming from developing countries: Kituyi, Mukhisa,, and Thomson, Peter, "90% of fish stocks are used up – fisheries subsidies must stop emptying the ocean," World Economic Forum. July 13, 2018; Marine Stewardship Council. *MSC Insights: Sustainable fishing, higher yields, and the global food supply.* January 2021.

few are recovering, many are rapidly depleting: "In Deep Water," *The Economist*, February 24, 2014.

between 86 or 130 million metric tons: Pauly, Daniel, and Zeller, Dirk, "Catch reconstructions reveal that global marine fisheries catches are higher than reported and declining," *Nature Communications*, 7(10244), January 19, 2016.

a culinary theme park: Aoki, Mizuho, and Osumi, Magdalena, "Koike announces Tsukiji relocation, plans to retain its cultural legacy," *The Japan Times*, June 20, 2017.

CHAPTER EIGHTEEN | A LEGACY BEQUEATHED

tons of large, fresh, healthy fish: NOAA Fisheries. *Final Rule to Increase Red Snapper catch limits in the Gulf of Mexico.* Accessed Oct. 5, 2024, https://gulfcouncil.org/press_releases_2023/2023/final-rule-to-increase-red-snapper-catch-limits-in-the-gulf-of-mexico; NOAA Fisheries. *Red Snapper: Species Directory.* Accessed October 5, 2024, https://www.fisheries.noaa.gov/species/red-snapper.

suffocates life at the base of the food chain: Schleifstein, Mark, "2017 Gulf dead zone is largest ever, size of New Jersey," Nola.com, Aug. 2, 2017.

flush down rivers out to sea: "The known unknowns of plastic pollution," *The Economist*, May 3, 2018; "Too Much of a Good Thing," *The Economist*, March 26, 2016.

and fibers, sickening reefs: Rader, Douglas. N. "New study published in Science quantifies growing threat plastics pose to coral reefs." Environmental Defense Fund. January 25, 2018.

and entering the food chain: Di Mauro, Rosana, Kupchik, Matthew, and Benfield, Mark, "Abundant plankton sized micro plastic particles in shelf waters of the northern Gulf of Mexico," *Environmental Pollution*, 230, 798-809, August 10, 2017.

more plastic than fish: Zoellner, Danielle, "Ocean plastic could triple by 2040 and outnumber fish by 2050," *The Independent*, July 23, 2020; Mathuras, Fon, "More plastic than fish in the ocean by 2050: Report offers blueprint for change," World Economic Forum, January 19, 2016.

discharge untreated microfibers into the semi-enclosed Gulf: Workman, James, "Plasticus Mare Balticum," IUCN Publishing, 2020.

concentrations of nutrient and plastic pollution on earth: Wear, Stephanie, "Missing the boat: Critical threats to coral reefs are neglected at global scale," *Marine Policy*, 74, 153-157, December 2016.

ecological thresholds or tipping points: Karr, Kendra, Fujita, Rod, Halpern, Benjamin et al. "Thresholds in Caribbean coral reefs: implications for ecosystem based fishery management." *Journal of Applied Ecology*, 52(2): 402-412, December 29, 2015.

resilience grows through responsible stewardship: Battista, Willow, Kelly, Ryan, Erickson, Ashley, and Fujita, Rod, "A Comprehensive Method for Assessing Marine Resource Governance: Case Study in Kāneʻohe Bay, Hawaiʻi," *Coastal Management* 44(4): 295–332, May 18, 2016.

an equally valid strategy as fishing: Bjørndal, Trond, and Guillen, Jordi, "Market competition between farmed and wild fish: a literature survey," *Fisheries and Aquaculture Circular*, 1114, Rome.

half of human demand for seafood: FAO, "The State of World Fisheries and Aquaculture 2016: Contributing to food security and nutrition for all," Rome, 2016.

fish eaten may be grown: "Fish to 2030: Prospects for Fisheries and Aquaculture" World Bank Report. December 2013.

shrimp imported from Thailand: Hodal, Kate., Kelly, Chris., and Lawrence, Felicity. "Revealed: Asian slave labor producing prawns for supermarkets in US and UK." The Guardian. June 10, 201; Greenberg, Paul. "10 things you should know about the US seafood supply." *Food Safety News.* July 14, 2014.

tilapia from China: Stewart, Jeanine. "US frozen tilapia market steady amid huge import volume drop." *Undercurrent News.* July 11, 2017.

Atlantic salmon from Chile: "Sustainable Seafood" NOAA Fisheries. Accessed October 16, 2024, https://www.fishwatch.gov/sustainable-seafood/the-global-picture.

It's not alone: Responsible Seafood Advocate. "Expanding mariculture 'vital' to world's food security, study finds." Global Seafood. May 3, 2022; Gewin, Virginia. "Is the US ready for offshore aquaculture?" Ensia. April 20, 2017.

Bush first authorized farms in the Gulf: Avasthi, Amitabh. "New Bill Seeks to Expand Fish Farming" *Science.* June 7, 2005.

mass equal to the region's wild harvest: "NOAA expands opportunities for US aquaculture." NOAA. January 11, 2016.

$20 billion "seafood trade deficit": "US Aquaculture." NOAA Fisheries. Accessed October 17, 2024, https://www.fisheries.noaa.gov/national/aquaculture/us-aquaculture; Davis, Christopher. G., and Rexroad, Caird. E. "US Seafood Imports Expand as Domestic Aquaculture Industry Repositions Itself." USDA ERS. May 22, 2024; "US Aquaculture." USDA ERS. Accessed October 17, 2024, https://www.ers.usda.

gov/topics/animal-products/aquaculture.

weaken the gene pool's resilience: Flatt, Courtney., Ryan, John. "Environmental Nightmare' After Thousands Of Atlantic Salmon Escape Fish Farm." NPR. August 24, 2017.

mangroves or wetlands are cleared for pens: "Preserve Habitats" Monterey Bay Aquarium Seafood Watch. Accessed October 16, 2024, https://www.seafoodwatch.org/ocean-issues/aquaculture/habitat-damage.

pose risks to human health: Hites, Ronald A. et al. "Global Assessment of Organic Contaminants in Farmed Salmon." *Science*, 303, January 2004.

disease spill: Lafferty, Kevin. D., Harvell, C. D., Conrad, Jon. M., et al. "Infectious Diseases Affect Marine Fisheries and Aquaculture Economics." *The Annual Review of Marine Sciences*, 7, 471-496. 2015.

domesticated carnivores, like salmon: Goldburg, Rebecca., and Triplett, Tracy. "Murky Waters: Environmental Effects of Aquaculture in the US." Environmental Defense Fund. 1997

in a federal lawsuit: "Fishing and Public Interest Groups File Challenge to Feds' Unprecedented Decision to Establish Aquaculture in Offshore U.S. Waters." *Progressive News Wire.* February 16, 2016.

if we make a mistake here: Lambrecht, Bill. "Feds open Gulf to fish farming, but opponents see big catch." *San Antonio Express.* Apr. 9, 2016.

filter-feeders to buffer and clean the water: Futures Centre. "The new fish farming: three ways innovation could revive aquaculture. *Medium*, Aug 31, 2017.

2017 paper, fish farming might: Levine, Jeremy. "Aquaculture ascendent: How farming fish could fix world hunger." The Bottom Line UCSB.

cleaning marine pollution: Rosenberg, Alec. "Can Farmed Fish Feed the World Sustainably?" University of California. December 8, 2017.

changing temperature, oxygenation, and salinity: Free, C. M., Cabral, R. B., Froehlich, H. E. *et al.* "Expanding ocean food production under climate change" *Nature* 605, 490–496, 2022; Responsible Seafood Advocate. "Expanding mariculture 'vital' to world's food security." Global Seafood Alliance. May 3, 2022.

habitat loss, disease, or pollution: Gunther, Marc, "Can deepwater aquaculture avoid the pitfalls of coastal fish farms?" Yale Environment 360, January 25, 2018.

for genetic purity or market price: Tresaugue, Matthew, "Agency's Non-decision Opens Gulf to Fish Farming," *Chronicle*, September 4, 2009; Lehner, Peter, and Rosenberg, Nathan, "Farming for the Future: The Science, Law, and Policy of Climate Neutral Agriculture," Environmental Law Institute, December 2021.

work together to market a US product: Lambrecht, Bill, "Feds open Gulf to fish farming, but opponents see big catch," *San Antonio Express*, April 9, 2016.

gifted few for the privilege: Bailey, Ronald, "Give a Man a Fishery and Soon You'll Have More Fish," *Reason*, May 30, 2012.

small hook and line fishermen: Rust, Suzanne. "System Turns US Fishing Rights Into Commodity, Squeezes Small Fishermen" NBC Bay Area. March 12, 2013.

fleet consolidation since at least the 1860s: Goldfarb, Ben, "The Catch 22 of New England Fisheries' Catch Share Scheme," *EarthIsland*, April 1, 2013.

harmed, and dismissed the lawsuit: Jud, Shems, "Judge dismisses attempt to halt west coast fishery," Environmental Defense Fund, August 9, 2011.

rose 30 percent to forty-seven million pounds: Brinson, Ayeisha, and Thunberg, Eric, "The Economic Performance of US Catch Share Programs" NOAA Fisheries Service.,August 2013; Whittle, Patrick, "Scallop Fishermen will be allowed to catch more next year," November 16, 2016.

vying against larger industrial fleets: Grasso, Thomas, "A Community Bank That's Helping Fishermen to Stay on the Water," Walton Family Foundation, May 30, 2019.

manage ocean resources more effectively: "Catch Together," *Multiplier*. Accessed October 16, 2024, https://multiplier.org/project/catch-together.

"stable stream of fishing revenue: Holland, Daniel, S., Speir, Cameron., Agar, Juan. *et al.*, "Impact of catch shares on diversification of fishers' income and risk," PNAS, 114(35): 9302-9307, August 29, 2017; Holland, Daniel, "Journal articles by Daniel Holland," ORCID. Accessed October 18, 2024, https://orcid.org/0000-0002-4493-859X.

goes for fifty-five dollars: Ropicki, Andrew, "Gulf of Mexico IFQ Pricing Report," *Sustainable Fisheries and Aquaculture*, July 2024.

ABOUT THE AUTHORS

JAMES WORKMAN is a storyteller, entrepreneur, and author of resilience strategies, including the award-winning book *Heart of Dryness*. Drawing on fieldwork with Indigenous Kalahari people, he founded AquaShares, a firm pioneering water credit trading. His writing has appeared in *The New York Times*, *Los Angeles Times*, *The New Republic*, *Orion*, *Trout*, and *Washington Monthly*. Jamie studied at Yale, Oxford, and Stanford, and taught at Wesleyan and Whitman. But his real education came from restoring wildfires, reintroducing wolves, blowing up dams, smuggling to dissidents, getting married and raising two daughters.

AMANDA LELAND fell in love with the sea at five years old, when her grandfather taught her to fish. As executive director of Environmental Defense Fund, Amanda brings stakeholders together to support healthy communities and economies while reducing climate impacts. She previously led EDF's Oceans program, a global team in fourteen countries focused on reversing overfishing while supporting those whose livelihoods rely on fish, triggering the dramatic economic and ecological recovery of US fisheries and beyond. An avid kayaker and scuba diver, Leland holds a master's degree in marine biology and lives with her family in Washington, DC.

TORREY HOUSE PRESS

TORREY HOUSE PRESS publishes books at the intersection of the literary arts and environmental advocacy. THP authors explore the diversity of human experiences and relationships with place. THP books create conversations about issues that concern the American West, landscape, literature, and the future of our ever-changing planet, inspiring action toward a more just world.

We believe that lively, contemporary literature is at the cutting edge of social change. We seek to inform, expand, and reshape the dialogue on environmental justice and stewardship for the natural world by elevating literary excellence from diverse voices.

Visit www.torreyhouse.org for reading group discussion guides, author interviews, and more.

Join the Torrey House Press family and give today at
www.torreyhouse.org/give.

SPECIAL THANKS

As a 501(c)(3) nonprofit publisher, our work is made possible by generous donations from readers like you.

Torrey House Press is supported by Back of Beyond Books, Bright Side Bookshop, The King's English Bookshop, Maria's Bookshop, the Ballantine Family Fund, the Jeffrey S. & Helen H. Cardon Foundation, the Lawrence T. Dee & Janet T. Dee Foundation, the McMullan/O'Connor Family Fund, the Stewart Family Foundation, the Barker Foundation, Kif Augustine & Stirling Adams, Diana Allison, Richard Baker, Karey Barker, Patti Baynham & Owen Baynham, Matt Bean, Klaus Bielefeldt, Joe Breddan, Karen Buchi & Kenneth Buchi, Betty Clark & Gary Clark, Rose Chilcoat & Mark Franklin, Linc Cornell & Lois Cornell, Susan Cushman & Charlie Quimby, Lynn de Freitas & Patrick de Freitas, Pert Eilers, Ed Erwin, Laurie Hilyer, Phyllis Hockett, Kirtly Parker Jones, Emily Klass, Rick Klass, Jen Lawton & John Thomas, Susan Markley, Leigh Meigs & Stephen Meigs, Mark Meloy, Kathleen Metcalf, Donaree Neville & Douglas Neville, Laura Paskus, Katie Pearce, Marion S. Robinson, Molly Swonger, Shelby Tisdale, Rachel White, the National Endowment for the Humanities, the National Endowment for the Arts, the Utah Division of Arts & Museums, Utah Humanities, the Salt Lake City Arts Council, and Salt Lake County Zoo, Arts & Parks. Our thanks to individual donors, members, and the Torrey House Press board of directors for their valued support.